Complete Home
Decorating

Complete Home
Decorating

A step-by-step guide to achieving the best results for your home

Phil Gorton

This is a Parragon Book
This edition published in 2005

Parragon
Queen Street House
4 Queen Street
Bath BA1 1HE
United Kingdom

ISBN: 1-40546-222-1

Printed in Indonesia

Produced by The Bridgewater Book Company Ltd, Lewes, East Sussex,
United Kingdom

Cover design by Fiona Roberts

Contents

Introduction

As the world enters a new millennium, people's lives have never been more stressful, their workstyles more fractious and time specific, or their lifestyles more fragmented. Relaxation at the end of a difficult day is consequently more of a basic requirement than ever before, and to be able to wind down in comfort and style in aesthetically pleasing decorative surroundings is not so much a bonus as a necessity.

Relaxing in familiar surroundings usually involves personal input to the area in question; favourite colours and textures, controllable lighting systems, displays and pictures and mementoes all act as a 'welcome home'. Whether 'home' is owned, mortgaged or rented or whether it is a house, cottage or flat, the decorative personal touch is essential if home is to be where the heart is.

Employing third parties to do decorating work is expensive, time-consuming, carries no real guarantees, and still requires a lot of personal input. Channel the energies of personal attention into the task itself, always being aware of its possible complexity, whether it is merely deciding on colour schemes for walls or whether it involves a complete makeover, so popular on television.

DIY programmes, in order to retain viewer interest, edit down technical job

sequences from hours to seconds, leading the unwary into the erroneous belief

that a decorating job can be done in the time it takes on TV. The most

important function of this book is to bring a sense of reality to the initial

discussions and scheduling, allowing decorating decisions to reflect a proper

timescale, and to take into account the available skill levels.

Throughout these pages a proper professional approach is encouraged, from

the drawing up of a detailed plan to the application

of top quality materials and power tools in a safe

and responsible manner. The tools required are

discussed at the start of each chapter, and step-by-

step sequences show each job in progression, and

can be easily followed and understood.

Whether these pages help with a simple painted

frame or a complex zonal plan, hopefully, after it is

completed, you will experience much greater

satisfaction in having done a quality job in the

home, rather than paying to have one done.

PLANNING

In today's highly competitive consumer-orientated marketplace, modern businesses must have carefully considered strategies and working schedules to ensure their survival and growth. You are probably aware of this requirement in your own daily working life and the same is no less true of planning home improvements. Most households already have some kind of general strategy for running the home smoothly, varying from a basic task 'duty roster' on a kitchen notice board to a complex time-specific system that includes family members and budgets, all logged onto a home computer. Forward planning is an essential part of running a home and is equally vital when it comes to making improvements, whether major or minor.

Practical considerations

No matter how small the job appears to be, forward planning is needed when you are considering refurbishing or decorating your home. Inspiration gained from a magazine or television 'makeover' needs to be turned into a plan of action if home improvement is to be successful. Here are some tips on what to think about before you start.

Clear brief

Imagine you have an independent builder taking on the job. What he would expect from his client is a clear brief, detailing all that is required from the finished work, which materials are going to be used and which colour scheme is required. Just because you intend to tackle the project yourself, don't skimp on the details when devising the plan of action. And beware: 'making it up as you go along' is liable to end in unsatisfactory results.

When planning a refurbishment, seek inspiration from a variety of sources, including magazines.

Measure the room, draw a plan, and collect colour cards, paint testers and material swatches.

Questions to consider

Whether you live alone or with others, it is worth considering the following questions:

- Is the planned change suitable for the particular room that you have in mind?
- Is it necessary?
- Is it practical?
- Will everyone in the house benefit?
- How long will it take?
- How much upheaval will there be?
- Can you live with it in the long term?

Budget

If the household members like the ideas and are happy to live with the works in progress, then you need to consider:

- How much will it cost?
- Is it affordable?

The job budget involves adding up prices taken from builders' and decorators' lists. You might need to include the cost of any new tools required (whether bought or hired), delivery charges for materials and/or rubbish clearance.

Skills and time

Presuming a reasonable skill level with a basic tool kit (the skills and tools required for each job are discussed throughout this book), try to devise a logical order of work, bearing in mind the following factors:

- The amount of work needed each day will depend on the size of the project, but don't take on too much in one go. Popular decorating programmes on television may give the impression that a room can be completely transformed in a mere 25 minutes, including a commercial break, but this is far from being the truth.
- Be realistic in assessing how long you think each part of the project will take.
- Cutting corners on any part of a job may lead to difficulties later on and may ultimately add to the time the job takes.

Implications of refurbishment

The eventual resale value of your property is not the only thing to bear in mind when assessing standards of workmanship. Removing period features from a room for 'modernisation' generally does not meet with approval today, so consider all the implications before you start. Sympathetic decorating and subtle changes can sometimes be more beneficial than wholesale refurbishment.

In years to come, you may tire of the changes you have made and seek to reinstate an earlier look, but if you have disposed of vital features, you may encounter considerable difficulty in replacing them. Give yourself time to come to terms with your plans; put them away for a while, then come back to them. Don't be afraid to change your mind or tone down some of the more ambitious aspects of the project.

Before

Ugly view

Sombre wall colour

Dark units

Obtrusive dresser

Stark display unit

Same-colour edging

Matt floor

Disjointed appearance

After

Blind hides view

Light wall colour

Light-coloured units

Dresser blends with units

Decorative jugs

Contrasting edging

Reflective tile floor

Cohesive appearance

11

Assessing room functions

If your work is not confined to one room and a complete makeover of the house is needed, then your plans must be more elaborate. Maybe you've just moved in or your family circumstances have changed dramatically. Whatever the reason, the first step is to assess the basic areas – living, working and sleeping – plus the role of the kitchen and bathroom.

Living areas

The living room must cater for all members of the household, who will use it for different reasons. Its main function is to provide a seating arrangement for family and friends where privacy is not possible. Several activities may take place in this room simultaneously, for example, reading, listening to music or watching television, family discussions and hobby pursuits, such as playing computer games. Decide whether an open-plan style is in keeping with this lack of privacy, or whether a breakdown of the living room into two separate functional areas is possible. In a period house, the downstairs living areas would usually have been arranged as a day room, near the cooking area for convenience, with easily cleaned flooring, and a separate evening area, with more luxurious fixtures and fittings, suitable for entertaining.

Working areas

What constitutes work, and what doesn't, may present an ever-changing issue in the contemporary household. Computers are used for schoolwork, business and family leisure activities. Digital interactive cables have transformed the television into a potential shopping mall and banking service. As certain areas become multi-functional, a study or home office may be a welcome retreat. This is a real necessity if you work from home full time; otherwise, professional commitments can easily spill over into everyday family life.

Sleeping areas

The younger members of a household often consider their

Living areas often benefit from being divided into separate areas for different functions.

This bedroom in the loft area of the house lends itself to several purposes at once: a sleeping area, with storage in the foreground, a sewing area and, at the back of the room, a shower area.

bedroom space to be out of bounds to anyone not specifically invited. These areas are already catering for several activities, and must be furnished accordingly. The bedroom used solely for its intended purpose is usually the parents' room, traditionally the largest. Consider the benefits of young children sharing this room instead. It will double as a nursery or play area, possibly freeing up a room elsewhere in the house. A good night's rest, however, relies on peace and quiet, so the location of bedrooms away from sources of noise is very important.

The kitchen

Generally the working hub of the home, the kitchen is frequently in use for food preparation, cooking, washing up and general cleaning. Home to many major labour-saving devices, such as the washing machine, dishwasher and food processor, it may need to accommodate several family members at the same time and to double as a breakfast or snack room. Easy access to other eating areas, such as a dining room, may be needed, so that cooked food reaches the table quickly. A large serving hatch between the kitchen and dining room may be the ideal solution, providing a practical and visual link.

The bathroom

In a large household, a second bathroom is a modern necessity, and builders' merchants stock all types of space-saving units with this in mind. If your main bathroom is fitted out traditionally (i.e. with a bath), a shower room would be a good idea, along with a second toilet, possibly incorporated in a downstairs cloakroom. If space precludes all these options, another possibility would be to divide the toilet off from the rest of the bathroom.

Interconnecting spaces

In an ideal world the home you inhabit would grow and change with you and your family. This is possible if the house layout is flexible. Corridors that have a decorative scheme encouraging adjacent areas to interact, rather than divorcing one from another, are a good start. The decor in any area becomes more interesting if flexible design allows the occupants to see through to another, different space.

Linking rooms does not necessarily have to mean sacrificing privacy, either. Decorative screens can be used to temporarily isolate parts of the open space as and when you wish. If you have the room to create open spaces in this way, however, try to avoid overcompensating by adding too much furniture.

Minimalism will not be an option for a family unit, of course, but too much clutter will rapidly reduce or destroy any feeling of spaciousness that you endeavour to create.

Opposite ideas often work well together. For example, a small apartment will appear larger if it is visually sparse. By contrast, a large loft apartment benefits from an aggressive colour scheme that is used to reduce the overwhelming impact of the space.

A balcony area surrounded by greenery creates a relaxed environment in which to work.

Making plans

Whether your plan is complex or simple at this stage, whether you intend to divide up a room space or merely paint a floor, you will find a detailed plan on paper makes life a lot easier. It doesn't have to be a work of art, but it does need to be accurate. If you have a computer with suitable software, you can draw up your plans and alter them using a grid system. You might even be able to put together a three-dimensional drawing.

Left: The essential tools required for measuring a room are graph paper, some coloured pencils, a notepad and pen, a clear plastic rule, a pair of scissors, a retractable steel measure and a calculator.

Below: Mark on the plan the room's basic dimensions, noting in particular any unusual shapes that distort the room's appearance, and all the doors, windows and other features such as cupboards.

Measuring up a room

To measure up a room, use a retractable steel measure of at least 5m/16½ft total length, with a lever to lock the tape at any given distance. Adding distances together from shorter tape measures, or using cloth tapes that are prone to sag, leads to inaccurate figures.

Measure the basic dimensions first – wall height and length. Measure the room from corner to corner to confirm that it is square, or at least square enough for your purposes. Add on any bay window and alcove areas, where necessary, and note down the sizes of the chimney breast, all built-in cupboards, window areas and doors, marking on your plan which way the doors open.

You will find it easier to write down initial measurements on a rough sketch. You can also add radiator positions and pipe runs, electric outlets and light fittings to this first drawing, even if they are not relevant to the final scheme.

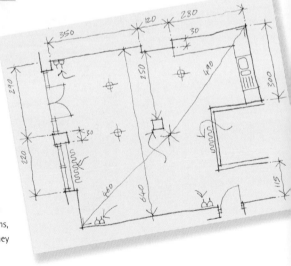

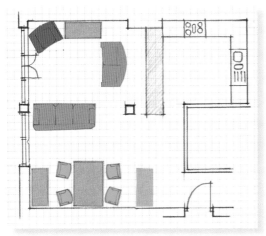

Transferring to graph paper

Using a pencil, not a pen (it's much easier to correct mistakes if you use a pencil as you can erase it when you go wrong), transfer your plan from rough sketch to graph paper and scale the area to size using the squares. Include only the items that you consider relevant from your comprehensive measurements. Simplify the plan as much as possible to reduce the risk of errors due to incorporating too much clutter.

If your room is furnished, or if you know what items of furniture will eventually be included, then represent these objects with small pieces of card cut to scale. You will be able to rearrange items of furniture at will, to establish their best position and to make maximum use of the available space.

Draw in shelving systems or new cupboards to go in alcoves, change access doors, and so on, until the plan is complete and you are quite happy with it.

A plan comes to life when the items of furniture are coloured in and you can see how they relate to one another and how they fill the space. Try moving them around to ascertain the ideal configuration.

Because of the positions of doors, windows and chimney breasts there are only so many combinations that will work in any given space. With trial and error you should finally arrive at the perfect solution.

COLOUR

Choosing the correct colour scheme for your home is vital to your sense of comfort and well-being. Individual tastes in colour are, of course, highly subjective, but there are also several important objective factors involved in the selection of colour schemes. In this chapter we look at the colour wheel, which will help in choosing contrasting and complementary colour schemes, and also discuss the importance of natural light, the psychological effects of particular colours and the visual tricks that can be achieved through careful colour scheming. Successful use of colour has the potential to transform rooms in an exciting and gratifying way, and in many instances involves no great expense to you, so it is well worth taking your time considering all the choices available.

Designer's notes

When making notes, the designer always considers the features that are
inherent in the original design of the room, and their current status and
condition. Whether these features are emphasised or visually disguised by
the new colour scheme will be a decision for the room's occupants,
influenced by some basic colour rules.

Designer's questions

Before you make plans for redecorating, imagine that you are an
independent interior designer looking at your home for the first
time and ask yourself the following questions:

- What is the aspect of the room (i.e. which direction does
  it face)?
- How much natural light comes into the room?
- Is there an original feature in the room. If so, is it to be retained?
- Will the room need joinery additions, such as built-in storage
  and shelving in an alcove, which will alter its basic shape?

- Can paint schemes be applied to existing features such as doors
  and windows?
- Will these items have to be replaced (for example, to restore a
  period feel)?
- Can the desired effect be achieved simply by cosmetic changes or
  is major work necessary?

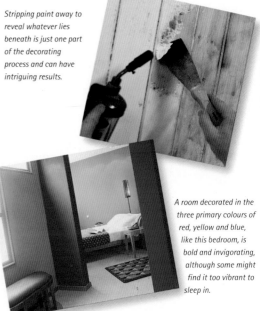

*Stripping paint away to
reveal whatever lies
beneath is just one part
of the decorating
process and can have
intriguing results.*

*Using a similar light colour on the
walls and furnishings opens up the
space and creates a feeling of*

*airiness. This scheme is cheerful and
uplifting and enhances whatever
light there is in the room.*

*A room decorated in the
three primary colours of
red, yellow and blue,
like this bedroom, is
bold and invigorating,
although some might
find it too vibrant to
sleep in.*

Bear in mind, however, that stripping a wall may involve you in a considerable amount of making good before it is suitable to be left exposed. The original mortar may be in poor condition and need repointing. Don't assume that every wall will be suitable for such treatment; in some cases, the underlying brickwork will have been laid carelessly and will never be attractive to look at. Be prepared to carry out some exploratory stripping of the plasterwork to ascertain what lies behind.

Other surfaces can also be stripped, such as floors. Here, the beauty of the grain of wooden boards can be brought out by careful sanding and varnishing. But again, repairs may be necessary. Always be prepared to amend your plans if it turns out that you can't achieve your desire.

You can make a feature like a fireplace into a focal point by surrounding it with intense colour.

Paint can be used to good effect to enhance original features, such as this attractive wooden door.

Colour for emphasis

You may feel that an old, ugly tiled fireplace is at odds with your twenty-first century ideal and want to remove it. On the other hand, you may have an older property suffering from 1970s 'modernisation' that needs the fireplace reinstated. Either possibility will involve a great deal of mess, in the form of soot, so obviously works of this nature have to be tackled first.

If you are in a position to undertake purely cosmetic changes, then you need to examine the features in the room even more closely. Working with what you have is always a good principle in home redecoration. This allows you to emphasise the best features of a room using colour. An old built-in cupboard, for instance, when it has been relieved of its multiple layers of paint, may reveal fine, sympathetically crafted woodwork. Using subtle dyes to enhance the grain can make a real feature of the joiner's art. A pale colour on the surrounding walls will emphasise the beauty of the wood and will not compete with it.

Decorating is usually seen as an additive process, which involves bringing paint, paper or some type of cladding/joinery to a room or replacing the existing scheme. However it can also be a subtractive process, for example, stripping paint off joinery. So, when you consider your intended wall scheme, you might think about removing wallpaper entirely in order to paint a wall a flat colour, or even hacking off the plaster to reveal the traditional brickwork that lies underneath.

The colour wheel

The colour wheel is a vital tool in the visualising and selection of colour schemes. It shows how all the colours of the spectrum act in relation to each other, and helps you to decide on contrasting or complementary schemes. The more advanced wheel shows how tints and shades of complementary colours can work together.

How colour works

When a white light source, typically the sun, consisting of different wavelengths passes through a prism, it splits to reveal the visible spectrum. It is often portrayed as a rainbow effect. The visible part of the spectrum runs from violet through to red. Ultra-violet and infra-red, either side of the visible spectrum, cannot be seen by the naked eye (e.g. we cannot see radio waves or X-rays). When the walls of a room receive this white light source, they absorb all the wavelengths except those of their own colour, which they reflect. The human eye responds to these reflected wavelengths and identifies them as colour. So, a wall absorbing all wavelengths except blue, which it reflects into the room, appears to the human eye as a blue wall.

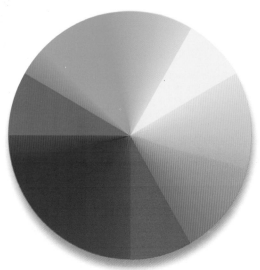

The wheel

The colour wheel is a circle based on the colour spectrum. The primary colours, red, yellow and blue, are opposite the secondary colours, green, violet and orange. Selecting colours that are opposite each other on the wheel, such as red and green, results in optimum colour contrast because you are using complementary colours. Selecting colours next to each other on the wheel, say blue and green, results in a more harmonious scheme because they blend into each other in the spectrum. Blending adjacent colours together creates a third set. The wheel is divided up into twelve segments that can be used to plan all your colour combinations.

Complementary colours

Complementary colours provide optimum contrast if used together in a room. They can make uneasy companions, however, if used in their purest form. All colours can be lightened by adding white to make tints or darkened by adding black to make shades of those colours. A more complex colour wheel shows not only the colours at their most intense, but also the tints and shades in a gradation. This is useful because it shows how the colour contrast is increased further if one of the colours is a tint or a shade.

A good example of this is provided by the use of red and green together in a room. Large expanses of these colours in their purest form cause problems for the eye, because they have a similar tonal value, meaning that they reflect similar amounts of light. If you imagine these two colours side by side in black and white for a moment, then they would appear as almost identical shades of grey – neither colour would advance or recede. Consequently the eye and the brain become confused. All colours from opposite sides of the wheel have a similar effect if they are of the same tonal value. However, using a tint or a shade of one of them can solve this problem. If you look at the second colour wheel you will notice how dark green will effectively partner red or a tint of red. Conversely, dark red combines well with a tint of green.

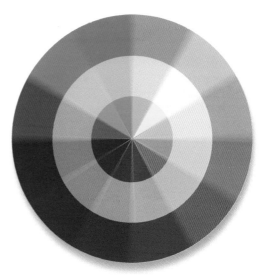

Complementary colours in the colour spectrum include red and green, orange and blue, and yellow and violet.

Being complementary colours, red and green work better in tint and shade combinations than in pure forms. But just looking at nature should be enough to convince us how well they can harmonise: think of pink wild flowers amid a meadow or of red berries against green foliage.

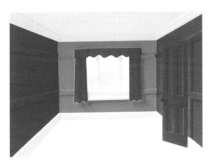

Using a darker shade with a lighter tint of its complementary colour avoids the visual problems caused when similar tonal values reflect similar amounts of light. Left: Red and green in pure form confuse the eye (neither advances or recedes). Right: the pale green recedes, allowing the darker red to appear dominant.

Light, colour and mood

Light and colour both play an important role in the way we feel – you have only to think of how much easier it is to get up on bright sunny days than it is when the skies are grey and overcast. So it is important to take into account both the direction that your room faces and the amount of light it receives when deciding what colours to use there.

Natural light

The amount of light reflected by a colour, and thus the intensity of that colour, depends on the light level that the colour receives from the sun. As available light recedes at the end of the day, colours will appear less and less bright, until finally they have no colour at all. With this in mind, consider carefully the amount of natural light that enters the room during the day, and what effect it will have. All the walls in the room will work in unison,

reflecting the available light received. Lighter coloured walls will reflect more light than dark ones, and will project it further. For example, a bright blue reflected into an otherwise white room will engender a cold blue tint, whereas a bright red will project a warm rose-like tint. When selecting colours, bear in mind that walls reflecting the same colour back and forth will intensify that colour considerably – otherwise you may end up with a much more powerful scheme than you envisaged.

The availability of natural light depends on the season. An important point to consider when choosing a colour scheme is the light level the room receives throughout the year. The more northerly the property location, the more extreme the difference between summer and winter, so a colour scheme reflecting warm summer days also needs to work during long winters under artificial light.

Aspect

Consider the aspect of all the rooms in your intended scheme. Light enters through windows or glass doors, so which direction do they face?

Northern aspect

A room facing north is usually cold, benefiting from direct sunlight only during the height of summer. A warm colour scheme will be essential in this room. Red, yellow and orange will brighten the winter days and reflect what little light there is. Cold blues and greens should be avoided.

Yellow walls will enliven a hallway
that faces north and can be rather
dark for much of the day.

Southern aspect

A room facing south is warm and sunny, with lots of natural light. You will not need to add to the light levels, so use darker colours, particularly green. When these are combined with lighter tints of brown, blue and green a summery feel can be created even during the winter months.

Eastern aspect

The powerful early light of sunrise becomes less potent as midday approaches, with no sunlight shining into the room in the afternoon and evening. A mix of colour works well here. Both cool blues and warm oranges together will offset the midday change in lighting conditions.

particularly in a child's bedroom, where colours that stimulate the mind will not be conducive to sleep.

There is a place in the home for earth tones such as brown and beige, and for neutral greys, especially in a work area such as a home office. Here concentration is needed and bright colours will be distracting.

A basement or garage workshop containing potentially dangerous equipment is another area where attention should be on the task in hand and not on the decor.

Likes and dislikes of colour effects are ultimately subjective. People who share the room space will have individual tastes and preferences, so canvas the thoughts of all the occupants before making a decision on a colour scheme.

In east-facing rooms, such as a nursery that receives light in the early morning, a blue scheme looks good and is also restful on the eye, lulling the child to sleep.

Work areas need to promote concentration, so neutral tones are often chosen in preference to vibrant primary colours.

Western aspect

This room will receive afternoon and evening sun, a sunset if conditions are favourable and dull light in the morning. Bright colours such as reds and yellows will overemphasise the warmth of the afternoon; a more neutral scheme involving greens and greys will work better.

Colour and mood

The psychological effect of certain colours in certain situations should also play a part in your colour scheme selection. Bright colours such as reds excite and invigorate. Cool blues and greens are much more relaxing. Make allowances for this in certain rooms,

Choosing colour schemes

There are various examples of colours and finishes to help you select the right combinations in your colour schemes, from colour paint cards to sample pots of paint. There are also certain visual tricks that it is worth being aware of, as they can help you make the most of your available space and maximise its potential.

Colour cards and sample pots

One of your first steps in selecting colours for your home decorating will be to consult a brand manufacturer's colour chart or card – but this may not be the best way to choose paint. The coloured rectangles on the card, while being as accurate as possible, may not be exact. They are very small and are positioned on a white background, which gives a slightly false impression of brightness. Remember, too, that the light reflected and absorbed by a tiny square or rectangle of colour will differ immeasurably from that reflected or absorbed by an entire wall of that colour. Yellows, for example, will seem much more powerful, because they reflect more light. Blues will appear darker because they absorb more light.

In response, paint-makers have introduced small sample pots of their colours. These provide an ideal way to experiment with your chosen scheme on the wall itself. Small pots of paint, swatches of curtain or furniture fabrics, carpet samples, wood off-cuts and wallcovering samples can all be used together to give a first impression of what the finished room will look like.

After choosing a colour from the card, buy a sample pot. This lets you evaluate a sizeable colour area on the wall you plan to decorate.

Visual trick colour schemes

Combining wall colours of different reflective qualities will allow you to play visual tricks with the size and proportions of the rooms and their interconnecting areas. Paint one wall red, for example, in an otherwise white room and that wall will appear to advance towards you, shortening the room. Conversely, painting one wall in a cool blue in an otherwise darker room will result in that wall receding visually and appearing to lengthen the room. If the ceiling is too high, paint it in a darker colour. You can lower it further still by painting the top part of the wall (above the picture rail, if there is one) the same colour as the ceiling. The opposite effect is achieved by painting a ceiling white to heighten it.

Walls can be made to appear higher if you paint the skirting boards the same colour as the walls. When all the walls and the ceiling are the same light colour, as in monochromatic schemes, the natural angles of the room are much less noticeable. This gives a feeling of increased space, almost as if the room were open plan.

If your rooms are linked by narrow corridors, as in many older properties, light colours will appear to increase the width. A darker colour at the end of a corridor will make it seem shorter. The most dramatic change in small or narrow linking areas occurs when the floorcovering is dark and the ceiling is painted in an advancing colour, which compresses the space vertically. To expand the horizontals, paint the walls white or use a receding colour. Using the same technique in all interlinking areas has a unifying effect throughout the property.

Red is the dominant colour in both these locations.

Left: The end wall advances, making a long corridor appear shorter.

Right: The tint and shade of red act together, appearing to the eye to change the shape of the room.

Receding colours are used visually to create a more spacious feeling.

Left: Subtle pale combinations make a corridor appear larger without appearing to alter any of the dimensions.

Right: However, a receding tint of blue on the far wall appears to lengthen an otherwise darker room.

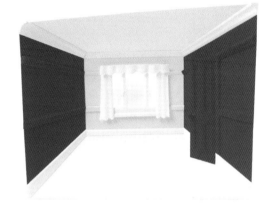

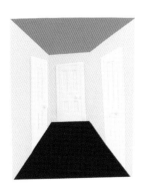

Vertically compressing space by using colour:

Left: In a neutrally coloured corridor, dominant red and orange appear to lift the floor and lower the ceiling, thereby expanding the horizontals.

Right: A ceiling is lowered visually by use of an advancing colour.

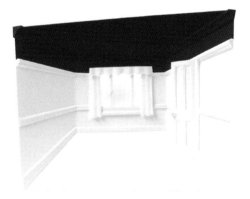

Monochromatic schemes

If you are considering a monochromatic scheme, that is, one colour only, then the colour you choose must form a strong relationship with the fabrics and soft furnishings, the woodwork and the flooring. Neutral greys, soft beiges, off-whites and creams are frequent choices because they offset and therefore enhance patterned fabrics, and look good with natural wood finishes.

The term 'monochromatic' is a misnomer, because patterns on floorcoverings and soft furnishings, wood varnishes and general household pieces have their own colour content.

An easy introduction to such a scheme is to visualize the room and its contents in black and white for a moment. A rough sketch of the room with everything white will allow you to position coloured fabric and carpet swatches, and colour in areas clad in wood, such as the fireplace. Adding a touch of harmonious colour to the previously white scheme is then straightforward.

Below: Colour scheming – sketch your room and its contents in black and white; then make colour substitutions from the chart.

Right: A beige and cream colour scheme works well in many rooms, complementing natural wood and giving an uncluttered look.

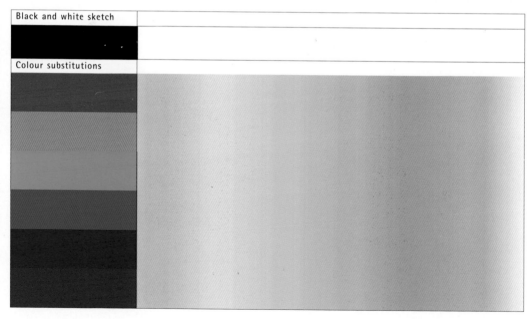

Black and white sketch	
Colour substitutions	

Schemes using contrasting colours, shades and tints are just as easy to approach in this way. A white room with one black wall, or a white-walled room with black skirtings, cornices and picture rails, shows the most extreme contrast achievable. Then, simply substitute your colours. Black may become dark green or mid-blue, and white can be softened into cream or pale yellow. The contrast is retained, but your choice of colours will define how dramatic that contrast is.

Schemes using a combination of colours side by side on the wheel would be represented in a black and white sketch by mid-grey. Colour contrast is not an issue because these are harmonious colours. There is no dividing line between the grey areas, so any two adjacent colours such as red and orange or blue and green can be substituted.

Swatch watch

When working on a room, designers will make up a swatch or sample board, consisting of colours, materials, fabrics, wallpapers and wood off-cuts stuck down onto a card to assist the decision-making process. All colours envisaged in the scheme are side by side on the board, and can be held in front of any of the walls for a suitability match. It is easy to put one together by collecting samples from shops. Use the material or paint you are considering, however. Never substitute a cut-out from a magazine because this involves a different printing process and will not be accurate.

When your board is complete, use it to compare differing available light levels, and note down the changes in colour in bright sunshine, dull, overcast or shadowy conditions and under artificial light. The artificial light should ideally be the lighting system that is going to be used in the room. If it is going to be different, then find the closest match you can.

To assist in planning your room scheme, make up a swatch board of sample colours and materials.

The great divide

A house is divided into many areas, and you may or may not have a preference for a colour linking system, that is to say linking all rooms on one floor by using the same door frame and skirting-board colour. You may wish to keep these natural divisions and, indeed, emphasise them by using different colour schemes. However, one-room dwellings, spaces for both living and working or popular city loft-style apartments are not compartmentalised. Therefore the same contrasting scheme or linking system is advisable throughout. Variations will work, such as substituting a cream finish for white on one wall with the same frame or trim colour, but they must not compromise the integrity of the overall scheme. Attempting too many colour divisions in an area designated as one space works against the original design concept and is doomed to failure. At best it looks fragmented, at worst it offends the eye.

This loft apartment has a pleasing cohesive look and is visually united by its wooden flooring and units, and by the consistent use of black as an accent colour: on the sofa cushions, piano and dining chairs.

PAINTING

O f the hundreds of weekend tasks that DIY enthusiasts take on in their homes, the most common is the simple paint job. A vast selection of paints and finishes is now available for all surfaces, and recent additions to paint-makers' ranges have increased the options considerably. This chapter guides you through the selection of paint, offers advice on paint schemes and shows you how to tackle your first paint job.

Designer's notes

To anyone approaching a makeover for the first time, the vast array of paints must be confusing. The latest paint technology has led to boasts that a professional finish can be attained by a novice. However, it is important to assess modern paints in terms of what they will do, and relate them to older-style paints that may have been used in the house.

Paint types

The paint in your tin will be either water- or solvent-based. Both types are made up of pigment, which provides the colour, and a binder that holds the pigment particles together. This combination in water is generally called *emulsion*. In a spirit-based solvent it is known as oil-based *gloss* or *eggshell*. Decorators have traditionally used water-based emulsions for interior walls and oil-based finishes for woodwork, such as doors and surrounds, because they are harder-wearing. Today's technology allows the manufacturer to offer the choice of water-based gloss or satin paints for woodwork, reducing the drying time considerably.

Traditional descriptions are altering, too. Silk vinyl emulsions are often labelled 'washable' or 'wipeable'. Matt emulsion is referred to as 'non-reflective' – also non-wipeable. Water-based gloss may be 'non-drip, no undercoat needed' or 'one coat only'. Often oil-based gloss is offered as 'liquid gloss', or, implying use by professionals, as 'trade' gloss. Don't be misled by the 'trade' label into thinking that this paint is superior in some way; it isn't.

Traditionally, water-based paints have been applied to interior walls, while oil-based gloss paint has been used on woodwork, but conventions are changing as new materials and finishes are now becoming available.

finish incorporates wood cladding, tiles, or even a powerful wallpaper pattern that is to be retained on some of the walls. Your paint scheme must take into account what the room inherits from its previous life, and combine with existing materials to achieve a matching or contrasting effect.

Old and new together

Retaining parts of someone else's room scheme may seem unappealing at first, but don't dismiss it out of hand. If the room has a particular feature that dominates it, then it may provide a better visual result if you work with it, not against it. If you like a particular characteristic, it makes no sense to remove or disguise it, and it can become the axis for the new scheme. In any combined scheme, remember that decorating can be done wall by wall, slowly

As you contemplate your choice of finish, consider only the durability of water-based versus oil-based paints. Oil-based is tougher, longer-lasting and easier to clean. Water-based paints are easier to use, environmentally friendly and the job is done in a quarter of the time. You will, however, need to repaint much sooner if you use water-based paints.

Choosing appropriate paints

On walls and ceilings, which are particularly large areas to paint, don't consider oil-based finishes unless you intend to apply a special effect such as ragging, in which case eggshell is ideal. Large areas of oil-based paint are unpleasant to apply, environmentally unfriendly and time-consuming to change. Emulsions are designed for the job, but make sure your wall surfaces are suitable first.

Once you have a colour scheme in mind, examine the room. What is the current state of finish? If it is a painted scheme on plaster, lining paper or wallcovering that can be painted, and you are merely altering the colours, your task is straightforward because paint is the major decorating factor. Perhaps the current

building up a new look. It doesn't necessarily have to be drastically altered all at the same time. In the same way that you must consider what effect the floorcovering, carpet or wood floor will have on painted walls, you have to view the walls themselves in relation to each other.

TYPES OF PAINT

Primers/Undercoats	Finishes/Top coats
Knotting solution/Primer	Vinyl matt emulsion
Wood primer	Vinyl silk emulsion
Aluminium wood primer	Eggshell emulsion
Alkali-resisting primer	Gloss emulsion
Penetrating stabilising primer	Gloss
Red oxide primer	Eggshell
Acrylic primer/Undercoat	Smooth masonry paint
Oil/Resin undercoat	Floor/Tile paint
	Ceiling paint
For detailed notes on paint types, see pages 246–247.	Textured paint
	Radiator enamel

Basic skills: guide to paint

There is more to painting than simply choosing your ideal colour. Sound preparation of the surface to be painted is a must, otherwise you risk having to redo it in the not-too-distant future and ending up with a patchy appearance. You also need to know how best to store your paint and use the tools that are vital to the process.

Wooden furniture must be properly prepared before it is painted. It must be sanded or washed down first, and will then require a coat of primer, undercoat and finally a topcoat in your chosen colour.

If you don't want your paint to soak straight into the wall you will need to use either a sealer or a primer before you apply any emulsion. This will stop the paint from being absorbed by the wall.

Before using the 'Paint: Types and Uses' table on pages 246–247 as a guide to paint finishes, consider your surface and what type of preparation, sealing and priming it may require. Emulsion on bare walls needs a sealer to prevent the paint from disappearing into the wall altogether. On old walls you should use a stabilising primer or a diluted mix of PVA. New plaster needs a plaster primer, although a stabiliser will do, but you must ensure that the new plaster is properly dry or you will be sealing in damp.

Before applying paint to either wood panels or wooden cladding, coat the knots in the woodgrain to stop them from seeping resin, which will show through the paint finish. Use knotting primer for this, followed by a primer, an undercoat and lastly a topcoat. Traditionally, primer was an oil-based paint, but acrylic primer and combined primer/undercoat have now gained in popularity due to their ease and speed of use, and also because they are environmentally friendly. The latest technology offers gloss or satin finishes in a 'non-drip' form that requires no undercoat, just a primer.

Paint pots

However good your paint job, accidental chips and scratches can occur, and a supply of retouching paint is always a good idea. A small amount of paint left in a can is best decanted into a suitable jar, with a lid, for storage. The more paint there is in the jar, the less air there is, and less chance of

Brushes, rollers and paint: the essential components.

a skin forming on the top.
Avoid getting paint around the
rim of the jar or inside its lid, otherwise
opening it some time later will be tricky. And don't forget
to label the jar.

A large volume of paint can remain in the original can. Many
tradespeople then store this upside down. If you do so, make sure
that the lid is hammered down securely or it may leak out. You
may prefer simply to invert the can for a few minutes in order to
allow the contents to run around the lid seal, and then to store it
the correct way up.

*Colour paint charts
are useful, but sample pots
will be more accurate.*

*Tongue-and-groove cladding might
be hiding a wealth of problems in the
walls behind, and it may be better*
*to leave it in place and repaint it,
rather than rip it off and have to
sort out the underlying problem.*

Tools and equipment

As with all tools of the trade, investing in cheap, badly made decorating equipment is a recipe for failure. There is nothing quite as expensive as trying to save money. An inferior tool can ruin a job or a finish by underperforming at a crucial stage, so invest wisely. Here is a selection to start off your essential toolkit for painting.

A palette knife, a filling knife and a scraper.

Tools and equipment

For walls and ceilings you will need a set of tools to take off the existing finish, and another set to put on the new scheme. Before you begin, always remember to protect the floor and furniture by covering them with large dust sheets.

Sugar soap and glasspaper

If you are repainting a papered wall, you only need to ensure that it is clean; household liquid soap applied with a soft cloth will remove grease. Make sure the wall is dry before you start painting. Repainting an emulsion on a masonry or plaster wall is easier if the wall surface is 'keyed' to receive the paint, so lightly abrade the surface with medium, followed by fine glasspaper. Before painting over a gloss, satin or matt oil-based surface, with either oil-, or water-based paint, use flexible wet-and-dry paper to remove the surface 'sheen'. Soak medium and fine-grade glasspaper in a bucket of hot water with sugar soap, an all-purpose cleaner. Abrade the surface as before, using lots of water. Rinse the surface and dry it.

Masking tape has numerous uses.

Brushes, pads and rollers

Good-quality paint brushes will apply paint evenly, and will not shed bristles all over the wall. Four sizes – 12mm/½in, 25mm/1in, 38mm/1½in and 50mm/2in – should suffice for any standard

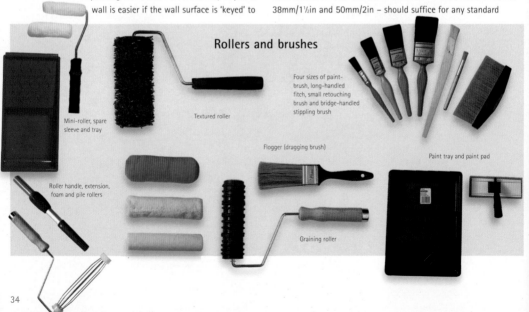

Rollers and brushes

Mini-roller, spare sleeve and tray

Textured roller

Four sizes of paint-brush, long-handled fitch, small retouching brush and bridge-handled stippling brush

Roller handle, extension, foam and pile rollers

Flogger (dragging brush)

Graining roller

Paint tray and paint pad

A heat gun with various attachments is useful for softening the paint on wooden surfaces so that it can be scraped off.

painting job. Larger sizes up to 150mm/6in are available, but they may make your hand and arm ache. For larger areas use a paint pad or roller. Always decant the paint into a kettle or bucket. Never paint straight from the can. The pad and roller will have their own loading containers, and as an option solid emulsion has its own tray.

The roller may be foam or fibre. Fibre rollers are available with different pile lengths. The more uneven the surface, the longer the pile you will need. For large areas use rollers, and to reach small awkward places use radiator rollers.

Other equipment

You can reach high ceilings by using an extension pole; however, high corners will have to be done with a brush. It is very important to make sure you are standing on a stable stepladder. An integral top platform is useful for placing your brush and paint kettle. Masking tape and paint masks can be used to protect adjacent areas of colour. If you do overrun, use a soft, damp cloth.

Maintenance

As soon as the job is done, clean the brushes, rollers and containers. Oil-based paints can be removed with white spirit, turpentine substitute or a brand-name brush cleaner and restorer. Water-based paint can be cleaned off in hot water and soap. After brushing out excess paint on old newspaper, work the cleaning solution well into the brush, as far up as the handle. Remove partly dried paint with an old comb. Rinse the brush and partly dry it with a soft cloth.

Never leave your brushes to soak overnight, because they will end up with a 'permanent wave' that will make accurate cutting-in of colours impossible. To remove excess paint from rollers and pads, simply wash them out in their respective trays. Squeeze the roller and then hang it up to dry; it contains metal parts, and rust will contaminate your next paint load if you do not dry the roller thoroughly.

Preparation materials

Butane gas torch

Bucket, soft cloth and sponge

Paint shield

White spirit and soft cloths

Dust sheet

Assorted fillers

Paint strainer

Paint

Paint remover, brush and wire wool

Shave hooks

General preparation

The finished job is only as good as your preparation. Walls and ceilings need very careful assessment before you reach for the roller and prise open the paint pot. They may need to have cracks repaired, and will need to be washed down (and possibly 'keyed') before you can apply emulsion or oil-based paint.

The qualities of paint

A thick coat of paint cannot be used to disguise a bad wall. Paint contains a binder, and the binder's job is to ensure that the coloured particles (pigment) dry together on the wall as a continuous protective film, on top of, but not hiding, any bumps, cracks or imperfections. Even thickening agents used in non-drip paints will not cause jelly-like applications to dry out any other way than flat on the wall. It is usually accepted that darker, glossier, more reflective colours show up imperfections more than pale, subtle tones, but this is not a recommended selection criterion. All flat areas of colour will emphasise wall damage, and the only proper course of action is to eradicate the problem during preparation.

Repairing damaged walls

Don't be unduly worried, however, if your walls are not in pristine condition. Cracks and crevices in plaster are commonplace. New plaster frequently develops hairline cracks as it dries out, often where large areas meet at an angle, such as a wall and ceiling. A slight settling of the building on its foundations, or a small amount of subsidence, will result in fairly obvious cracks appearing in the plasterwork on the walls and ceilings. Check all around the room thoroughly if this is the case. You may find other evidence of settling, where skirting boards meet the walls, and around door frame mouldings.

    All these cracks can be easily made good, using a decorator's pack of all-purpose filler, which comes in white powder form to be mixed with water. Cracks caused by movement that is likely to recur, where the stair skirting joins the wall in the stairwell, for instance, should be repaired with a flexible filler. These fillers are available pre-mixed in cartridges, are usually applied by means of a simple-to-use cartridge gun, and have a nozzle that can be cut to fill a specific width.

Holding the cartridge gun at an angle to the wall, squeeze the filler into the crack, before smoothing it out with your finger or a filling knife. Once dried, the filler can be sanded down flush with the wall.

Use a shave hook to rake out any loose material and dirt in the crack, and to undercut it slightly to give the filler a good grip. Then press the filler firmly into the crack using a filling knife.

If the walls have an oil-based paint finish, eggshell or flat oil, then in addition to washing them down, you will need to provide a 'key' for the new paint finish to adhere to. Lightly abrade the surface using abrasive paper wrapped around a sanding block.

Use medium paper for gloss and fine paper for eggshell. Alternatively, you can combine both operations by keying the surface while it is wet, using flexible wet-and-dry paper. Soak the paper in a bucket of soap and hot water for at least five minutes, while pre-washing the wall using a sponge. Using plenty of water, lightly abrade the wall surface to remove the sheen. Finally, wash down the wall with clean water.

Preparing paint

Always read the manufacturer's instructions, and familiarise yourself with the information on the side of the can. Make sure the top of the paint can is clean before you open it, otherwise any dirt there may fall into the paint. Insert a screwdriver blade horizontally under the lip of the can and turn it slowly until it is vertical, repeating further around the rim to prise off the lid. This minimises damage to the lip, and makes re-sealing easier. If the can is half-empty, carefully remove any top skin and stir the paint. Any remaining tiny pieces of skin or debris must then be removed by straining the paint. You can do this by decanting it into a paint kettle or bucket through a piece of stretched stocking.

Overpainting

Overpainting wall areas with emulsion, whether in the same colour or not, is a common task in the home. Provided your walls are sound, you only need to ensure that they are clean and free from contamination by dust, dirt and grease. Usually, household liquid soap, hot water and a sponge will do the job. However, if a wall or ceiling has an unsightly stain caused by a leaking roof or upstairs appliance, you must seal it or it will quickly show through the new paint finish. The easiest way is to paint over the stain with oil-based gloss or eggshell in an appropriate colour, allow it to dry and then apply the emulsion. Alternatively, stain sealers are available in spraycan form.

Sand an oil-based surface lightly with abrasive paper to provide a 'key' for the paint to adhere to.

Then wash the wall down using hot water, liquid soap and a soft sponge to remove any excess dirt.

Remove the lid of the can using a screwdriver. Old paint may need to be strained into a kettle or bucket.

37

Abrasives

The generic term 'sanding down', referring to surface abrading as a vitally important part of decorating preparation, is still in common use, even though 'sandpaper' as such has not been commercially produced for many years. The modern equivalent – glasspaper – and all other suitable abrasives are in stock at your local DIY store and are outlined here.

Never cut abrasive paper with blade or scissors. Fold a sheet into quarters and tear it along the edge of the table.

Preparing the ground

Quality preparation is the key to a quality result, and a smooth surface is essential for a paint or varnish finish. This means rubbing down with the correct abrasive, because using the right materials speeds up the laborious task and gives the best result. Some surfaces must be rubbed down dry (bare woods, surfaces containing water-based fillers), some wet (gloss paint that is being recoated), and some, such as floorboards, are suitable for both applications. Common sense and personal preference should also play a part in your decision. Wet abrading of water-soluble materials, including fillers, often leads to little more than a paste-like mess; dry rubbing of dirty, greasy surfaces will clog the abrasive in no time, be ineffective and expensive because the paper cannot be re-used.

Wet or dry?

Traditionally, rubbing down was a dry process, starting with coarser grades and finishing with finer ones, the finest grade of all often being referred to as 'flour' paper. With the legislation of the Lead Paint Act (1926) as a spur, whereby the dry abrading of lead-based paint was made illegal, manufacturers introduced a waterproof paper so that a lubricant could be used with the abrasive. Initially not a popular choice, because of its cost, it was used in coach finishing and other high-quality work, and general decorating workers continued to dry rub. Today, silicon carbide used with a lubricant is recognised as a real alternative to dry papers. It is faster and more efficient because of its cutting action, lasts longer, doesn't clog easily, and can be rinsed clean in a bucket on site. This offsets its higher cost (it is four times the price of glasspaper).

Green aluminium oxide is generally suitable for heavy-duty and machine use.

Left: Cloth sanding belts are available for all belt sanding machines, DIY and heavy-duty machines alike. The abrasive is aluminium oxide; the belt is full resin cloth, flush joined at a 45 degree angle to give maximum life.

Right: Yellow aluminium oxide sheets (here torn from a standard 115mm roll) are suitable for hand and block use. You can clearly see the difference in grit sizes.

Abrasive sheets

Conventional glasspaper: coarse, medium and fine grades in standard sized sheets.

Waterproof, latex-backed synthetic silicon carbide, commonly called wet and dry paper.

Aluminium oxide

This is used dry, available in sheets, 280mm x 230mm, or in rolls 115mm wide and sold by the roll or in metre lengths cut from a roll or in precut sizes ready-made for machine sanders. Graded in grit sizes, 40 grit (coarse) to 240 (very fine). Electro-bonded, with a grit size giving a more controlled cut, it is frequently used instead of glasspaper in the same type of application because of its longer life.

Silicon carbide (wet or dry paper)

This can be used dry or lubricated; if regularly rinsed in the wet application it is long lasting. Available in sheets 280mm x 230mm, graded 100 (coarse) to 1200 (very fine), but frequently found in DIY stores as a 'decorator's pack' containing a couple of sheets of coarse, medium and fine flexible papers. Tough, flexible and long lasting when lubricated, it should be a first choice for painted surfaces.

Steel wool

This can be used either dry or lubricated, available as boxed rolls about 70mm wide, or as pads. Graded from 5 (coarse) to 0000 (very fine), often packed as a kit containing coarse, medium and fine pads. Can be used as a cleaner or degreaser on flooring to scour wood following the use of water-washable paint remover, or to apply waxes to prepared surfaces. Always wear gloves when using this material.

Today's cutting edge

The home decorator is able to make the same choices in buying and using as the working professional:

Conventional glasspaper

This is used dry, available in sheets 280mm x 230mm, graded 3 (coarse) to 00 (very fine) or simply labelled coarse, medium and fine, depending on the manufacturer, suitable for hand or machine use. Cheap but clogs very easily and selection of inappropriate grades can result in scratching of the workpiece.

A roll of steel wool. Always wear gloves when you handle this product and, as with other abrasives, wear a dust mask.

Rubbing blocks

Use an abrasive with a sanding block to maintain an edge on the corners of the work. Always sand in the direction of the grain, particularly if you intend to apply a varnished finish, because cross-grain scratching will show up badly.

How to paint

It might appear that painting is a perfectly straightforward procedure, but there are numerous tips – on the selection of your brush, roller, pad or aerosol – that can make the task much easier. If you know how to apply the paint properly and what sort of stroke to use, the result will be much more pleasing.

Using a brush

Always select a brush of a suitable size for the job and make sure that it is clean. Ensure that the bristles are in good condition by working the brush up and down on a dry surface. This will cause any dust and defective or loose bristles to fall out.

For very small wall areas, for blending in and for finished detail work on roller painted walls, use a small brush, 38mm/1½in or 50mm/2in size. Hold it between your thumb and fingers on the metal casing, or ferrule, which encases the bristles.

Larger brushes, although quicker initially, will soon become tiring and difficult to control, and are no substitute for a roller. However, if you decide the large 150mm/6in brush is for you, then you will find it easier if you hold it by the handle.

If emulsioned surfaces, the easiest to paint, do not dry out uniformly flat, simply apply a second coat. Oil-based finishes must not dry out at the edges before the entire surface is finished, or the brush strokes will be obvious, so blend in the wet edges continuously as you move from side to side across the surface. Frequent changing of the direction of the brush stroke will result in a more even distribution of paint.

Using a roller

A paint roller is the most time-efficient way of applying a water-based finish to a large area. The only shortcoming is that you cannot butt up to other colour surfaces or into corners, and you will need a small brush to complete the job. Oil-based paints are equally easy to apply, but they will retain some of the texture of the roller in the finish, whereas emulsions all dry flat. If an absolutely dead flat finish is needed in an oil base, use a brush.

- Select a suitable roller sleeve for your wall, remembering that the smoother the surface, the shorter the pile required.
- Pour the paint of your choice into the reservoir of the paint tray, level with the ribbed rolling area.

For maximum control of a small or medium-sized brush, hold it by the ferrule, or metal casing, dip it into the paint to one-third of the bristle depth and use long, sweeping strokes to apply the paint.

Roll out excess paint on the ribbed area of the paint tray before applying a roller to a wall.

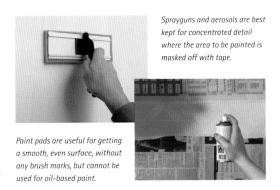

Sprayguns and aerosols are best kept for concentrated detail where the area to be painted is masked off with tape.

Paint pads are useful for getting a smooth, even surface, without any brush marks, but cannot be used for oil-based paint.

- Immerse the roller sleeve in the reservoir, then roll it out gently on the ribbed area to ensure an even distribution of paint.
- Apply the roller to the wall using even pressure throughout, in vertical overlapping strokes.
- Finish off by changing to horizontal strokes, which will ensure an even coverage.
- Don't try to cover too big an area each time you load the roller. You may find it helpful if you visualize your wall broken down into imaginary squares and then fill one at a time.

If paint spatters onto adjacent surfaces as you roll out the paint, it's not because the roller is overloaded, it's because you are driving it too fast. This is always a temptation, particularly when using an extension pole to paint a ceiling. So, slow down and remember that paint splashes from above can land on your head. Always wear eye protection.

Using paint pads

Paint pads come in a variety of sizes and the larger ones can be used with an extension pole to reach ceilings. Edging pads are available to cut into corners and angles. Pads come with their own paint tray and special loading roller. Simply pour in your paint, and load the pad by running it back and forth across the ribbed cylindrical loader. Paint in vertical overlapping strokes to achieve a smooth even coat. While paint pads are simplicity itself, bear in mind that they carry less paint per loading than a brush or a roller, so an extra coat is likely to be required.

Aerosols and sprayguns

Universally available in solvent or water-based form, aerosols are very useful for spraying small areas as special-effect patterns on a plain painted wall, such as coloured stripes or squares. They are expensive, however, and require accurate and detailed masking. They are not suitable for spray painting an entire room. For this you would need to hire an electric airless spraygun with a changeable paint reservoir from a local hire centre or builders' merchant. These guns have a viscosity measuring cup to ensure that the paint for the reservoir has been thinned down correctly. Useful accessories include a flexible extension nozzle, for spraying a ceiling, and more powerful models have a fine adjustment control for flexibility of spray volume. It may look simple in the hands of an expert, but unless you are experienced in the use of guns, you are advised to choose another application method.

A roller on an extension pole is ideal for painting ceilings, although you will need to use a brush to fill in corners.

TOP TIP

Using your second finger as a pressure guide on either the handle or ferrule of a brush can quickly result in a blister, particularly if you have soft hands. An astutely positioned sticking plaster, or even a length of masking tape wound around the finger, will protect against rubbing. Try to keep the brush handle and ferrule free of sticky, semi-dry paint or varnish at all times, because this exacerbates the problem.

Special effects: glazes

Glazes are semi-transparent paints that allow the underlying base colour to show through. They have become increasingly popular because they can be used to create a whole range of different effects and are relatively easy to use. With a little practice, you will be able to emulate the look that a professional painter can achieve.

Decorative finishes for walls, from simple rag-rolling to more complex crackle glazing, can be undertaken successfully on correctly prepared wall surfaces. It is always a good idea to experiment on a spare piece of board first. It's a lot easier to throw out a scrap piece of board if you don't like the colour or the effect, than to re-do an entire wall or room.

Preparation

Whether your intended finish is based on oil or water, a correctly prepared surface is essential. Since several popular effects are common to both oil and water bases, you do have a choice. However, oils are easier to work with because they dry more slowly and are much more resilient. Water bases dry quickly, which is helpful only if you are attempting a multi-layered build-up of colours. To achieve the same longevity as oils, a water-based surface needs several coats of varnish.

Rectify any wall defects, cracks, crevices and holes, as you would for a straight emulsion roller job. For an oil-based finish on bare plaster, prime the surface with all-purpose oil-based primer-sealer. For water-based finishes you can use water-based primers or PVA thinned with water. Sand the surface of previously painted plaster walls to provide the necessary 'key', using a medium-grit abrasive paper. Now apply the underlying coats

The walls in this sitting room have been painted porcelain blue with a white glaze swirled in.

Apply your base coat to the wall in the normal manner, using long sweeping strokes.

Abrade the surface of the wall between coats with fine grade glass paper.

Blend a little colour with turpentine and mix it into the glaze, avoiding lumps of colour.

that will partly show through your glaze. One or two coats of oil-based eggshell will suffice for oil finishes; one or two coats of water-based undercoat or emulsion for water-based finishes. If you decide to add a second coat, lightly abrade the surface of the first using a fine grade of abrasive paper, to remove any irregularities.

Choosing and making glazes

Most finishes require oil-based glazes. A slow drying time allows you to handle the medium easily, even when attempting more ambitious effects. Water-based glazes are thinner and dry very quickly. Colourwashing and sponging techniques aside, they are unsuitable for most finishes. Water-based glazes are simply made up from coloured acrylics thinned with water, or a water-based emulsion glaze, often with the addition of white emulsion to tint the colour. Oil-based glazes consist of scumble glaze, available from good paint retailers, which can be diluted with a mixture of linseed oil and white spirit, or with turpentine. In both cases more scumble in the mix slows down the drying process, and allows more time for playing with the effects.

Start with a basic ratio of 50:50 if you are mixing scumble glaze with turpentine, adding more turps to thin down the mix, and the finished glaze, if preferred. When linseed oil and white spirit are used instead of turpentine, more

TOP TIP

Photographs in magazines and books may appear to show exactly the effect that you want, but bear in mind that these are reproduced by a four-colour process that is not necessarily an exact colour match, particularly where metallics are concerned.

white spirit will thin the glaze and shorten the drying time. Increasing the amount of linseed oil will result in a smoother, oilier finish. The exact proportions are a matter of personal preference, and some experimentation may be useful.

If you are happy with the consistency of the glaze, add the colour of your choice, a little at a time. Any oil-based colour can be used, but remember to mix specialist artists' oil paints carefully with a small amount of glaze to start with. This will show you whether the colour is what you expect, and will prevent the mix from being lumpy.

A selection of oil-based glazes showing the mixed-up version and the combed out glaze.

Sponging and colourwashing

Two of the simplest, and most widely used, paint effects are sponging and colourwashing. Both of these broken-colour effects work over the underlying base coat that has been applied to the wall, although sponging involves dabbing on additional colour, whereas colourwashing creates effects and texture in a coloured glaze.

Apply the larger sponge lightly to the wall, trying not to make the resulting pattern look too regular.

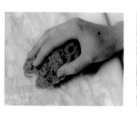

Reload the sponge as necessary, changing its position and adding more colour in some areas.

When the first colour is dry, dab on the second colour with the smaller sponge until the effect looks right.

Colourwashing

Colourwashing, also water-based, is similar in principle to waxed textured finishes. You can use this technique to create a rustic effect, with subtle colour on a roughened surface. Similarities end here, though, because the wall must be sealed with two coats of emulsion as a base. Then the watered-down colours are brushed on, before being worked into the wall with a dry brush. Ageing and distressing techniques can be applied if desired, using watery white to achieve a dusty, chalky feel. If similar colours are used on textured walls, contrasting colours used on smooth, flat surfaces give an entirely different result with almost the same technique. Emulsion the wall as before, brush on the coloured glaze, and then use a very wide, dry brush to create long, sweeping strokes in a haphazard manner. The base coat underneath will show through.

Sponging

Sponging is a very simple paint finish and the variations open to you with this technique are endless. Applied on a plaster, lined or papered wall it should be water-based, but if you try sponging on a wood-panelled or cladded wall use an oil base, such as eggshell, because it will last longer. You will need natural or marine sponges for this technique. Select a large one that is easy to hold, and a smaller example in another shape to put on a second colour or add patches of different colour intensity. Pour your coloured emulsion into a small tray or kettle, and partially immerse the sponge. Dab it onto a sheet of paper to remove any excess and to check the effect. If you are completely satisfied, dab the sponge onto the wall base colour. Vary the angle and try to avoid making it look too uniform. When it is dry add a second colour with the other sponge.

Apply a base coat to the wall in the standard manner, using long, sweeping strokes.

Add a liberal coat of coloured glaze. The best effects will be created by using a contrasting colour.

Using a dry, wide softening brush, work over the glaze in a random direction, using long strokes.

Stippling and rag-rolling

Two additional techniques are stippling and rag-rolling. Stippling with a brush is a one-off finish, which creates a pleasingly mottled appearance on a wall. Rag-rolling, which is also known simply as 'ragging', can be built up in layers, provided that each layer is left to dry completely before the next one is added.

Brush the glaze onto the underlying base coat. The stippling action will remove any brush marks that show.

Hold the stippling brush at right angles to the wall and stab briskly at the surface.

Two-colour finishes

Both of these techniques produce a two-colour finish and are best used with oil-based glazes. Both require similar wall surfaces and give a pleasingly subtle result. Two coats of eggshell are required as a base colour in both cases.

Stippling

To achieve the best finish, stippling needs an even glaze on the base coat, because the aim is to remove all brush marks from the surface. A special stippling brush is best purchased specifically for this task, although you can experiment with any large, reasonably stiff brush.

The object of stippling is to hit the painted wall surface with the end of the bristles. The bristles must be reasonably dry, however, or you will simply put glaze back onto the surface, so unload your brush regularly by stippling onto a clean rag.

Stippling gives a rich, powerful finish. It is ideal for emphasising bright, strong colours, so choose your combinations bearing this in mind. It needs to be done relatively quickly, so it is best to have someone else help you.

Rag-rolling

Ragging involves dabbing a dry, crumpled-up ball of cloth onto a glaze coat, to remove parts of it before it dries. As you roll the rag across the glazed surface, irregular patterns will be created. A design can be created using a variety of contrasting materials. Softer or harsher patterns can be made, resulting in quite different visual effects, depending on the fibres in the cloth.

Often these two techniques are combined, with a surface that has been earmarked for ragging being stippled first in order to remove all brushmarks.

Make sure you have plenty of rags and keep turning each rag to expose a clean surface as you work. When a rag becomes clogged with glaze, replace it. Work on small areas at a time, otherwise the glaze may become too dry.

Brush the glaze over the base coat in a random manner, so that some of the base shows through.

Using a crumpled cloth, dab at the wall to remove some of the glaze while it is still wet.

Vary the direction and change the rag as necessary, so that you end up with an irregular pattern.

Woodgraining and dragging

These techniques are variations on the same theme; woodgraining is merely an extension and amplification of dragging. However, dragging will show up any imperfections in the wall, so it is best kept for surfaces that are perfectly smooth. Woodgraining effects can look stunning in the right situation and will add interest to an otherwise plain interior.

Both of these techniques involve pulling or dragging a dry brush through an oil-based glaze to create irregular linear patterns. Skilled decorators can achieve imitation wood finishes in this way, by raking long, narrow strokes with special straight-haired brushes called floggers. You can use any dry brush, however, and many irregular patterns and line widths can be achieved, depending on the condition and age of your brush.

To woodgrain, apply glaze generously over the base coat, working parallel to the grain on wooden surfaces.

Dragging through a wall glaze using a fine, soft brush results in a subtle fine-line finish. Adding a graining-comb finish to distort and offset these lines can give the appearance of exotic wood. This technique works well on furniture and wood panels.

A woodgrained blue wall with stencilling applied to the beams is offset by the simple table and ceiling in this dining room. Woodgraining is often most effective when done on just one wall.

Using a dry flogger, drag a series of parallel lines in the glaze to create the pattern of the grain.

Use a graining comb to manipulate the parallel lines and make interesting patterns.

To drag a surface, once you have applied the glaze over the base coat, draw a dry flogger over it, working from the top to about halfway down.

Then drag the brush upwards from the floor, meeting at different points along the wall. Don't worry if the lines are not perfectly straight.

Dragging

Dragging is, in reality, the first part of woodgraining, but if you select an entire wall for this effect, only drag half the wall at a time – otherwise the brush will overload because it picks up too much glaze from the surface. Always keep the brush as dry as possible – you may find this easier if you drag the second half of the wall upwards from the floor, meeting in the middle. Lessen the pressure as you move through the join, and don't meet in exactly the same place as you move along the wall. Try to vary this by 30cm/12in or so.

Other effects

A variety of effects involving oil-glaze graining and dragging can be achieved using manufacturers' paint-effect kits, consisting of base coat, top coat and effect applicators. For example, you can create your own blue-jeans wall finish in this way. A denim-blue top coat is rollered over a dry, very pale blue base, and then dragged with a long-haired flogger brush, which can be used to create a denim jeans-effect, from ceiling and floor to the middle of the wall. Follow the kit instructions because a protective final coat may be needed.

On modern, smooth walls, a floor-to-ceiling denim effect adds a cool, unusual feel. Or, if you prefer, the traditional blues can be replaced by other colour combinations.

Woodgraining

Using the woodgraining technique, you can make your surface look like the raised grain on planed timbers. Select your eggshell base coat carefully, for example, using a mid-yellow base showing through an orange glaze to imitate pine. Other combinations will give an appearance similar to other types of wood. Use a 50:50 mix in your chosen oil-based glaze and brush it on evenly. Any brush marks that are left visible must run in the final direction of the grain.

When you are satisfied with the even colour, drag a dry brush through the glaze, leaving veins of base colour exposed. The width of the grain effect will depend on the age and condition of the brush. Rubber rockers and graining combs can be used to imitate the peculiarities of a natural timber surface, such as the fibres, grain spirals, bands of paler tissue and so on.

To create a denim effect, first paint the wall surface with a very pale blue base coat.

Then paint the surface with a denim blue, which should contrast well with the underlying colour.

Drag a long-haired flogger over the wall from top to middle and bottom to middle to create the look.

Spattering

Spatter effects, sometimes called speckling, are achieved professionally by using a spraygun fitted with a special decorators' spray head at very low pressure. The colour is not atomised and hits the wall as a series of tiny splashes. You can imitate this finish by flicking single colours onto a surface with a brush, slowly building up the overall colour.

Making a splash

For spattering you can use water- or oil-based paint. Oil will last longer, but a sealer can always be applied to emulsioned surfaces. Whichever you use, you need to carefully mask and protect the adjoining surfaces. By applying small splashes of red, yellow and bright blue from separate cans in a dense pattern, you can make a wall look dark brown; only close inspection will reveal the secret.

Method

The technique consists of sharply tapping a paint-laden brush against an offcut of wood, directly in front of the wall. The size of the splashes will vary, depending on how near you are to the wall, and the quantity of paint on the brush. You can experiment on a large piece of scrap card to get a feel for the technique.

Flick bright yellow paint onto a white base, carefully building up an intense pattern of irregular splashes. Clean the brush and repeat with bright red, and then bright blue. Although the paint on the wall is in reality a kaleidoscope of coloured dots of varying shapes and sizes, viewed from the other side of the room it will appear to be dark brown. This build-up of colour is similar to that in a printing process, and you can try out different combinations.

Begin spattering by tapping the brush against a piece of wood to flick the paint onto the wall.

Spattering can be applied to all kinds of surfaces, not just walls. Here it has been applied in a highly expressive way to a radiator. Remember to use heat-resistant paint suitable for this purpose.

Start adding the second colour, in this case red, in the same manner, building up an even coverage.

Finish off with a spattering of blue. When viewed from a distance, the finish will appear as a brown.

Spatter blue on a yellow base to make green. Try a black and white scheme using black and grey splashes to achieve a dull finish, and then liven it by adding white. If the combined effect is deemed unsatisfactory, you always have the option of adding another colour. You can do this without waiting for the others to dry.

This technique is somewhat haphazard, the size and shape of the spatter effect being difficult to control. Experimentation with scrap board or card is essential. If you find it very difficult, try dragging an old blunt knife along the bristle tips of a large wall brush. Hold the brush bristles down, and run the knife towards you. As the bristles spring back, paint is flicked onto the near surface.

Do not confuse this technique with multi-colour finishes. These are special trade paints that achieve a spattered effect in one coat. Such industrial paints have pigment particles that remain permanently in suspension. They don't bind in the usual way, and as a result must be sprayed conventionally. Airless and hot sprays are unsuitable methods of application; neither are brush and roller an option. This a special purpose finish which is best left in the hands of professionals.

You can create a soft focus effect in your home by using the spattering technique.

Depending on the colour scheme you select, the effect can be cool or, as shown here, warm.

Marble finishes

Marbled paint effects are time-consuming and complicated to apply. However, careful consideration of the chosen surface, a suitable piece of marble, or picture, that can be used as reference, attention to detail and sympathetic use of colour in the rest of the room can transform any area in an attractive fashion.

Bathrooms and shower areas

Bathrooms and shower areas will benefit from a marble makeover, but be selective and don't overdo this effect. Smaller wall areas, bath panels, shower sides and other places where tiles might be found are all suitable targets for experimentation. If you attempt to recreate the ultimate Roman bathing room, however, you may find the overall scheme a little intimidating.

Marbling is ideal for bathrooms, giving a feeling of opulence. With practice, you should be able to achieve very realistic results. Don't overdo it, though, as the effect can be overpowering.

Method

To begin, find a piece of marble to copy. A tile, for instance, in the appropriate colours, is a good starting point. If you intend to marble a bathroom wall, first ensure it is completely flat and in prime condition. Make good any defects, and coat the wall with oil-based eggshell. Now brush on a contrasting glaze, using equal portions of scumble and turpentine mixed with the artists' oil colour that matches your scheme. You need only a thin coat, then add more or a different artists' colour to the glaze. Apply this to selected parts of the wall, creating random areas of different colour strengths. Blend these areas together by dabbing lightly with a soft cloth or natural sponge, or by stippling the surface. As this removes the glaze, it creates lighter tones in part. To

With care, you can copy the veins and colours of marble in paint.

create the marble veins in contrasting colour glazes, use a small artists' brush and vary the width, sharpness and direction of the veins across the wall. Complete the wall by adding more oil glaze to some of the veins, stipple more colour onto selected areas and lighten others until you are happy with the result. Leave your wall to dry completely, then apply at least two coats of clear oil-based varnish in satin or gloss, depending on whether you prefer a polished appearance or not.

Begin by painting the wall with an oil-based eggshell paint and allow it to dry.

Working on a manageable area at a time, brush on the coloured turpentine and scumble glaze.

After adding a third colour, dab a cloth into the glaze to blend the colours together.

Paint in the veins with a small brush. Vary their thickness and direction as in real marble.

Add more glaze as necessary until you are happy with the result. When dry, add a clear varnish.

Alternatives

As an alternative to an overall varnished finish, if you find a panelled pattern that suits the room, it is relatively simple to transfer the design to your finished marble effect wall using masking tape to define the panel shapes. Adding different colour tints to the satin or gloss varnish will alter or enhance the colours of panels making up a geometric shape. Several coats of tinted varnishes can be applied to the same areas, building up the depth of the design. Allow your geometric panel design to dry and finish as before with two coats of clear varnish. As an alternative to gloss, satin coat can be polished to achieve a sheened finish.

Varnish over paint

Building up a depth of finish, using several layers of varnish to give a 'coach' finish on top of the colour-tinted glazes and varnishes, protecting the geometric patterns created, is a technique not confined to marbling. Any wall finish can be overvarnished, thereby creating apparent depths in the finish. It is essential that the wall is in good condition.

- Prime the surface, roller on a flat colour of your choice and allow it to dry. Divide your wall into geometric areas, stripes or hoops of horizontal stripes, or be more adventurous with squares or different sizes of interconnecting rectangles. Brush on clear gloss varnish over the shapes you want to define.

- Use one coat for some, and two or three for others so that you build up a pattern of definition. Special paint finishes can work well if they are accentuated in this way.

- You could try using a metallic paint, such as copper, but remember to stir the paint throughout the operation. Varnish on top adds either a slight sheen or a spectacular mirror effect, depending on the number of coats you apply.

Varnished finishes have been popular throughout history, as evidenced by this beautiful lacquered cabinet from China.

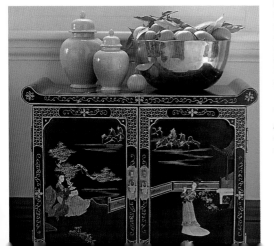

Stamping and stencilling

Both these techniques are perfect for adding a unique character to your decorative scheme, an individual touch that defines the room as yours and yours alone. Symbols, simple cut-outs, silhouettes, abstract shapes and caricatures can all be stamped or stencilled as a painted finish, in a continuation of the colour scheme or as a complete contrast.

You can buy ready-made stamps for creating decorative patterns.

Stamping

Stamping involves rolling colour onto an individual raised surface, a stamp, then offsetting the colour onto a wall, forming a deliberate pattern or random marks. This technique is best suited to decorative borders and for framing larger areas of colour.

Ready-made stamps, in a variety of designs, are widely available from art suppliers and decorating stores, and generally come in kit form with a selection of paints and a small applicator roller. You can, of course, make your own stamp, drawing a design or image onto foam rubber about 5cm/2in thick, and cutting around the external shape. The internal details can then be cut out and removed to a depth of 25mm/1in with a craft knife. Try using your design to form a two-colour creative border; use strips of tape to mask the edge of a wall stripe, and paint the stripe in a complementary colour to the rest of the wall. Remove the masking tape when the paint is dry. Roll the second colour of your choice onto your stamp, and gently press it onto the wall stripe at regular and equal intervals, starting in the middle.

Emulsion is the best paint for stamping. Remember to roll colour onto your stamp evenly, and try a test-pressing first to remove excess paint. Never dip the stamp directly into the paint.

Stencilling

Stencils, like stamps, are usually associated with edgings and borders, such as dados, or smaller decorative panels, but you could use this versatile technique over an entire wall.

You can stencil by brush or sponge, applying paints or crayons onto a surface, through shaped areas cut into a mask that removes areas of background, onto sections defined by masking tapes, or through holes in paper and card. Anything that partially masks your working surface can be referred to as a stencil.

Commercial stencils are available from artists' suppliers, either in a transparent plastic film or flexible waxed card. Waxed card is easier to cut and cheaper. Card is opaque, so consider film if your design is complex, because you can see through it. Trace your design onto the stencils, making a different stencil for each colour. To copy from an original, size it by using a photocopier and either use it as a mask or trace it down, using carbon paper or tracing paper from an art shop. To ensure that the colours all fit together in the finished design, you will need to use a registration system to

Stencilling is a very effective method of adding decorative borders and paint features to a room. Either buy stencils ready-cut from DIY stores, or buy the raw materials and make your own.

To form a two-colour border, begin by masking off a stripe on the wall and paint it a contrasting colour.

Complete the stripe with a darker shade to create a sunset effect and remove the masking tape.

Draw the stamp design on card, cut it out and use it as a template for cutting out of a cork tile.

Brush or roll the desired colour of paint onto the stamp, making sure it is evenly coated.

In this sunny yellow room, stencilling has been used to good effect to enliven the plain coloured walls and outline the doorway. It is ideal for decorative framing and for use as a border.

Press the stamp onto the coloured stripe to create the pattern, re-coating with paint as necessary.

place the stencils one on top of the other on the wall. Either cut an 'x' through all the layers when they are correctly positioned, one on each side, or cut notches in the sides. If you are using transparent film, you have the option of lining up the stencils visually.

Stencils can be used to decorate entire walls; for example, a patterned tile effect for a bathroom as shown here. The finished area is sealed with an exterior quality varnish to waterproof it. Decide on your tile design and size, draw it onto acetate stencils, one for each colour, and mark the tile size as a black outline. Draw the tile size in grid form on the wall using a waterproof marker. Stencil the design onto the tile grid, completing the wall in one colour before starting the next. Use the method of your choice, but for a large wall a stencilling brush and quick-drying stencil paint is fastest. Redraw over the tile grid with a waterproof marker, using a matching colour, to indicate lines of grouting. A border, if needed, can be easily added using masking tape to stencil straight horizontal lines.

Trace your selected design onto the stencil material, making a separate stencil for each colour.

If you want to create a tiled effect, set out a grid with a waterproof marker and straightedge.

Apply the first colour, taping the stencil in place and adding the colour with a stippling action.

When the first colour has dried, add the second in the same way, aligning the stencil carefully.

Murals and one-wall effects

Often used to decorate children's rooms, murals can also be
considered as a way of decorating main living areas, too.
By using a grid system to scale up the design, even
large expanses of wall can be treated
with great success.

Creating a mural

You may find inspiration for the mural in a magazine or newspaper
or want to use an old photograph as reference. To draw or paint
your chosen design onto a wall you will need to 'scale it up' first,
Scaling up can be done by drawing a grid of squares over the
picture you want to copy. Use a tracing-paper overlay if you don't
want to mark the original. Now draw a similar grid of squares onto
the wall at the increased size, and copy the design over square by
square. You must be accurate when transferring the marks, paying
attention to detail where lines leave and enter the squares. If this
appears too complex, technology is at hand. Specialist shops that
offer a photocopying service can produce an enlarged image over
several sheets of A3 paper that can be stuck together. A feeder tray
loaded with heavyweight tracing paper (90 gsm or heavier) will
produce an image that you can see through, assisting the
positioning. Photocopy specialists may have colour machines that

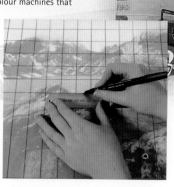

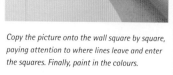

To scale up a design for a mural, first of all
lay a sheet of tracing paper over the
picture you want to copy.

Draw a grid of lines over the reference picture
you have selected. Then draw the same number
of squares on the wall to the desired size.

Copy the picture onto the wall square by square,
paying attention to where lines leave and enter
the squares. Finally, paint in the colours.

can reproduce an overhead visual on film from your image or design. This is then enlarged onto the wall via an overhead projector, and traced. Any of these methods can help you build up a series of images into a wall mural.

Combination images

Projected images can be used in conjunction with other, simpler paint techniques. A garden mural, for instance, may incorporate trelliswork diagonally masked out by 25mm/1in tape. Stipple pale blue and white emulsion into a sky effect, combining your stencil and colourwashing skills, or create an illusion of depth by washing over backgrounds with a thinned-out white emulsion, so they disappear into the mist. Painting in stronger colours to the foreground base will emphasise this three-dimensional effect.

Collage and montage

More accurately a paper finish, images from posters can be stuck onto painted walls to create a unique mural. Try cutting out figure images of a favoured sporting team and positioning them on a grass green wall in playing formation to liven up the decor of a hobby or work room. Tramlines marking out playing areas can be masked out with tape, or backgrounds of spectator enclosures stencilled in, all adding to the graphic effect.

This technique can be used to produce a wide range of interesting and decorative effects. Make sure that the edges of the images are firmly stuck down, then when the glue has dried paint over them with one or two coats of varnish in order to provide a hardwearing finish.

Murals need not be confined to children's rooms; they can make very effective decorative effects in your home's main living areas too.

In this case, the floor-to-ceiling garden scheme has even been extended to the window shutters with great success.

Images of sports stars, cut from magazines or posters, can be used to liven up a sports field mural.

Using red paint, add 'mud patches' to your green football field after masking off tramlines with tape.

When the paint has dried, carefully remove the masking tape to reveal the tramlines.

Paint in the figures of spectators to give the appearance of a football game in progress.

PAPER FINISHES

The decorative styling and design features that are built into the modern dwelling differ in visual and practical ways from the basic amenities in the house that our grandparents lived in. A more time-conscious lifestyle, a greater reliance on electronics and labour-saving devices, the need for security and an eye for fashion have all contributed to visual change in the home. One of the few things that has not altered, not even updated, is the use of wallpapers as the prime means of decoration. The versatility of the wallcovering, from cosy decorative feel to disguising poor surfaces, ensures its continued popularity.

Designer's notes

Selecting a suitable paper for a room surface, be it in a Victorian terraced house or a part-finished loft apartment, is an intimidating task. As multiples of choice do not usually simplify selection, it is a good idea to approach the pattern books with a clear concept, otherwise you will face a bewildering array of shapes, colours, patterns and styles.

The Victorian love of wallcoverings often ran to two different papers on a single wall, separated by a dado or paper border. Visually breaking up the wall height in this way can be very effective, provided the patterns do not compete for attention. A thin stripe and a bold, heavy stripe together, or a standard small-patterned paper on top of a heavily embossed one can work well. Many embossed wallpapers are specifically made to be overpainted, and they are very hard-wearing on the bottom half of the wall. Consider, too, on a half-and-half wall, wood cladding or

Wallpapers offer a wide range of decorative effects, from exuberant floral patterns (left) to subdued stripes (below) and everything in between. Choose carefully to reflect the style of room you want.

The interior designer today is faced with more choice in wallcoverings than ever before. Hand-blocked, nineteenth-century designs can be bought, but most wallcoverings are descendants of machine paper runs begun in middle of that century. Factory production techniques, cost-effective paper runs and new colour dyes opened up the Victorian marketplace for wallpaper.

Just as paint-makers have introduced period colours to modern paint systems to allow for environmentally friendly historical colours, wallcovering manufacturers have re-introduced popular papers of the past. You can find simple Georgian hand-blocked designs and Regency stripes, as well as the familiar large patterns and floral designs of Victorian taste and the subtle, pale colour combinations of the Edwardians.

Wallpaper with vertical stripes can be used to create the illusion of greater wall height.

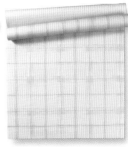

Choose a horizontally striped paper to make walls appear lower und wider.

Many wallpaper manufacturers offer ranges that duplicate Georgian, Regency and Victorian patterns, allowing you to recreate the original look of rooms in a period property. Although more expensive than standard papers, they are worth considering.

panelling on the bottom half. It does a similar visual job while protecting the wall from knocks, and is a useful asset in entrance halls and corridors. If this combination appeals, try cladding the base of the wall with vertical tongue-and-groove (TGV) woodstrips finished with a horizontal shelf or dado. Then paper the top half in a subtle stripe that suggests a repetition of the joins in the TGV.

Consider the design carefully: bold designs always work better on larger wall areas.

Papering the top half of the wall and adding wood cladding to the lower half can be very effective.

Visual tricks

Unlike wall areas of flat colour, patterned wallcoverings use deliberate placement of designs and shapes to attract more, or less, attention. Visual illusion is caused by the arrangements on the surface area, not the area itself. Just as walls painted in different colours will advance or recede, papered surfaces use small patterns to create an illusion of space. Larger, more powerful designs can produce a highly dramatic impact. Place a sample of a delicate small repeat pattern next to a large colourful design, and you will see how this works.

When choosing paper, ask yourself the same questions about room sizes that you would if you were painting the walls. If your ceiling is low, heighten it with a vertical stripe. A hoop or horizontal stripe will appear to lower the ceiling and increase the width of the wall. A small patterned paper will increase the feeling of space in a small room. Using bold colourful motifs will make the wall area look smaller and nearer. Vigorous small designs that are good at hiding wall deficiencies are also easier to hang,

Use paper to create visual illusions: a large pattern will make a room seem smaller.

If you want the appearance of greater space, choose a small repeat pattern.

because mistakes are disguised. A wall that is out of true unfortunately will be emphasized by symmetrical stripes. When hanging more than one paper in a room, consider which paper carries the overriding or dominant colour, and use this colour as a match or contrast for the woodwork paint scheme.

Basic skills: choosing wallcoverings

Be aware of the job you are asking your wallpaper to do, and consider your requirements. Perhaps its purpose is to be purely decorative, or it might have to disguise a badly cracked wall. It might get accidentally wet, in a bathroom area for instance, and so need to be water-resistant, or it may get dirty and you might have to be able to wipe it clean.

Certain paper types are intended for specific purposes. For example, heavy-duty wipe-clean vinyls are designed for use in kitchen areas, which are prone to steam and condensation. Your local decorating supplier or superstore will carry a range of all the popular paper types. But if you want something a little out of the ordinary there are specialist suppliers offering proprietary papers with period designs, hand-made papers and hand-blocked or screened untrimmed rolls. If you are in search of a unique or unusual paper, start with the small ads in the back of fashionable home interior magazines. If you are starting with pattern books, simplify the selection process by dividing the papers into two main categories, those that are made to be overpainted and those that are not. Wallcoverings intended for overpainting will usually, but

Hand printing of wallpaper is an expensive process and is used for short runs only.

not always, have a relief design, having either a textured finish like woodchip, or a raised surface pattern like moulded or embossed papers.

Wallcoverings that have a printed pattern that is not meant to be painted can be further divided, into washable (frequently ready-pasted) and non-washable papers.

Lining paper

As the name suggests, this is used to line the wall, providing a sound, uniform surface prior to hanging top-quality decorative or heavy-duty embossed papers. It is useful for improving uneven walls and disguising recently repaired surfaces. It comes in various weights and can be easily painted.

Machine-printed paper

Multi-coloured and available in different weights and qualities, this is the most common wallcovering. 'Pulps' are cheap papers where the printing inks sit on the paper surface. 'Grounds' are more expensive machine papers where inks sit on a prepared surface, coated with a 'ground' of colour. These are both produced in bulk and are therefore more economical to buy.

Lining paper (left) provides a good surface for papering. Machine-printed papers (right) are the most common.

Hand-printed paper

Whether block-printed by hand or screen-printed through a frame, this is more expensive because of the labour cost. Large-scale designs and special colours can be incorporated on very short runs.

Woodchip paper

The cheapest of the relief papers, this has small wood shavings (chips) sealed between two layers of paper. The resultant rough textured finish works well on substandard surfaces, disguising cracks and imperfections. It is sometimes called 'oatmeal' paper.

Embossed paper

With various registered tradenames, this has a relief pattern pressed into it when damp. A pattern is produced by pressure from an embossing roller. Colour can be added simultaneously, or the

peel off the top layer to leave the backing paper behind, which must be stripped in the normal manner. Otherwise, they must be scored to allow moisture to reach the backing – a laborious task.

Flock paper

Originally an expensive hand-made paper where a blocked adhesive print had wool or silk fibres dusted onto it, it is now available as a more economical machine paper. The elaborate design has a velvety, raised pile on a backing paper, and synthetic fibres are used to produce vinyl papers with a flock pattern effect.

Washable paper

Machine-printed designs with a film of protective, transparent plastic on top, this wallcovering is often found in convenient, ready-pasted form.

Hand-block printed papers are at the quality end of the market and often recreate historic designs.

Woodchip sandwiches wood shavings between layers of paper to make a cheap relief paper.

Embossed papers have a raised pattern and are often supplied white for overpainting.

Flocked paper has a raised pattern formed from velvety fibres bonded to a backing paper.

paper produced with a white finish for overpainting. Damp embossing, as opposed to dry, enables the relief to retain its shape better when receiving paste.

Vinyl paper

Also available in heavy-duty, hard-wearing formats, vinyl paper consists of simple designs printed onto plastic or vinyl film with special inks, bonded onto a backing paper. It is tougher than washable paper, but more expensive. Some varieties need a heavy-duty wall adhesive.

This paper can be difficult to remove, since the moisture of normal stripping won't penetrate the vinyl surface film. If you can lift a corner, it may be possible to

Washable papers are protected by a thin plastic film and are often ready-pasted for easy hanging.

Vinyl wallcoverings provide a tough, hard-wearing surface, but need special adhesive.

Tools and equipment

Paperhanging equipment is not expensive or difficult to source, and many items serve other decorating purposes too. Only specialist brushes, a pair of paperhanger's scissors, single seam roller, plumb line and paste table are unique to this job. The remaining multipurpose items will form a useful part of your household tool kit.

Dust sheet
and goggles

If you are painting, access to ceilings or high wall areas can be simplified by the use of extension arms, or a simple stepladder. Paperhanging is a more difficult task. You need to be able to reach the top of the wall safely while carrying the pasted paper roll. For ceiling work you need a platform giving 20cm/8in head clearance that allows you to hang an entire length without getting down.

A stable stepladder will suffice for the wall, but a sturdy platform is required for the ceiling. Use two scaffold planks tied together side by side across adjustable trestles, which you can hire. For stairwells, a combination of extension ladder, plank and adjustable stair or multipurpose ladder will be needed. Cover the area with protective dust sheets, and use a retractable measure, spirit level and pencil to mark starting points and horizontals. You will also need a plumb line to line up your first roll, a bucket for paste, a stick to stir the paste and some string stretched across the top of the bucket to wipe off excess paste from the brush. If your paper is ready-pasted, you will simply need a wallpaper trough filled with water.

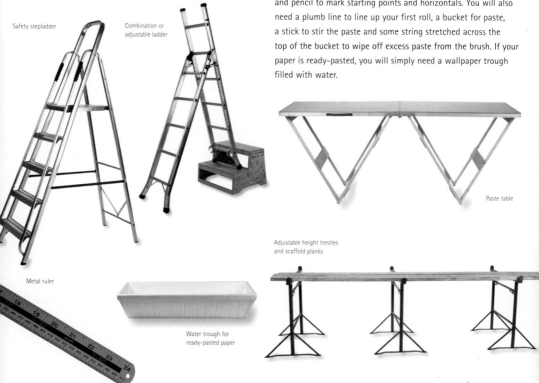

Safety stepladder

Combination or
adjustable ladder

Paste table

Adjustable height trestles
and scaffold planks

Metal ruler

Water trough for
ready-pasted paper

Scraper, filling knife, dispenser and filler

Bucket, sponge
and sugar soap

Long-handled fitch

You will also need:

- pasting brush
- folding paste table (which you could hire)
- paper-hanging brush
- paperhanger's scissors (30cm/12in)
- fitch (a small brush used to add extra paste to seams)
- seam roller (to re-stick seams after extra paste has been added)
- sponge (to remove excess paste)
- craft knife
- gloves to protect your hands and the paper
- eye protection when mixing paste
- measuring jug to ensure paste is mixed correctly.

Measuring up

There are several ways to count up the number of rolls you will need to paper a room or wall, and one or two extra factors to consider. Use a roll of paper to measure all around the skirting board, and count up the number of full lengths, ignoring short lengths under windows and above doors. Now measure the room height, to see how many full lengths can be cut from each roll, allowing for pattern wastage. Now divide the first figure by the second, the number of full lengths by the number cut from each roll, to give you the total of rolls required. Part of a roll must be reckoned to be a complete roll. Or you can work out the surface area in square metres

Wallpaper stripper, misting
handgun and all-purpose filler

(multiply height by depth) and calculate one standard roll per 5m/16½ft square, or use the standard table for your wall height and length. The chart (see page 247) assumes the roll is 10.05m/33ft long and 520mm/20½in wide. Handmade papers vary, so check the total surface area of the paper you are using, and adjust as necessary. The standard chart assumes an average door and window area per room. If you have large windows reduce the quantity accordingly. Papers with a repeat pattern or design will produce more wastage as you line up, so add the pattern depth to the height of the room when calculating. Very large patterns will need an increase of one roll for every five.

When calculating the number of rolls for a ceiling, use the first method described above, measuring the length of the ceiling and working out how many of these lengths can be cut from a single roll. Using a roll of paper, count up how many lengths will be needed, and calculate the total number of rolls. When the mathematics are completed, buy your rolls at the same time and from the same batch. A batch number is included for this purpose; slight colour variations are possible between batch numbers. Your retailer can also supply the manufacturer's recommended adhesive, which may be heavy duty.

Protective gloves

Wallpaper scissors, plumb line,
chalk line, Stanley knife
and seam roller

Above: Bucket and string,
brush, mixing stick,
sponge and measuring jug

Stringed bucket, kettle
and hook (for use when
working on a ladder) and
paperhanging brush

Spirit level

Preparation of surfaces

If your wall surface is not stripped plaster in good condition, you have a job or two to complete before papering. First, place dust sheets on the floor to collect debris and protect the carpet. You may need to strip off old paper, make good parts of the surface, wash down and key a painted surface, or simply seal and stabilise the plaster.

Previously papered finishes

Papered walls have to be taken back to the plaster. Leaving on old paper or vinyl backing leads to an unsatisfactory finish, because it may not bond well to the wall. Over-papering can cause it to lift away and form small air pockets. If the existing paper is vinyl or washable, it won't adhere. Stripping printed wallpapers is time-consuming and messy, but is not difficult. In older properties you may find yourself removing several layers of paper at once, and a great deal of patience is needed. The greatest danger is that when the last layer comes off, it pulls off old plaster with it, so try to avoid digging the scraper into the wall. Be very careful at this point; it may save you a lot of time spent filling and sanding later.

Soaking or stripping with hot water

Hot water will penetrate and soak printed wallpapers, but to speed the job up, mix stripper, in powder or tablet form, with the correct amount of hot water in a bucket. To aid water penetration, run a spiker or scorer over the surface of the paper. Wearing eye protection and gloves, soak the wall, a little at a time or it will start to dry out before the scraper gets to it. Allow the solution to penetrate fully and then remove the paper gently with a broad-bladed scraper. On stubborn areas you will have to repeat the process. The scraper has a stiff blade, not to be confused with a flexible filling blade, so try not to scratch the wall surface. It's a good idea to clear up the mess as you work, otherwise it dries out where it falls and sticks to the dust sheet and your shoes.

Dry-stripping vinyls

The two layers making up the paper can be separated fairly easily by carefully lifting the top layer at the corner, and pulling up and away from the wall to free it from the backing paper. It is inadvisable to leave the backing paper on the wall. It doesn't double as lining paper, so you should ideally strip it off the wall using hot water.

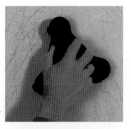

To aid penetration of the stripping solution, go over the papered surface with a scorer.

Working on small areas at a time, brush the paper with the solution and allow it to soak in.

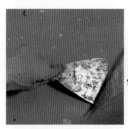

Use a scraper to remove the soaked paper from the wall, taking care not to gouge the plaster.

A scorer has sharp wheels that cut through the surface of the paper, improving penetration of water.

Scrapers

You can hire a steam stripper for major jobs.

while scraping off the steamed paper. The best results will be achieved by scraping with your writing hand and holding the steamer pad in your other hand.

Wall furniture

Permanent wall furniture, such as a radiator, is best removed, if possible. Isolate the radiator from the water supply at the valves, drain the water into a shallow bowl and lift it off the wall supports. If this is not possible, however, a long-handled radiator roller can be used to press the pasted paper into the problem area. Electric switches and sockets must be isolated from the supply before the faceplate screws are loosened, if this is neccessary to strip away the paper behind. Curtain rails can be left in place, and pelmets need be removed only if they interfere with paperhanging around the window area.

Using a steamer

This speeds up the process. Steam penetrates the surface under the pad, lifting the paper away from the wall. You can hire a steam stripper fairly cheaply, but familiarise yourself with the machine before you start. Prime the reservoir with hot, not cold, water, switch it on and wait for it to boil. Wear protective gloves, a long-sleeved shirt and glasses or goggles. Position the steam pad on your starting point. Hold it for about half a minute, then move along the wall to the next position

A steam stripper provides an effective means of stripping wallpaper quickly. With practice, you can hold the pad to steam one area of the wall while scraping paper from a previously treated area. Remember that steam can scald you, so take care and wear protective clothing.

Go over the wall looking for cracks and other damage. Mark them all so that you don't miss any.

Use the blade of a scraper to rake out all the loose debris and undercut cracks slightly.

Repairing walls

Once the wall is back to the plaster, you need to inspect the surface. Look out for cracks, holes and deep scratches in the plaster surface as a result of the stripping, or because removal of the paper has revealed previous damage. All these imperfections will have to be made good. To avoid missing any when filling, mark them all clearly as you find them using a watercolour felt-tip pen.

To prepare the crack for filling, carefully rake it out with a scraper blade, so that no loose debris remains, and clean the damaged area with a dusting brush. Using a small paintbrush, dampen the entire area with water so that your filler bonds with the wall plaster, and ensures that the wall does not draw too much water out of the filler too quickly, causing it to shrink and fall out. Mix up your filler, using a proprietary 'decorators' pack'. Following the makers' instructions, try to achieve a smooth, but

You will need a scraper, filling knives, a brush, filler and gloves.

firm, consistency. Don't mix up too much at once; the makers claim a workable time of one hour, but this is less on a hot day. Fill the damaged area using a flexible filling knife, overlapping the edges slightly and leaving the filler raised proud of the surface. This allows for shrinkage when drying, and for sanding back. Make sure

the filler is completely dry before you abrade the surface. Deep cracks will be dry on the surface long before they are dry all the way through. Sand back with the abrasive of your choice until the filled area is uniformly smooth and flush with the wall surface.

Decorators' packs and other general-purpose fillers are suitable for all peripheral wall damage. Deeper crevices can be filled if they are 'layered'. Apply a little at a time and allow each 'layer' to dry. Don't attempt to save time and try to fill a deep crevice all in one go. The filler will be unable to bond properly, and will slide out, forming a bulge.

Larger cracks and holes are best filled with plaster. You can buy small amounts 5kg/11lb of multi-finish from your local builders' merchant. Don't assume plaster is like filler and apply it the same way. The mixing is the same, but that's all. Plaster is stronger and must be applied with a trowel,

Safety goggles

not a flexible knife. Plaster surfaces are not meant to be sanded, either, so a flush, smooth finish must be your aim. Old wall surfaces will be very dry. If you apply plaster without a sealer, the wall will draw all the water out of the mix and the plaster will fall out. Splash a solution of one part PVA diluted with three parts water liberally in and around the damaged area, and leave it to dry, preferably overnight. Repeat this just prior to plastering. Not only have you sealed the wall, but the area is 'keyed' and the plaster will bond better. Use a trowel to smooth the surface flush. If you are not confident that you can achieve this, leave the plaster just shy of the top surface, and complete the job with decorators' filler, which you can sand back when dry.

After raking out, use a brush to remove any remaining dust from the cracks.

Dampen the area with water to prevent the filler from drying too quickly and falling out.

Fill the cracks, applying the filler with a flexible-bladed filling knife. Press the filler well into the cracks

and leave it slightly proud of the surrounding surface. Allow plenty of time for it to dry.

When the filler has dried, sand it flush with the surrounding surface using abrasive paper wrapped

around a sanding block. You may need to add a little more filler here and there to finish the job.

Large areas of damage are best repaired with plaster, and you can buy special packs for the purpose.

First treat the area with a PVA solution to seal it and help provide a good bond with the new plaster.

Mix the plaster with water and trowel it into the hole. Use the trowel to strike it off flush with the

surrounding surface, or leave it just below the surface and finish off with normal filler.

Cracks caused by movement around doors, or where skirting boards meet the wall, particularly on the stairs, should be filled with a flexible filler. This will allow for a certain amount of continual movement. Flexible fillers are available in ready-mixed tubes and are applied with a dispensing gun. Once dry, they are easy to sand back.

Finally, as with all home decorating projects, it is important to consider the health and safety aspects. Remember that sanding filler will produce a lot of dust, so protect adjacent surfaces with dust sheets and wear old clothes. Wearing a dust mask and a pair of protective goggles is a good idea, too, in order to avoid irritating or damaging your eyes while you are working.

Washing, sealing, stabilising and sizing

The wall surface should be cleaned thoroughly, using a solution of sugar soap and hot water. Wearing gloves, sponge down the wall. Rinse it with clean water and allow it to dry overnight.

Old wall stains can eventually show through the wallpaper, so they need to be sealed with a coat of oil-based primer to stop them ruining your finish. If the stains are a result of an old (and cured) damp problem, oil-based primer or a damp sealant will prevent any further stains from appearing. However, if the patch is still damp to the touch, or you suspect that it is still active, you must investigate the cause of the trouble before proceeding. On no

Wash the wall thoroughly using a solution of sugar soap and hot water. Rinse it well and allow to dry completely.

account attempt to seal over it, and don't ignore it. Consult a professional builder.

Stabilising the surface results in an equal amount of suction on all parts of the wall, preventing problems caused by shrinkage due to patchy, uneven drying. Walls that are very dry, and therefore very porous, should have a thin coat of PVA adhesive diluted with water. Mix this up one part to five. Once it has dried, run the palm of your hand over the surface. If white powder comes off onto your palm, the wall needs a second coat.

When the wall is ready, apply a size to the surface. A coating of size will allow you to manipulate the paper on the wall, enabling you to slide it carefully into position and line up the pattern. Without size, the paper will stick to the wall immediately, and moving it on the surface will be difficult, often resulting in a tear. If you are working on a lined wall, size the lining paper just as you would a bare wall, before you wallpaper over it. A coat of thinned-down wallpaper paste can be used instead of size.

Wall defects

While damp areas that are still active demand professional advice, areas of mould or fungus caused by moisture can be cleaned using a fungicidal wash. Investigate the cause of the moisture before proceeding. It is most likely to be poor or non-existent ventilation. If mould containing live spores is present on the underside of the paper you are stripping, you must take precautions to stop the mould infecting the new finish. Parcel the old paper up and discard it immediately, or preferably, burn it.

Treat the wall with a PVA solution to stabilise the surface and reduce the amount of suction, which could cause shrinkage problems.

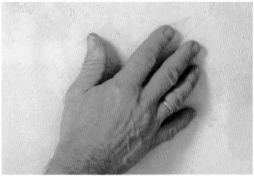

When dry, run the palm of your hand over the wall. If it becomes coated in white powder, a second stabilising coat will be required.

Sizing the wall will make it easier to slide the paper into position. Mix the powder with water.

Brush the size onto the wall, making sure you cover it completely, and allow to dry.

Condensation produces damp patches on walls and encourages mould growth. Improved ventilation should provide a cure. Treat mould with fungicide.

Condensation encourages the growth of mould, particularly in older properties not built for today's central heating systems. Make sure you have adequate ventilation and air circulation. It is interesting that wall paints that 'breathe', like distemper, are becoming popular again in older houses because they do not trap damp below the wall surface.

Fluffy white deposits on plastered walls are the result of soluble salts coming to the surface as the wall dries out. Called efflorescence, this surface problem can simply be brushed away, but it must be done with a dry brush. If you use water, the salt will dissolve, become re-absorbed into the wall and the problem will reappear later. If the wall suffers from flaking paint, either the finish cannot adhere to the surface because of under-preparation, or a damp area has been painted over. Once the cause of the damp has been determined, the wall area must be properly sealed.

Water penetration causes brown stains on ceilings and walls. They remain even when the cause of the problem has been dealt with. They may show through paintwork and light-coloured papers, so cover with an oil-based paint to seal them before papering.

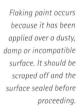

Staining is caused by damp penetration and the cause must be found and cured before proceeding. Treat stains with an oil-based paint to prevent bleed-through.

Flaking paint occurs because it has been applied over a dusty, damp or incompatible surface. It should be scraped off and the surface sealed before proceeding.

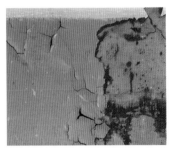

Efflorescence is caused by salts within the brickwork being carried to the surface as the wall dries. Dry brushing should remove it. Don't try to wash it off.

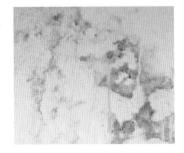

Damp patches that remain active must be investigated and dealt with promptly. Seek professional advice; don't try to cover up the problem, as this may make it worse.

Lining the walls

If the surface is still not ideal for hanging the patterned wallcovering directly onto it, you need to line the wall. Use a plain paper roll, about 35mm/1⅜in wider than the standard patterned roll. It is hung in the same way as the final paper.

Lining paper is available in several weights, either as an uncoated pulp or with a smooth finish. It helps to disguise wall imperfections, and some particularly rough areas can be lined twice. If you do this, make sure the seams are not in the same place, or hang the first paper vertically and the second horizontally. It is better to butt-join lengths at a room corner, rather than take a narrow strip the height of the room around the corner. If the walls are not square, there will be a slight, uneven gap where the vertical lengths don't quite meet. You can disguise this by smoothing a length of flexible filler into the corner.

You will need to take a narrow strip around a chimney breast. The breast face should be lined in the opposite way to the walls; if the room is lined vertically, then line the breast face horizontally. The walls may not be square, so line horizontally first and wrap the paper around the corner each time. The next vertical length sits on top of these overlaps, and you need to cut the paper from ceiling to floor 36mm/1½in from the edge, parallel with the corner line. Use a craft knife and a steel ruler for this. Remove the overlaps after peeling back along the length, so that you do not have a double weight of paper, and smooth the vertical length back into position with the paperhanger's brush, to achieve a butt join.

Cross-lining – hanging lining paper horizontally and wallpaper vertically – is not mandatory. If lining a wall horizontally, start at the top; the widths won't divide into the wall height exactly and pasting on specially cut widths is easier at the bottom of the wall.

Lining a wall

Adding a lining paper to a wall before papering it is a good way of improving the surface and is essential when hanging high-quality papers. In some cases, it may be necessary to hang two layers of lining paper to disguise surface imperfections.

Hang lining paper horizontally so that the seams don't coincide with those of the wallpaper.

When doubling up layers, fold back the edges and tear them off later to prevent ridges.

Butt-join lengths of paper at internal corners. If they don't quite meet, add flexible filler.

Lining a chimney breast

Chimney breasts need treating slightly differently to the rest of the room because of the narrow reveals on each side. Horizontal lengths of paper should be hung on the face of the breast and wrapped around over the reveals and onto the adjacent walls.

Cut paper long enough to span the breast, cover the reveals and lap onto the adjacent walls.

Overlap the next vertical length and cut down through both layers of paper, removing the waste.

Brush the edges of the paper down and they will meet in a perfectly butted seam.

Use a steel tape and waterproof pen to mark the paste table in 30cm/1ft increments. This will speed measuring the paper.

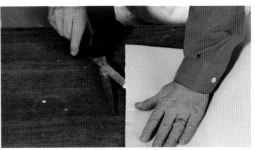

Allow for a slight overlap of paper on each length, fold the paper and use a scissors blade to slice along the fold.

Lay the paper on the table and paste it, working out from the centre. Overlap the edges of the table slightly to keep the table free of paste.

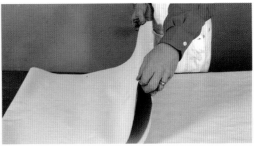

As you paste, gently fold the paper back on itself in concertina fashion to make the length manageable for hanging.

Using the paste table

- Set up your paste table in the centre of the room.
- Paper lengths will be longer than the table, so make sure you have enough space at the ends. Working in a confined space is more difficult.
- Keep your buckets of paste and water under the table where they can't be accidentally kicked over.
- The paste table will double as a measure if you mark it out along the edge. Use a waterproof pen so that you don't wash the measurements off. Mark in increments of 30cm/1ft, depending on your preference.
- Keep the paper square on the table. This reduces the risk of inaccurate cutting when using the edge measure.
- Cut the lining paper, leaving a small overlap at each end for final trimming on the wall.

- Apply the paste evenly, starting at the centre of the paper and working outwards.
- Keep the table clean at all times. Washing down with a warm wet sponge, and drying with a clean cloth, after pasting each length minimizes the risk of paste getting on the wrong side of the paper.

Papering walls

The key to successful paperhanging involves preparation, so that the bare surface provides uniform suction and manipulation (the final positioning of the paper on the wall) is easier. Never skimp on the preparation, because ultimately it will affect the final result, and although you have an expensive wallpaper, you may not have an expensive-looking finish.

Checking colour

Printed wallpapers carry a surface pattern printed by machine, and variations in colour can occur, even if the batch numbers are the same. Checking for colour at the start is crucial, otherwise the first time you will notice a colour variation between lengths is when the wallpaper dries out in position, and then it will be too late. You cannot do this as the hanging progresses because when the paper is more difficult, because you have to match up the patterned design. The easiest way is first to cut a wall length with the repeat pattern height added on at the top and bottom. This lets you position the pattern and trim it to fit. Before any pasting takes place, cut several lengths at the same time, lining them up on the table and matching each to the previous length before cutting.

When working with a repeat pattern, cut one piece to length and match others to it.

Line up the lengths of paper on the table and check that the pattern will match.

Cut each length with the scissors, allowing the repeat pattern height at top and bottom.

Pasted paper should be folded concertina fashion, pasted face to pasted face.

is wet with paste, the colour will be slightly different. Open and unroll the first length of each roll on the table. Set them out so that about a quarter of the length is visible, one behind the other: any colour discrepancies will be obvious. Should you have any cause for complaint, return the rolls to the shop.

Cutting

Using the measuring guide you marked on the table when lining, cut the lengths required. If the paper is cut too short it is useless; if it is too long it is wasteful. Add on a small amount top and bottom for trimming in position. Cutting a repeat pattern to length

Mark your cutting lines in pencil on the face of the paper, using a long straightedge as a guide. As you cut each length, make a pencil mark on the top so that when hanging you don't inadvertently hang a drop upside-down.

Pasting and folding

Paste should be mixed according to the maker's instructions, but do ensure it is not too thin, otherwise sliding the paper on the wall during precise positioning becomes very difficult. Line up the paper's edge with the paste-table edge, and apply paste by brushing from the middle to the edges, which reduces the possibility of paste contaminating the face of the paper. If paste does accidentally meet the patterned face, wipe it off immediately with a damp cloth or sponge.

As you finish pasting an end, fold it over on itself as if you were starting a concertina, and carry on pasting the rest of the length. Fold the remainder to complete the concertina. Set the paper aside to allow it to absorb the paste before attempting to hang it. The manufacturer's data sheet will tell you how long the soaking time is for your paper, which is usually ten to fifteen minutes. It's a good idea to write down the length number and the hanging time, and leave this next to the concertina, ensuring it goes onto the wall at the right time and in the right order.

Hanging the paper

The most important length is the first one you hang. It must be plumb vertical and in the correct place in the room. If the room has a chimney breast, any repeat patterned paper must be centred on it, so you need to hang your first length here. If pattern centring is not a requirement, start by dropping a plumb line to

one side of the main window and work away from the major source of light. Starting with the first length centred on the chimney breast requires accurate measuring to each side. Subtract the width of the paper from the width of the breast, and halve the figure. Measure in this amount from either edge, and mark by drawing along a vertical spirit level. Line up the first piece using this guide, and paper the entire breast first.

To start at the window, drop a plumb line from ceiling to floor. If the frame is plumb vertical, start at the frame. If it is not, drop a line just less than the width of the paper away from the frame, mark the line at several points with a pen, and join up the marks using a straight edge. You will need to paper three sides into the last corner, return to your starting point and paper in the other direction to finally join in the window corner. This corner will best disguise a non-matching join, as the wall contains the major source of light.

Having decided on your starting position, check to see whether the pattern is designed to be hung in a specific direction. This may or may not be obvious. Some designs appear to be truly abstract, but an initial impression can sometimes be wrong. When such patterns are hung as a complete wall, you may discover there is a definite top, and bottom, to the image. Time taken getting the first length plumb vertical, the pattern centred satisfactorily over the wall depth and trimmed equally at both ends, will be well spent because the following lengths can be positioned more easily.

When hanging the paper, begin at the top of the wall, brushing it into place with the paperhanger's brush and gradually unfolding the concertina as you go. Make sure that the first drop is aligned perfectly with the guideline, as this will affect the position of all subsequent drops.

Use a plumb line to establish a perfectly vertical guideline for hanging the first length of paper.

Carefully align the edge of the first length with the guideline. This is essential for a good job.

Work down the wall, unfolding the concertina of paper and brushing it flat to remove air bubbles.

At the ceiling, crease the paper into the angle with the scissors, then cut along the crease.

Make release cuts in the paper so that it can be fitted around, for example, architraves.

Use a seam roller to flatten any seams that have lifted, adding more paste if necessary.

At the corner of an architrave, make a diagonal release cut and paste the paper onto the wall around the frame.

Crease the paper with the scissors, pull it away slightly and trim along the crease to fit. Finally, brush it into place.

Wall obstacles

Hanging lengths against a straight wall is simple, so long as your first length provides a good template. Papering around obstacles such as window or door architraves involves cutting a diagonal into the corner where the moulding meets the wall. Now crease a cutting line along the frame edges with the scissor points. Be sure to take the weight of the excess paper when you do this or it will tear. Pull the paper away from the frame edge, and cut carefully along your crease line. Paperhanger's scissors are the best tool for this, but if you use a craft knife make sure the blade is sharp. You must keep it clean because paste drying on the blade will blunt it, and consequently tear the paper. The craft knife is very useful for

the intricate detail to either side of the mantlepiece, however. Drop the paper from the ceiling, and allow it to drape over the front of the fireplace. Using the paperhanger's brush, crease the paper into the right-angled join along the mantlepiece and trim to each corner. You will need to support the weight of the paper again, and smooth the side papers into position, making a series of cuts into the side moulding details. Crease a cutting line around the mouldings and the sides, and trim the sides with scissors. You may find the sharp knife is better for cutting around the edges of the detailed mouldings.

Electrical fittings

To paper over a square surface fitting, indent the paper with a finger to mark the edges. Cut a hole in the centre, cut diagonally towards all four corners and bend back the paper to expose the fitting. Trim the paper sufficiently so that it will fit neatly under the faceplate, and isolate the fitting from the supply. Loosen the two screws and push the paper underneath. Or, you can trim the paper to fit flush with the edges of the fitting. This will be your preferred method if the faceplate is not flush. Wipe any excess paste off the electrical fitting with a dry cloth.

Pasting the wall

Some papers are made to be hung dry, directly from the roll, onto a pasted wall surface. Mix up your paste, following the

At a mantlepiece, crease the paper into the angle with the wall and cut it to size.

At the sides, make a release cut in the corner and brush the paper onto the wall.

Use the scissors to make a series of release cuts around the detail of the fireplace surround.

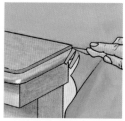

Brush the paper into place, removing the slivers of paper with a sharp knife.

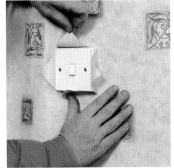

When you encounter a light switch, drape the paper over the top and make diagonal release cuts out from the centre.

Fold back the paper flaps and brush the paper flat onto the wall around the switch. Turn off the power supply and remove the faceplate.

Slacken the mounting box screws and pull the box away from the wall. Trim the flaps and brush them under the box. Replace the switch.

instructions, and use a pasting brush to coat the wall. Paste an area slightly wider than the roll width, and smooth it out evenly. Hang the paper from the roll or, if you prefer, cut it to length and match the pattern in the usual way first. A fitch is useful to re-paste seams if you hang by this method.

Ready-pasted papers must be soaked in water. You can either place the trough at the foot of the wall and hang directly from it, or pull the paper onto the table and fold it in the normal manner.

Pre-pasted papers

Vinyl or wipeable papers normally come pre- or ready-pasted. There is a dried coating of paste already on the back of the paper. The manufacturer's recommended soaking time is given with the roll. A water trough, usually supplied with the rolls, is used to soak the paper, paste side out, which is then positioned on the wall. Many patterns can be hung directly from the trough if it is placed at the skirting below the intended position, and moved around the room as hanging progresses. You still need the paste table, though, and when you are cutting and matching large designs, you may prefer to place the water trough at the side of the table. This allows you to check the pliability of the soaked length before hanging by folding inwards in conventional concertina style on the table. If you are satisfied that the paper is ready, carry it to the wall as normal.

It is quite acceptable to apply your own paste to ready-pasted papers, treating them as conventional machine-printed papers. Many decorators are of the opinion that self-pasting gives better control of the paper, especially during manipulation on the wall, and the data sheet supplied with the roll may acknowledge this.

Papering a ceiling

Don't avoid this job just because it looks difficult; in many ways a ceiling presents fewer problems than a wall does, because there are no radiators, electrical sockets or frames; a ceiling rose will probably be the only complication. Remember that a good working platform is essential and, if it's your first time, make sure you have a helper.

Do not feel intimidated by this task. The pasting, folding and carrying technique used to position and brush paper onto a ceiling is the same as that used when covering a wall. In fact, a ceiling will have fewer obstacles to paper around. There are no doors, radiators, windows or switches to make life difficult, merely a central rose, and not even that if you have wall lights. The only difficulty is that working over your head, your arms get tired, particularly if they are supporting a long length of heavy pasted paper, so a second pair of hands is very useful. Of prime importance is a safe means of access that allows you to reach the ceiling without having to stretch and to hang each length without continually having to move ladders.

Decide which direction you are going to paper in. You may think it's easier to paper the shorter ceiling width, but if there are two of you it will be quicker to start with the longer lengths. Professional decorators will paper parallel to the window wall, or if there is more than one window, parallel to the bigger light source. This means that they will start at the window wall and paper away from the light.

Starting the job

Set up your working height platform underneath the proposed first length. Under no circumstances try to over-reach on a stepladder. The best arrangement is two scaffold boards tied into position across two adjustable trestles, with a step-up stool at each end. This arrangement allows access to the complete paper length as it is unfolded along the ceiling, and is stable and safe to use. The cornice or angle on the window wall will not give an accurate line for your first length, so measure out from each end of the wall 50cm/20in, and join these two points with a chalk line. This will give you your starting line, with a small overlap onto the window wall for trimming off. Position the pasted concertina at the starting point, allowing for a small wall overlap, tightly against the marked line so that each loop opens out as the length is pasted across the ceiling. Make sure each loop is brushed firmly into the correct place before releasing the next. A second pair of hands to hold the pasted concertina simplifies matters considerably. If you are working alone, support the folds on an unopened roll of paper. Crease and trim the length and width to the cornice or wall angle.

Papering a ceiling is not as difficult as it may seem, especially if you have someone to help you. Some form of access platform is essential, but otherwise the techniques are much the same as for normal wallpapering, and you will encounter fewer obstacles.

Use a chalked stringline to snap a guideline onto the ceiling for hanging the first length.

Have your assistant hold the concertina of paper while you align its edge with the guideline.

Work across the ceiling, one of you opening out the paper while the other brushes it into place.

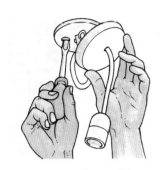

Before you begin papering, turn off the power supply, remove the ceiling rose cover and release the baseplate from the ceiling.

Allow the rose to hang on its cable and brush the paper onto the ceiling behind it. Then replace the rose.

If you can't avoid the rose being in the middle of a length of paper, work up to it and make a small cut in the paper at the centre of the rose.

Pull the flex and bulb holder through the hole, taking care not to tear the damp paper. Brush the remainder of the length into place.

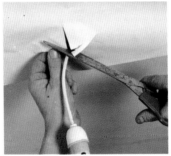

Return to the rose and make a series of release cuts out from the hole to the edge of the rose. Brush the paper tightly into the angle.

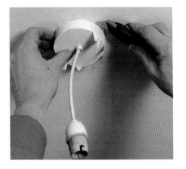

Finally, use a sharp knife to trim off the slivers of paper to leave a neat finish. Clean any paste off the rose with a damp cloth.

This first length will be a difficult, time-consuming job, but having completed it, a marker will have been established on the ceiling, and the remaining lengths will be easier.

The ceiling rose

By measuring out from the window wall to the rose centre, it is possible to arrange the paper lengths so that a seam join runs through the middle. A larger overlap on the window wall may result, but it will simplify things in the centre of the room. Either make small cuts in the edge of the paper, starting from the rose centre, to allow a cutting line to be marked with the point of the scissors and then trimmed off, or, if possible, remove the fitting. Isolate from the power supply if you do this, unscrew the cover,

and remove the retaining screws. The fitting can be allowed to hang from the wire for a minute or two while the papers are smoothed into position and the screw holes marked with a point. Replace the screws in their original positions and put back the cover. Should you reach the rose with the middle of a length, mark the position on the paper where the wire will drop, and cut a small hole, supporting the paper as you do it. Pull the wire through and brush the remainder of the length into position. Now make a series of outward scissor cuts starting at the centre of the rose, to allow a cutting line to be marked at the rose circumference. Exchange your scissors for a craft knife and trim. Wipe off any surplus paste with a clean, dry cloth. Never use a wet cloth on an electrical fitting for safety reasons.

Papering problem areas

Whether your problem area is a simple light switch or electrical outlet, or an intimidating stairwell where the drop is the height of the house, there is a technique to help you. Even difficult jobs are simplified if you approach them in the right way. However, safety must always be paramount when using platforms, so make sure they are quite safe.

Stairwells and landing areas

The biggest problem areas in your house will be the stairwell and landing, particularly in older properties where the stairwell drop is the entire depth of the house. There are no more difficulties in papering technique here than you have already encountered elsewhere, apart from the length of drop. Here a second pair of hands is needed to support the pasted concertina, or it will tear under its own weight as you hang it from the top. The real problem is one of access to the walls at a convenient working height. However, small, interlocking scaffold towers that will fit a stairwell

are available for hire. As an alternative you can combine ladder, stepladder, combination (multipurpose) steps and trestles with scaffold planks in an ingenious arrangement to allow you to complete the job successfully and safely. Set up your platform, using any variation of the examples shown here, with safety uppermost in your mind. Remove all stair carpets and underlays, and clear the area of all obstacles. If the ladder feet rest on a stair tread, nail or screw a batten support in place to prevent the feet from moving, and tie a soft cloth around both head ends where they contact the wall, to prevent marks. Double up scaffold boards to minimise sagging, and tie them to each other and to the supporting ladders or steps.

Survey the task ahead. Identify the edge of the longest length you have to hang and drop a vertical plumb line from the ceiling to

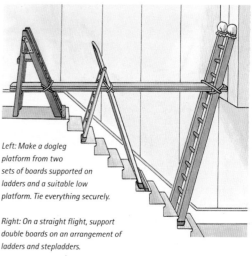

Left: Make a dogleg platform from two sets of boards supported on ladders and a suitable low platform. Tie everything securely.

Right: On a straight flight, support double boards on an arrangement of ladders and stepladders.

Begin by marking a vertical guideline on the wall with the aid of a plumbline.

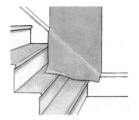

Remember to allow for the fact that each drop will have a long edge and a short edge.

Make small triangular cuts in the paper to fit it neatly against a curved skirting.

Make a vertical cut beneath a banister, shape the paper around the rail and paste to the wall.

the skirting. Make a mark with a pen and a straightedge to establish your guide for the first length. It is crucial that this length is correctly positioned and plumb vertical, because it will be a template for what follows. When you calculate a drop onto stairs, remember that the paper has two edges of different lengths; you must measure the longer edge, or the paper will come up short. For this reason it is better to paper up the stairs, not down, as a mistake in calculation can be re-sized further up the wall. It can even be the next length if you are not matching a pattern and the stair skirting rises consistently.

One or two difficulties, usually unique to the stairwell, will have to be overcome. For example, the skirting and the strings are likely to be shaped, and the banister rail on top of the balustrade may be joined to the wall on the landing. If your skirting curves around at the top of the stairs, then the paper must curve as well. Make a series of triangular cuts butting up to the skirting, and smooth the paper around the corner. If the banister does not butt to the wall at the edge of a paper length, cut from the bottom of the length parallel with the side so that the two strips can fit each side. Make a series of small cuts from your initial slit outwards, then shape the two pieces around the banister with the paperhanger's brush and trim carefully with the scissors.

Take a small margin of paper from the face wall onto the arch, then paper the arch itself.

When papering an arch, cut two strips of paper that will meet in the middle, otherwise the pattern will be upside-down on one side. Strong patterns will make the seam more obvious.

Arches

It is not really possible to match a pattern into an arch. Papering the inside of the arch is done in two sections, one from each end with a straight butt join at the arch centre. The best approach is to take the patterned paper from the face wall around the corner into the arch, trimming to leave about 25mm/1in overlap. A sequence of small triangular cuts in the paper edge will allow you to wrap around the curve. Paper the inside of the curve with a one-piece heavyweight lining paper. Cut it flush to the facing wall. Paint the lining paper in a matching or opposite colour.

Special effects

Use a matching or contrasting (by colour or pattern design) border strip, as a decorative dividing line between different papers, as a paper dado on a half-and-half wall, as an outline to emphasise a window recess or as a simple mitred frame around a serving hatch to add an attractive and stylish feature to your home.

Patterned borders can enliven newly papered walls.

Patterned borders

Borders can dramatically change the look of your newly refurbished room. Small patterned wallpapers with an overall base colour can have the effect of that colour emphasised or muted by a border. Small rooms that need plain, pale walls to make them appear larger can still have a decorative effect in miniature. Apart from the obvious colour and decorative qualities, placing a border or frieze at the ceiling/wall junction will appear to lower the ceiling, and bordering a window will make it look larger.

To save expensive mistakes, try positioning the border with masking tape first, so that you can study the effect. When you have determined your border position and height, use a spirit level and pencil (not a pen because it may show through the design) to draw a line around the room. Take care to maintain a dead level; nothing looks worse than a sloping border. If the ceiling or skirting has a pronounced slope, don't add a border anywhere nearby, as this will emphasise the slope even more.

Wallpaper manufacturers produce some border designs to complement a range of their own papers, and you can select both

at the same time by looking through the pattern book. There are several widths available, and two application methods. One involves using backing paste like conventional wallpaper, and the other is self-adhesive. You simply peel off the backing paper to stick down the self-adhesive type. But take note; it is not designed to be repositioned should you place it incorrectly. Printed borders applied using wallpaper paste can be manipulated on the wall just as wallpapers can, but beware of paste getting onto a non-wipeable paper because it can stain the face. You can always wipe clean water-resistant coverings with ease, but you require a special adhesive, available from your decorating store, to stick the border onto vinyl or wipeable finishes. In all instances, if you use a seam or small roller to flatten the border onto the surface, protect both border and existing paper with a tear sheet of lining paper, and roll on top of that.

Mitred corners

These are simple, provided your border angles are square. Even if the window you are outlining is slightly out of true, measure and

Mark the position of the border, using a tape measure and pencil. Make light marks only.

Using a spirit level, mark out a continuous horizontal or vertical guideline for the border.

Apply paste to the border, folding it concertina fashion in the same manner as normal wallpaper.

Brush the border onto the papered surface, aligning it carefully with the pencil guideline.

draw a positioning line in pencil that has 90-degree corners; do not follow the window shape. Paste up the top horizontal border strip first, followed by either vertical, adding on 5cm/2in or so at each end. Overlap the lengths at 90 degrees, then draw a guide line from corner to corner, using the 45-degree angle of a set square. Cut through both strips together with a sharp craft knife, and carefully peel away and discard the waste pieces.

Matching a bold, obvious pattern at each angled join will not be possible, so you could consider smaller, intricate or more abstract designs that will serve to camouflage rather than to emphasise any discrepancies.

Paste on the horizontal and vertical borders so that they overlap at a right angle.

Pull back the ends and remove the off-cuts. Finally, brush the ends back for a neat mitred seam.

Patterned borders have many uses, but they can be particularly effective when used to create a dado rail effect. In this case, they match the height of the banister.

Paper dividers

Some of these do the same job as a dado rail and can be used for a purely decorative effect, acting as a border to separate two different designs or styles of paper, or they can have an important function. Running a paper divider up the stairwell at the same height as the banister rail allows you to replace the bottom section of paper (and the border), while leaving the top part intact. As the bottom of the wall is more likely to suffer human traffic damage, and the top section is the one that causes all the difficulties, this can save much time and money. In a divided room, hang the two different papers together, completing the bottom paper run first, butting up to the guiding line around the room. Overlap the top paper by the exact width of the border. Now hang the border on top, using the paper join as a base guideline. However, if the lower part of the wall is to be covered by a vinyl paper, you will need to overlap this onto the upper paper, and use the join as a top guideline. The reason for this contradiction is that ordinary paste is not an effective adhesive on vinyl, and when running the border you must use border or overlap adhesive.

Using a steel rule and sharp knife, make a diagonal cut down through both border strips.

WOOD, BRICK AND TILE FINISHES

Repainting existing wood finishes and hanging new paper on the walls of a room are cosmetic changes, and, although a facelift results, the area is not radically altered. Removing the plaster to reveal and emphasise original brickwork, using hand-made tiles or wood panels on complete or half-and-half walls or building panelled shelving and storage into a recess have a much more far-reaching effect. The nature and 'feel' of the room are changed, as different materials have been brought together in exciting new combinations.

Designer's notes

Changing the feel of a room space by using new materials, building in a purpose-designed storage solution, or uncovering or cladding wall areas require you to accurately assess your constructional capabilities. As always, a scale drawing of the scheme is a good first step, before starting on any minor or major construction work.

Changing the colour of your walls or repapering a surface to upgrade the appearance of an internal area are really cosmetic alterations. Cosmetic paint and paper alterations utilise the existing features in the room, and any decorative change they make is on the surface. If you decide to physically change an area of your home, then you must progress from decorative techniques to basic carpentry and building work. Spare a few minutes, initially, to consider space and how it is perceived in a room. Any form of clutter, particularly on the floor, will make a room look smaller. Simple steps such as racking magazines, putting books onto shelves and tidying up generally may create the feeling of spaciousness you desire. Co-ordinated seating arrangements and plain flooring, rather than a mix of mismatched chairs and brightly coloured rugs, can give an ordered, somewhat geometrical feel, which assists the impression of spaciousness. The issue of spaciousness becomes more important as property becomes increasingly expensive. Families are often forced to accept smaller living areas and need to maximise the available area and yet create a spacious feel. Everyday clutter needs storage space in cupboards and shelves, so that the main room area can be free from obstruction. If you are able to create this space without altering your room dimensions, however, and thereby make good use of previously 'wasted' areas like alcoves, you have the ideal solution.

Co-ordinated seating and a plain floor will help to create the impression of space and order.

Storage solutions

Do not think of a storage solution as several shelves, units or cupboards in a room, think of your solution as an integral part of your new scheme. Not only can you achieve a matching decor, but you can visually disguise the true function of any storage unit that matches and continues the line of the wall surface. Even a unit constructed from different materials will instil a sense of geometric order, provided it does not interrupt the wall line.

Other possibilities include half-wall units, preferably floor standing, with the ceiling line recessed, allowing the top half of the recess to be panelled, tiled or taken back to the brick. This is, visually speaking, little more than a practical development of half-wall finishes, where the dado rail divides two different decorative effects, or where the bottom half of the wall is clad for protective purposes. Shelving utilising the top half of the wall, with the floor line interrupted, is also possible, but somewhat self-defeating as anyone using the floor space is in danger of banging their head. For this reason the area underneath tends to become a more obvious and unsightly storage area itself, so you might as

Left: In a kitchen, make the most of available space with built-in storage units.

Above: Freestanding, half-wall-height cabinets can be used to good effect in alcoves.

well include it in the plan in the first place. As always, a sketch or drawing of the intended scheme is a good first step because it will allow all interested parties to voice an opinion on its viability. Measurements should, of course, be precise. A storage unit that does not house certain items because they are too big for it is no use at all.

Once you have worked out the kind of storage you need, consider whether you will buy it ready-made or build it yourself. There are many storage systems and items of furniture on the market, but to make the most of the available space, you may be better off constructing something that meets your needs exactly.

Using colour with different finishes

Which base colour is most suitable to match a pine wood finish in a bathroom? How can you emphasise the subtle colours of a local stone? Which wood finish best complements hand-made tiles in earth colours? The answers – you will not be surprised to discover – indicate that natural materials have their own colour associations.

In sketching out your scheme for consultation, consider the effect the raw materials could have on the finished room decor. Woods, whether solid planks or veneered man-made boards, can be varnished or oiled to enhance as well as protect their colour characteristics. Wood colours like dark reds, oranges, browns and yellows will look their best alongside green and blue schemes. They are at their most familiar and friendly too, because we associate trees with green fields and blue skies. Any natural materials that you use in your own environment will have colour associations that are dependent on their source, and you should consider these, without feeling restricted by them, when making colour decisions. An obvious example is to place pine cladding on the bottom half of

a yellow wall. Because pine is predominantly yellow the colours will match well, but the impact will be lost and the cost of the raw materials wasted. Far better to take the darker green of pine needles, or the mid-brown of a pine cone as your contrasting colour for the top half of the wall, thus emphasising the yellow textures in the wood.

A colour scheme that allows the timbers to be the focal point is essential if you decide to use sawn, unfinished lengths (i.e. not planed), for a rustic, more traditional look.

If you strip off the plaster to reveal a wall made of local stone, as opposed to brick, find out about the soil in the area. Is it red, sandy or brown in colour? A tint of the local colour will be a

Left: Combining exposed brickwork and woodwork can produce a charming country kitchen feeling.

Above: You can achieve a Scandinavian look by incorporating plenty of pale varnished woodwork.

Exposing rough-sawn ceiling joists by removing the plasterwork can produce an eye-catching ceiling.

Team it with sturdy wooden furniture to create a harmonious decorative scheme.

A chimney breast will often be the focal point of a room. You can emphasise it by stripping off the

plaster to reveal the brickwork. Exposed wooden lintels can also make dramatic statements.

natural partner for the stone, and the finished scheme will be pleasing to the eye. Back-to-the-brick finishes are focal points. Mixed yellows contain subtle colourings that will be wasted if they are juxtaposed with vivid or abrasive colour. The scheme will be more successful if you use white as a base mixed with a hint of the brick colouring as it allows the brick finish to tell its own story.

Using colours with wall tiles

The way that you consider colours when they are used with wall tiles must generally differ from considerations made for wood and stone because the clay of the tile is not in its natural state. Original tiles are available that use earth oxides, for example, or tiles that have a matt finish on pale blue clays, but these are hand-crafted exceptions. Commercial mass manufacture has introduced an extra process, a coloured glaze fired onto the surface of the original clay. Colours created in this way can be matched or contrasted in the same way as painted walls, because nature's colours have been superseded. Blue and white may have come to be regarded as the classic tile colours through the years, but they are not the original colours of the raw material. Consequently, unless you source a hand-made tile from a specialist limited-edition workshop, your colour scheme will be man-made. This allows all kinds of decorative patterns and designs to appear on a tile, more suitable, perhaps, for smaller wall areas.

Splashbacks above and behind basins and sinks, bath panels and shower areas are ideal places for tiles. They practical, being waterproof and easily cleaned, and in a confined space and need not dominate the room. Pick a wall colour to match a specific hue within the tile for a co-ordinated room scheme, or note the overall base colour of the tile and pick its opposite on the colour wheel for your wall.

A tiled splashback behind a kitchen worktop provides a wonderful opportunity to make a statement

with colour while taking care of the need for a hygienic, easily cleaned surface.

Basic skills: wood

The strength to weight ratio of wood makes it the most versatile
of constructional materials, as well as the most attractive. Your
wood merchant holds timber stocks and man-made boards in specific
sizes, and before you start to draw up and price a project you need
to find out what they are.

Measuring up

A sketch of your intended construction serves as more than just a
discussion piece. As you add accurate dimensions it becomes a
working drawing, allowing you to calculate how much timber you
will need, and what sizes you should buy. This is not quite as
straightforward as it seems because timber is cut at the mill and
the size given is the original sawn size. If you are buying sawn
lengths, this is fine. If you require finished timber, machine planed
all round (PAR), however, then the nominal size still applies. Always
remember that the finished size includes the discarded machined
waste. Strange measurements have resulted from metrification,
too, because wood sizes given in metric are conversions from
traditional imperial sizes. For example 12.5 x 38mm equals ½ x
1½in. Calculating for machine waste adds another complication.
Nominal size 25 x 101mm, 1 x 4in imperial, actually arrives at your
door as approximately 19 x 95mm/¾ x 3¾in. If you calculate a
reduction of 4mm/⅙in on all sides, from the given or nominal size,
then you won't be far wrong. DIY superstores carry wood stocks in
finished metric sizes, but specialist smaller woodyards may accept

imperial, although they will convert to metric at the till to conform
with European trading standards. Don't mix the two systems as the
risk of a mistake is great, but use a retractable rule that has
imperial and metric markings, so you can convert.

Buying considerations

The raw materials you source can be placed in one of three
categories: hardwoods, softwoods and boards. Hardwood, such as
oak, beech and birch, is cut from deciduous trees, is difficult to
find and very expensive. Good timber merchants will usually stock

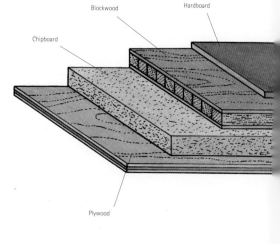

Blockwood

Hardboard

Chipboard

Plywood

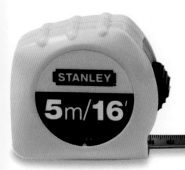

*Man-made boards
come in a variety of
types and sizes. Always
take a tape measure
with you when buying
timber or boards.*

STANLEY

5m/16′

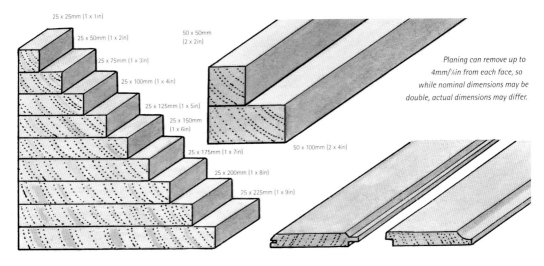

25 x 25mm (1 x 1in)

25 x 50mm (1 x 2in)

50 x 50mm
(2 x 2in)

25 x 75mm (1 x 3in)

25 x 100mm (1 x 4in)

25 x 125mm (1 x 5in)

25 x 150mm
(1 x 6in)

25 x 175mm (1 x 7in)

50 x 100mm (2 x 4in)

25 x 200mm (1 x 8in)

25 x 225mm (1 x 9in)

*Planing can remove up to
4mm/⅛in from each face, so
while nominal dimensions may be
double, actual dimensions may differ.*

*Softwood is sold in a range of standard sizes. However, the quoted size
is the original sawn dimension, not the finished size.*

*Cladding boards may be tongued-and-
grooved (left) or shiplap (right).*

mahogany, but again, prices may be prohibitive. Softwood is
cheaper and is stocked by all wood merchants. Redwood, spruce,
and yellow and white pine are all fairly common, but they are
simply sold as 'softwood', and not by individual name. Pine may be
the exception, however, particularly parana pine.

Cladding is machined from softwood with a tongue on one edge
and a matching groove on the other, and is thus easily joined
together for panelling. Sizes will vary, but 12.5 x 101mm/½ x 4in is
popular. Deal and cedar are good choices for TGV. Plywood boards,
man-made from real wood veneers, are sandwiched together with
glue so that the grains alternate at 90 degrees. Blockboards are
similarly surfaced with a real wood veneer, but sandwiched inside
are small irregular blocks of scrap wood. This can lead to different
cutting resistances during the same sawcut, and this board is not
as popular as plywood. Both these boards are normally supplied in
2440 x 1220mm/8 x 4ft external dimensions, and 6, 9, 12.5 and
18mm/¼, ³⁄₈, ½ and ¾in in thickness. The top layer of veneer, or
facing, varies. You can buy birch-, beech- or oak-faced boards,
usually one-sided, and the price varies according to quality. Other
man-made building boards are available, such as chipboard, which
is used as a substitute for wooden floorboards, and hardboard,
useful for lining floors.

Choosing and cutting

Timber merchants stock in sizes, depth x width. When you draw up
a plan for the job, a knowledge of standard sizes will be invaluable.
Select linear timbers carefully; try to avoid knots – particularly
dead ones as they fall out – and look for lengths cut from the
centre of the log. These have growth rings closer together than the
rest of the stock. Look down the length to see if it is distorted,
bent, warped or twisted. If it is, reject it. Merchants will cut exact
lengths if pressed, but it is to your advantage to pick pieces
slightly longer than you need, which you can cut to the exact
length on site. This allows you to cut off ends damaged in transit,
or suffering from shakes (splits along the grain, caused by uneven
shrinkage) and splits in the endgrain. When buying large boards,
make sure the yard has a machining service. They may charge extra
for this, but your boards will be professionally cut to the right size,
saving you time and trouble. If you are starting a big job, or one
that utilises wood taken out of another room which involves lots
of cutting, consider hiring a dual-purpose 'flip-over' saw. This
machine cuts to length and mitres on one side of its table, and,
when rotated, cuts as a conventional table saw on the other side.
Not only can this save on cutting charges at the woodyard, but it
will allow you to resize materials as you need them.

Tools and equipment (basic)

It may be true that 'a bad workman blames his tools', but it is also true that first-class results cannot be attained with substandard and inaccurate equipment. Always buy the best tools that you can, maintain and look after them, because in most cases they are an investment that should last a lifetime.

Compass saw

Tenon saw

Rip saw

Coping saw

Floorboard saw

Bead saw

Hack saw

Cheap and badly made equipment is a bad investment. High-quality hand tools will enable you to produce first-class results, and will last a lifetime if you look after them. Poor work, inaccurate fixings and amateurish finishing are all you can realistically expect from badly made tools. Do not attempt a job without the correct tool, either. Improvising takes longer and puts current and previous work at risk.

Ensure guidelines are level with a spirit level and mark them with a high-quality steel straightedge. Use a retractable steel tape to measure larger boards and linear timber, and a steel rule for smaller dimensions. Square up with a try square or engineer's square, and mark mitre cuts with a combination square. A good-quality combination square will include a detachable steel rule and a carpenter's level. Non-standard angles can be measured and transferred using a sliding bevel. Cutting lines for boards should be made with a carpenter's pencil, but a marking knife must be used for small cuts and wood joints. Keep a conventional pencil and a general-purpose craft knife in your kit as well. Saw timber across the grain with a crosscut saw; when sawing with the grain use a rip saw. A panel saw is, in effect, a smaller crosscut saw, used for cutting boards. The more stable-bladed tenon saw cuts large wood joints. Smaller or restricted-access cuts need a small back saw.

You can cut holes in panels with a padsaw. Make right-angled cuts on the bench supported by a bench hook, and cut mitred angles in a mitre box. Sink panel pins and moulding pins with a pin hammer or joiner's hammer, pull out pins using a claw hammer or pincers. Counterpunch pin heads below the surface with a nail set or punch. Use a bradawl to make starter holes for small screws, and a tee-handled gimlet for threaded pilot holes, remembering that the correct bladed screwdriver is needed to drive

Mitre saw

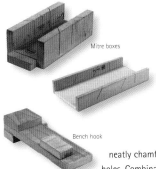

Mitre boxes

Bench hook

screws. Large woodscrews require a drilled pilot hole. To do this, use a bradawl and twist bits, or a self-starting auger bit in a hand drill or brace. A countersink will ensure the screw head is below the wood surface, and a plug cutter will produce neatly chamfered plugs to fill screw holes. Combination drill-drivers that are powered by mains lead or rechargeable battery can combine these jobs, particularly if fitted with a Screwmate or combination screwsink. Any power driving into masonry will need a drill-driver with a hammer action, usually called a combi-drill.

Rebate waste wood can be removed with a mortise or firmer chisel, driven by a wooden mallet if necessary. Keep sharp chisel blades in their protective plastic casings; if they are blunt or chipped, sharpen them using an oilstone.

Always secure the workpiece with a G-cramp or bar cramp, and use a sash cramp to hold glued joints until dry. Small pieces of waste wood can be positioned to protect the workpiece from cramping indentations. Smooth edges using a jack plane or smoothing plane, and keep all edged blades sharply aligned. Along with chisels, drill bits and planes can be sharpened. Your local ironmonger's will be able to provide this service.

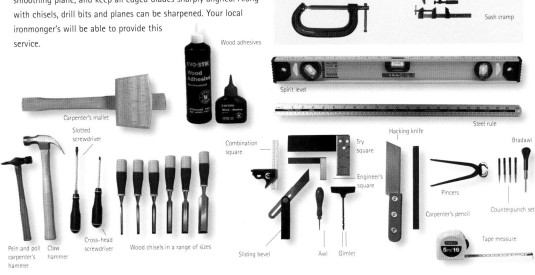

Basic toolbox items

Brace

Rotary hand drill

Countersink bits

Masonry and wood bits

Twist drill bit set

Yankee screwdriver and bits, ratchet and changeable tip screwdriver

Plug cutters and cylinder bore

Combination screw sinks

Retractable Stanley knife

Corner cramps

'G' cramps

Screw cramp

Sash cramp

Wood adhesives

Carpenter's mallet

Slotted screwdriver

Spirit level

Steel rule

Pein and poll carpenter's hammer

Claw hammer

Cross-head screwdriver

Wood chisels in a range of sizes

Combination square

Sliding bevel

Awl

Gimlet

Try square

Engineer's square

Hacking knife

Pincers

Carpenter's pencil

Bradawl

Counterpunch set

Tape measure

Tools and equipment (advanced)

Power tools are 'boy's toys' and cheap versions of drills and saws are on special offer in every do-it-yourself superstore. But don't be tempted – remember that inaccurate, badly made power tools merely do a poor job even faster. Buy a brand name with a good reputation, and go for the top of the range. It will be worth it.

Mains-powered jigsaw

Power drills

Drills feature in the basic tool kit either as hand drills, or possibly as small DIY-quality cordless drill-drivers. These portable units have become very popular due to their ease of use and price. They will allow you to take on small jobs around the home, but will be found wanting if you attempt to tackle anything heavy-duty. Even the drill-drivers of a professional standard are intended to penetrate only wood, plastics, plasterboard and block. Drilling into masonry is left to the combi-drill, which is basically a drill-driver with a hammer facility for driving into brickwork. Cordless drills are rated by the battery-pack voltage; DIY units are often 9.6v or less, while professional hammer drills for high performance in concrete will be 24v. A good cordless combi-drill for the home kit would have a 14.4v battery pack, and have a drilling capacity of 13mm/½in in masonry and 32mm/1¼in in wood. The price is high,

Cordless drill with battery pack

though, and a compromise may provide the answer. If you already have a DIY drill-driver, you could extend your capability by adding a traditional, top-quality hammer drill, which is powered by the mains, at considerably less cost.

Power saws

Two basic types of power saw are available: the jigsaw and the circular saw. The jigsaw will cut curves and irregular shapes, while the circular saw cuts in a straight line. The jigsaw has easily interchangeable blades that are designed to cut different materials, and a tilting sole plate for bevel cutting. The saw cuts with a powerful reciprocating motion, and better models have an orbital-action blade. Variable speed control is a real advantage. Try to find one with a top knob handle so that you can use both hands. The circular saw also has changeable blades, but it is a more complicated tool, and a unit usually comes supplied with a tungsten-carbide-tipped blade for cutting both hard and soft materials. The depth of cut can be adjusted, and the base

Cordless circular saw

PSB 750-2 RE

Mains-powered hammer drill

TOP TIP

Always adopt a safety first policy with powered equipment. Wind leads around handles when not in use and never let them trail across the floor. Store tools in their carry cases or in a locked cupboard, out of the reach of children.

Belt sander

into tight corners and confined spaces. Belt sanders are used primarily for more heavy-duty abrasive work, such as levelling surfaces, rounding off corners and reducing timber widths. An interchangeable sanding belt moving at a continuous speed removes wood stock very quickly.

'Snip-off' mitre saw

A 75mm/3in belt is a good width, and is available in coarse, medium and fine grades. Better machines have variable speed control. If you intend to sand the surfaces of boards, invest in a sanding frame to ensure even removal.

plate tilts to make bevelled cuts easy. A blade diameter of 185mm/7¼in is ideal. Make sure your saw comes with a guide fence. Mitre saws are basically 'pull-over' circular saws mounted on a swivel turntable on a mountable base. The saw cross cuts and swivels up to 45 degrees to mitre cut. Better models have soft start, a fence clamp, adjustable debris guard and a dust collection bag.

Power sanders

Orbital sanders are sanders used for fine surface finishing. A rectangular base holds the abrasive paper, and is driven in an oscillating motion by a motor, thus 'orbiting' the sanding surface, usually in a

Palm sander

6mm/¼in diameter. The abrasive paper can be changed quickly, from medium to very fine grades for the ultimate finish. All-purpose random orbit sanders come with a supply of quick-fit perforated sanding discs. The standard size is 125mm/5in, and a flexible dust skirt and dust extraction bag are also provided. Multi-sanders that use circular discs and triangular bases allow access

Finishing sander

Routers

An electronic plunging router will cut a rebate, channel a groove or cut a mortise. The router bit is driven in a clockwise direction, plunged down into the wood through the hole in the centre of the face plate, and carefully guided

Plunging router

from left to right, cutting into the workpiece. Slow-start and variable speed are real assets, giving more control. These tend to be features of only the more expensive machines, however.

Electric planers

You can shape linear timbers to fit against uneven wall surfaces with an electric planer. It can be used to rebate, chamfer, bevel and smooth. It is faster than a manual tool, so beware of removing too much wood – you can't put it back! A blade width of 82mm/3¼in and cutting depth up to 3mm/⅛in is adequate for household projects. Make sure yours has a setting gauge and fence guide.

Electric plane

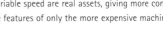

Bench planes

Basic wood techniques

The basic requirement in cutting wood to fit is accuracy. Ensure that you measure, mark and saw the wood carefully. You don't need excessive strength, but you do need patience, a stable workpiece and a sharp saw. Drilling also needs a secure workpiece, a marked starting point and a sharp bit. In neither case should undue force be necessary.

Measuring and marking

Remember the woodworker's basic rule: measure twice, cut once. Measure at right angles if you are measuring across a board, and parallel to the edge when measuring along its length. Don't let tapes sag or kink. Mark cuts to be made across boards with a carpenter's pencil, and cut on the waste side of the line. Blow away sawdust if it obscures the line as the saw moves through the

If you need to cut at a right-angle to an edge, use a try square and pencil to mark the guideline.

Using a marking knife to mark cutting lines severs the surface grain, preventing splitting.

When marking out angled mitre cuts at 45 degrees, use a combination square.

To make an accurate mitred cut, place the wood in a mitre box, which has slots at 45 degrees.

piece. If you use a circular saw, remember to calculate for the width of the blade. Mark cuts across the grain with a marking knife, and cut on the waste side of the marked line. Simple halving wood joints are marked accurately by using one half as a template to mark the other, so you only need to measure the one half. If you mark a mitre, use a combination square at 45 degrees, then transfer the workpiece to a mitre box or saw.

Cutting

The first rule of cutting is to have a stable workpiece. Any movement or slipping of the wood causes inaccuracy and is potentially dangerous. Secure your board with cramps when possible, supporting any overhang on a trestle or something similar. Adequate support is also needed for long sections of timber, but shorter pieces cut on the bench can be stabilised by a bench hook.

When making cuts with a large hand saw, whether cutting across the grain (cross cutting) or along the grain (ripping) of timber stock or cutting man-made board, hold the saw at an angle to the workpiece throughout the cut. Establish the cut with backstrokes first, and then cut using the entire blade length, with your index finger pointing along the top edge of the saw. This will help keep the saw straight and aligned with the cutting line. Keep just to the waste side of the line; if you centre the blade on the line, your finished piece will be too short. You can always plane or sand the sawn piece back to the line.

Tenon saws have a rigid back, so the blade is stable when you make a cut. Establish the cut as before, but as you progress gradually lower the blade until it is cutting horizontally through the workpiece. Don't cut all the way through the wood, as the grain will tear and splinter as the blade breaks through on the

Secure the wooden board with a cramp before you start to saw.

When cutting smaller pieces of wood with a tenon saw, stabilise them on a bench hook.

Establish a saw cut by holding the blade at an angle to the edge and pulling back a couple of times.

Cut with the tenon saw blade horizontal, cramping the work to scrap timber to finish off.

underside. Stop the cut just before completion and cramp the workpiece onto a scrap piece of timber. Now continue the cut through into the scrap to achieve a clean finished cut.

Drilling for screws and dowels

This is a very simple technique for joining wood pieces, provided you use the correct size of bit. To insert a screw, you first need to drill a small pilot hole (to guide the screw thread), then a hole the same diameter and depth as the screw shank (the shank clearance hole) and finally the countersink (to take the head below the wood surface). Some screw types do not have a shank, because the thread is continuous, so the shank clearance hole can be dispensed with. Always drill a pilot hole, however, otherwise the screw is unlikely to run straight and may bind so much when you insert it that it becomes impossible to turn. A finishing hole is essential for a countersunk screw, otherwise the head will end up slightly proud of the surface. Countersunk heads can be filled before painting. As

an alternative, use a combination screwsink that will drill a pilot, shank and counterbored hole at the same time. Insert the screw and fill the hole with a plug of the same wood cut to the size of the hole with a plug cutter. Drilling holes to join wood pieces with dowels needs a self-starting auger bit with a rubber depth stop. Adjust the rubber ring to indicate the correct depth of hole if you are using fluted dowels. If you intend to drill completely through the wood, cramp it to a scrap piece of wood. Drill straight through to the scrap, minimising damage as the auger bit leaves the hole, otherwise you risk splitting the grain. You must be sure to use the correct sized auger bit. If you buy a pack of fluted dowels, however, the bit is usually supplied in the kit.

Examples of tools and equipment are shown below, and they are as follows: a number 12 masonry drill and wallplug fixing used to screw a number 8 screw into the wall; a number 8 combination screw sink and number 8 CSK screw for wood; and a 7mm slotted driver blade fitting a number 8 CSK screw.

(Top to bottom): Wallplug fixing and number 12 masonry drill; number 8 combination screw sink and screw; wallplug fixing and slotted driver blade.

Drill large holes with a self-starting auger bit. It has a sharp point to allow easy centring of the bit on the hole position.

A rubber depth stop can be attached to the bit and adjusted so that you can drill holes to an accurate depth.

Advanced wood techniques

Joining wood pieces together is an art form in itself. If you don't feel confident about tackling an open mortise and tenon, start with a simple halving joint. Accuracy is everything in producing good wood joints, so it is a good idea to practise a little on an offcut first.

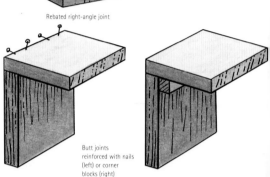

Rebated right-angle joint

Simple wood joints are not difficult, provided you measure and cut accurately with correctly set, sharp tools. Use a marking knife, not a pencil, and use one half of the joint as a template for the other to ensure a tight fit. Joints and housings that are identical, but cut from separate wood lengths, can be clamped together and marked for simultaneous cutting to ensure uniformity. Cut the wood precisely and assemble it 'dry' to check the fit, remembering that a loose joint has no strength. Do not rely on excessive amounts of wood glue acting as a filler in a badly crafted, ill-fitting joint.

Butt joints reinforced with nails (left) or corner blocks (right)

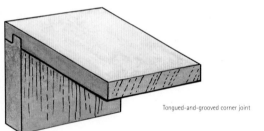

Tongued-and-grooved corner joint

Use dowels to reinforce any of the following joints:
- butt joining, L-joints and block reinforced joints
- tongue-and-groove joint (for panels, bought pre-machined)
- halving joint
- rebated joint
- 45-degree mitre joint
- bridle joint/open mortise-and-tenon.

L-shaped butt joint   T-shaped butt joint

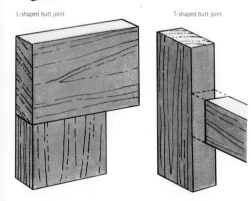

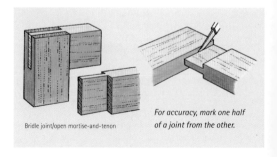

Bridle joint/open mortise-and-tenon

For accuracy, mark one half of a joint from the other.

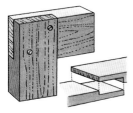

Halving or lap joints can make right-angled and inline connections.

For an exact fit, cramp the pieces together and cut them both at the same time.

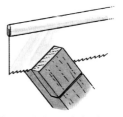

Clamp each piece to the bench and begin cutting down the grain at an angle.

Finish the cut with the saw blade parallel to the cut across the grain. Check the fit of the joint.

TOP TIP

Removing waste wood from a cut housing is simplified by making several parallel cuts side by side to the housing depth with a small back saw. You will find it much easier to remove slivers of waste wood one at a time with a 6mm/¼in chisel than to try to chisel out the housing in one piece with a larger blade.

Boards sold for cladding have a simple machined joint system with a tongue on one edge and a groove in the other. When the boards are assembled, the tongue fits into the groove. They are secured by nails driven through the tongues.

For strength, glued butt joints should be reinforced. One method is to drive nails through one piece into the other. However, wooden dowels are far better and can be concealed within the joint in blind holes. If visible, their ends should be trimmed flush with the wood. If hidden, careful marking out is necessary to ensure the dowel holes coincide exactly.

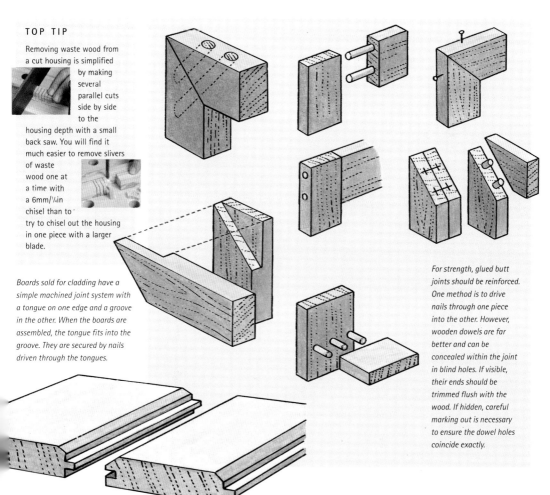

Wall fixings and hardware

Wall fixings and hardware are now so widely available that your hardware shop and even the local store will have a selection on sale; there is no need to visit the DIY superstore. The difficult task is discovering the type of wall you are trying to fix into, and trial and error is just about the only way to find out.

To attach constructed wooden pieces to a wall, or to start a 'built-in' project with wooden battens on the wall surface, or simply to put a screw in the wall for a mirror or bathroom fixture, you will need the appropriate wall fixing. This involves selecting a plug to receive the screw, and the type of plug will depend on the original construction of your wall, usually whether it is solid or cavity.

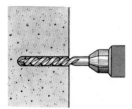

When you are using wall plugs, you need to drill a hole of the correct size and depth for the plug in the wall.

Push the plug into the hole until it is flush with the surface. It is important not to hammer it, as this may distort it.

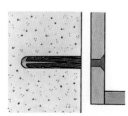

Offer up the fitting to the wall and align the screw hole with the wall plug. You can then insert the selected screw.

Tighten the screw. When the screw enters the plug, the latter will expand, gripping the sides of the hole tightly.

Solid walls

If your wall is solid all you will need is a simple nylon or polypropylene wall plug. This type of plug has grabbing lugs or pointed teeth to stop it turning in its hole as you insert the screw. You will need to pre-drill a hole, and you must be very accurate in lining up and marking. Plug manufacturers have a colour-coding system:

- yellow plugs for small to medium size screws
- red plugs for medium to large
- brown plugs for large, normally described as 'heavy-duty'.

You will find that the drill, plug and screw sizes are all related. Plugs sold in packs have the required drill size and recommended screw shank acceptance size pressed into the plastic centre strip. Frame fixers are long-shanked screws in their own sleeves and do not need previously marked and drilled wall holes, allowing you to drill through the wood directly into the masonry. The plug is fitted directly through the wood piece, and, as the screw is tightened, anti-rotation lugs open out to grab the wall. The sleeve is designed to eliminate distortion of the wood during tightening. Some forms of frame fixer are designed to be hammered home, which speeds installation. A screwdriver may be required for final tightening and to remove the screw to allow removal of the framework.

For a really heavy-duty fixing in solid masonry, an expanding bolt should be chosen. It works on the same principle as a wall plug, the segmented steel body of the fitting expanding in the hole as the bolt is turned with a spanner. Removing the bolt leaves the body of the fixing in place.

Cavity walls and plasterboard

Plugs designed for these walls are to be pushed through a hole in the wall until the petals or arms reach the cavity and can open out

Types of fixing

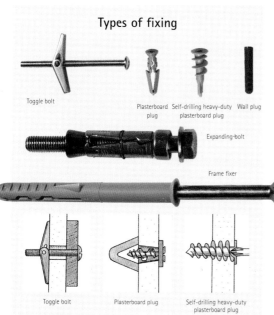

Toggle bolt

Plasterboard plug

Self-drilling heavy-duty plasterboard plug

Wall plug

Expanding-bolt

Frame fixer

Toggle bolt

Plasterboard plug

Self-drilling heavy-duty plasterboard plug

to spread against the back of the wall as you turn the screw. They are simple to insert, but not very strong. Heavy-duty expanding fixings, which consist of a metal sleeve around a central bolt, will take more loading. The sleeve fits the hole precisely and expands outwards when the bolt is tightened, gripping the sides and back of the hole. Spring toggle bolts have metal wings that are pushed through the hole into the cavity and spring open. Then, as the bolt is tightened, the wings grab the back of the wall. This fixing has a

drawback in that the hole must be quite large, because the wings pass through it, but the open wings spread the load effectively. It is often recommended for walls of low structural strength. Self-drill plasterboard fixings are plugs with a screw thread. You simply make a pilot hole and insert them with a screwdriver until they are flush with the wall surface. After this you can treat them as you would any wall plug. A screw is supplied with the plug, but longer ones of the same type will be needed for battens.

Hinges and catches

Cupboard doors and shutters built in to your new room will need hinges. Butt hinges, which need to be recessed to fit flush, are the most common and are available in every size, format and finish. Flush hinges are designed for lighter load-bearing duties. Their advantage is that they are designed to screw to the surface, and no cutting in is necessary. Small matching cupboard doors that are fiddly to align often utilise concealed adjustable hinges, adjustments being possible after the doors are hung. These hinges were primarily designed to allow doors not inset into the frame to open at right angles in confined spaces. Some concealed adjustable hinges are spring-loaded to keep the doors closed. For other hinge styles, you will need to fit a catch. Magnetic door catches are easy to fit, usually being an enclosed magnet case screwed to the cupboard, which attracts a small metal plate fixed to the door. More difficult to fit, requiring accurate positioning, is the automatic latch. This excellent device allows you to open the doors if both hands are full, and makes handles and knobs unnecessary. The mechanism is cased inside the cupboard unit, and the latch lever is lined up on the inside of the door. You simply press the outside of the closed door to unlatch it, and it swings open.

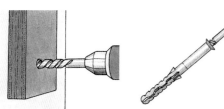

Frame fixers allow you to hold the timber framework in place and drill straight through into the wall.

The fixer comprises a long, heavy-gauge screw and long expanding plastic plug.

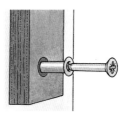

Pass the fixer through the timber into the wall so that the end of the plug is flush with the frame's face.

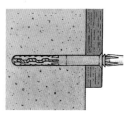

Tighten the fixer's screw to expand the plug and secure the frame to the wall in one operation.

Screws, nails and adhesives

There are an amazing number of screws on the market in all types, sizes and finishes, with slotted or cross heads in countersunk, raised and round-head form. Nails, too, come in many different types and sizes for specific purposes, while there are plenty of glues to choose from to meet your do-it-yourself needs.

Screws

Despite the confusing array of types, hold onto the basic principle that screws are used to draw together and join two previously separate items. This may be two pieces of wood for permanent fixing or it may be holding a batten against a wall by gripping the inside of a plug, or simply holding hardware, such as hinges, against a wooden surface.

Of the types you may find in your local store, slotted screws have been used in carpentry for many years, manually driven by a matching bladed screwdriver. Screws with crossheaded slots, like Phillips, require a matching cross-slotted driver, and many users claim that this type of driver is less likely to jump out of the slot.

Cordless drill-driver users rely on cross-slotted screws, particularly Pozidrivs and Supadrivs, partly for this reason, and partly for speed. The length and 'grab' of the thread varies. Conventional woodscrews have a shank, the diameter of which determines the size number (e.g. 6 or 8). Crossheads have a continuous thread that can be quite pronounced with a high 'grab', and are often similar in appearance to self-tappers. The head can be countersunk, intended to be driven below the work surface, unless a screw cover is used.

The other head shapes are domed (round), often used with washers and when the screw may be removed periodically, and raised, when the head is set in a cup for decorative effect.

Screws can be steel or brass; brass may look better, but steel is stronger. Steel screws may be stainless, bright, galvanised, zinc-plated or chrome-plated for protection against rust.

Screws

Whether you need a screw for a strong hidden fixing or one that can be exposed as a decorative feature, you'll find what you need.

Roundhead screws

Countersunk head screws

Screw seats

Use the correct blade size for the screw head. A blade too small for the head will damage the slot and jump out; a blade too wide will damage the workpiece as the screw is inserted.

Modern nails and pins

Nails, brads, pins and tacks

Modern nails, brads, pins and tacks are the distant relatives of hand-forged nails produced in the smithy; they had tapered, sharp-cornered bodies or shanks. These original fasteners held better than today's machined round nails, because the sharp shank cut through, as opposed to spreading, the wood grain. Buying cut floor or floorboard nails is as close as you are likely to get to a piece of history, however, as today's manufacturers prefer to offer hundreds of different types and sizes of round nail.

Nails have different heads, lengths and thicknesses (gauges), and you will find that the reference name usually describes the use. For general use about the house, a work-box could contain round lost-head or finishing nails, 40 to 75mm (1½ to 3in), oval brad or lost-head ovals 25 to 100mm (1 to 4in), and a selection of panel pins and moulding pins (available in small boxes). Hardboard nails, masonry nails and plasterboard nails, all self-descriptive, can be bought for more specific jobs.

Glues

Wood glues, particularly when used in conjunction with pins or screws, will give a very strong joint. Jointed surfaces must be supported, either by screws, G-cramps, sash cramps or similar, while the glue dries, usually overnight. Both waterproof and non-waterproof glues are available in handy sizes, starting with mini-packs and 125ml/4oz containers with easy-to-use applicators, up to 5 litre/3 quart professional packs. Mouldings are sometimes glued to the wall surface with a rapid setting, fast-grab panel adhesive. This is a high-strength gap and filler adhesive. It is usually available in a tube, which comes with a dispenser similar to a skeleton gun.

Wood adhesives are available as waterproof and non-waterproof.

Interchangeable driver bits

Cut floor or floorboard nails

Cut floor (floorboard) nails have sharp-cornered bodies designed to cut through the wood grain.

Timber mouldings

Wooden panel mouldings and architraves provide a finishing flourish to offset a sometimes functional piece. For this reason, they have long been used as decorative features on built-in room units, doors and cupboards. Mouldings can line recessed panels, provide a decorative edging to shelves and hide screw heads around fixed frames and room panelwork.

Softwood mouldings

Most wood mouldings are routed from softwood. Skirtings and picture and dado rails will all be familiar, as will door and window architraves, and they can be found in a multitude of shapes and designs. Period styles with ornate patterns or more austere, modern chamfered lengths are available to suit or match any room. A few basic examples are shown here. They vary in moulding detail from supplier to supplier, so you need to buy from the same source.

The growth in the refurbishment market has led to some period designs being available 'off the shelf', but you will need to find a specialist supplier for more unusual and imaginative designs. Some suppliers may be able to match your existing moulding if you provide them with a sample. Panel mouldings that give a finishing touch to plain surfaces and decorative pine strips for smaller areas like cupboard doors can be found at most DIY stores and good timber yards.

Hardwood mouldings

Hardwood mouldings are for edging the outside of boards and the inside edges of cutaway panels, where the layered sides of the board would otherwise be visible. Boards with a hardwood veneer can thus be edged with a matching strip, and oiled or varnished. Small hardwood mouldings in ramin or mahogany can be employed as decoration for cabinet doors, as contrasting finishing lengths on panelwork and frames, or as internal edging on right-angled corners.

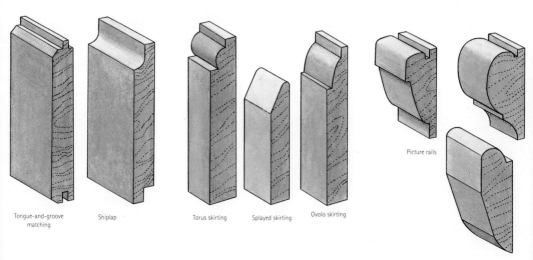

Tongue-and-groove matching

Shiplap

Torus skirting

Splayed skirting

Ovolo skirting

Picture rails

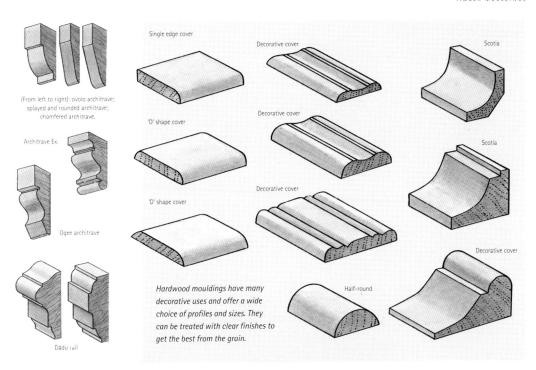

(From left to right): ovolo architrave; splayed and rounded architrave; chamfered architrave.

Architrave Ex.

Ogee architrave

Dado rail

Single edge cover

Decorative cover

Scotia

'D' shape cover

Decorative cover

Scotia

'D' shape cover

Decorative cover

Decorative cover

Hardwood mouldings have many decorative uses and offer a wide choice of profiles and sizes. They can be treated with clear finishes to get the best from the grain.

Half-round

Left: Dado rails tend to be chunky to withstand knocks from chair backs and other furniture.

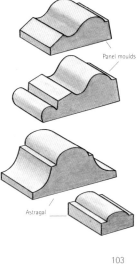

Panel moulds

Astragal

Wall Panelling

Wood has a unique way of altering the look and feel of a room.
As a natural material, it has an aroma all its own and a visual
elegance second to none. Whether you opt for vertical or horizontal
cladding, pick an appropriate finish, not only to go with the room
decor, but to enhance the natural beauty of the wood itself.

Prepared timber lengths for cladding a wall can be bought from
DIY superstores, usually in shrink-wrapped packs priced per
metre/yard. You will find them under a variety of names.
Traditional cladding is intended for interior use only. Constructional
and shiplap cladding can both be used outdoors. Alternatively, buy
your wall cladding from your local wood merchant. Both TGV and
shiplap will be priced per 30cm units or per foot run. Before buying
specific lengths, be sure you know whether the cladding is to run
horizontally or vertically. This way you will minimise wastage when
cutting to size on site.

Wall surface

Before you start any planning, examine the wall that you plan to
batten. If it is damp, even very slightly damp, the panelling will
exacerbate the problem and fungi will form on the reverse side of
the wood. Simply fitting vents in the cladding will not solve the
problem. You will need to cure the damp at source, and will require
professional advice. Whatever the state of the wall, a coat of
timber preservative on the wood cladding is recommended.

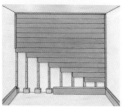

*When cladding walls, boards can be
run vertically and horizontally. The
supporting battens always run in
the opposite direction.*

*On an external wall, trap a damp-
proof membrane behind the
battens, then add the boards.*

*The ends of boards should reach
halfway across the batten to ensure
adequate support.*

Wood cladding should be
pinned to softwood battens
fixed to the wall. An ideal size
for the battens is 50 x 25mm/
2 x 1in. These must be
horizontal for vertical cladding,
and vertical for horizontal
cladding. Fix the battens to the
wall, approximately
460mm/18in apart, using the
same spacing for the fixing
points. If you are driving into
bare masonry you can use

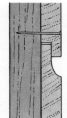

*Tongue-and-groove boards should
be 'secret nailed' through their
tongues, shiplap through the face.*

masonry nails. Plastered surfaces, however, require plugs and
screws; countersunk 50mm/2in number 8 are ideal. The framework
of battens must be in a true vertical plane. You can check this by
placing a spirit level on the uprights and on a long straightedge
held across the horizontal sections. If the wall is very uneven, pack
out the timbers with strips of cardboard or thin plywood.

Skirting

Whether you retain the skirting board or not is your choice. If the new cladding is intended to fit flush from ceiling to floor, then the existing skirting merely becomes part of the battening because it is the same depth. If the skirting is part of the new scheme, however, then it must be carefully prised off. Position a batten so that you can nail the skirting back in position to complete the job.

Vertical cladding

Centring vertical lengths on your chosen wall requires precise mathematics. You need to measure the visible width of the wood first. A popular size is 90mm/3½in. Divide this figure into the wall length. If you are lucky the cladding will fit exactly or fall very slightly short, allowing a slight opening of the fit between tongue and groove to take up the space. Otherwise an equal amount should be taken off each end, effectively centring the wood lengths on the wall. If this does not worry you, or the cladding is continuing around the corner, simply start at one end. With the exception of the very first piece, which is pinned through the centre of the face, TGV cladding should be invisibly pinned through the tongue, the groove in the next length hiding the fixing. This means that whichever end of the wall you start, the groove must butt to the wall. Shiplap starts the same way round, but is fixed through the face of the wood, just before the lap. The pin needs to

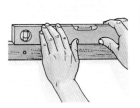

When attaching horizontal support battens to the wall, check with a spirit level that they are accurate.

At switch and socket positions, nail a framework of battens to the wall around the mounting box.

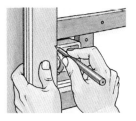

When you reach the switch or socket with the boards, mark them and cut them to fit around it.

Screw the faceplate to the mounting box so that it overlaps the cut edges of the boards.

be punched below the surface and the hole filled. The first length must be plumb vertical. If the wall is not, plane the wood to fit. Build up the cladding with successive lengths until you reach the end of the wall; the end piece may require planing to fit in the same way as the first piece. If the cladding fits flush, a decorative panel moulding around three sides will complete the job. If not, nail the skirting back into position on top of the cladding.

Horizontal cladding

The same principles apply to horizontal cladding. Start with the groove against the ceiling line, using a spirit level to ensure it is straight. If not, and the ceiling is slightly bowed, plane the length to fit. Retaining the horizontal level line, pin the lengths down the wall to the floor. The final piece must be cut or planed lengthways to fit flush, and panel mouldings added to finish. Or you could stop just below the level of the skirting board. In this case, pin short offcuts onto the remainder of the battening, down to floor level, and reposition the skirting, nailing through the offcuts onto the battens.

Timber wall cladding is a versatile means of providing a room with a unique look. You can stain it or paint it to suit the style you want.

Plywood panelling

This kind of wallcovering gives you an opportunity to explore the concept of cladding further, either by matching the veneered surfaces and the woodstrips, using a stock such as beech, or by using a mix of different woods to make up the wall area and running different water-based stains into the grain.

Plywood 6mm/¼in thick can be found in a variety of finishes, from fairly crude exterior grades to one-sided hardwood-veneered interior panels. You can buy sheets of 2440 x 1220mm/8 x 4ft and have it machine cut to size. Or you can purchase smaller panels of 1827 x 607mm/6 x 2ft or 1220 x 607mm/4 x 2ft. The smaller sizes are made for DIY purposes and are consequently more expensive, but usually have a good veneered finish. The concept is to produce a wall that looks like old-fashioned panelling, but at a fraction of the cost. This style is very effective in study rooms and home offices, giving your home-based business centre the appearance of a traditional library.

Positioning and centring

Sheet panelling must be pinned into position on battens, in the same manner as TGV lengths. This time, however, the battens must form a horizontal and vertical grid, making an identical grid to the finished panel work. The reason is that when the finishing strips are pinned through the veneered sheet onto the wall battens, all board joints will be hidden under the strips. The grid you choose can be to any dimensions that suit your purpose or the wall effect you desire, provided the battens and finishing strips line up and the joints are concealed.

Battening

Attach 50 x 25mm/2 x 1in battens to the wall, using 50mm/2in number 8 screws and countersinking. Masonry nails can be used if the wall is bare brick. Vertical battens must be positioned so that their centres coincide with the joints between boards: for example,

Although plywood is a very functional material, with a bit of imagination and effort, it can be transformed into stylish wall cladding.

Painted panelling offers a simple and effective means of concealing a lavatory cistern.

a board machine cut 2440mm/8ft x 607mm/2ft wide requires a batten centrepoint 607mm/2ft from the starting wall edge. The horizontal batten centrepoints are the same, and the 2440mm/8ft edge will fall in the middle of one. You will need to decide whether your panelling design should be centred on one wall, or could turn one corner to partly clad the next. Whatever the dimension of the vertical batten spacing, replicate it exactly when positioning the horizontals, so that the finishing strips which conceal the joints form a pattern of a square.

Finishing

When the batten grid is complete, check the system for accuracy by offering up a board, making sure the joints will be covered. Mark the position of the grid on the face of the board with a carpentry pencil. Apply panel adhesive to the batten grid, and pin the veneered sheet into position with 18mm/³⁄₄in panel pins,

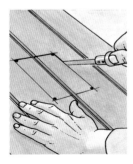

Make a cut-out for a switch by drilling a small hole at each corner and joining them with a padsaw.

Fit battens around the switch mounting box and offer up the panel; pin it in place.

punching flush with the surface. Position the remaining boards. Following your marks on the surface, draw the grid again to act as a guide for the finishing strips to make up the squares. Glue and pin the strips into position using 25mm/1in moulding pins. Some 50 x 12mm/2 x ¹⁄₂in vertical strips with butt joined horizontals will give a square, right-angled finish, but it is worth attempting a moulded panel finish. Try a finishing strip size of 25 x 12mm/ 1 x ¹⁄₂in centred over the battens, butt joined as before, forming squares. Select a small decorative panel moulding, no larger than 25 x 12mm/1 x ¹⁄₂in, and cut and mitre to size to fit the inside angles of each individual square. Glue and pin at an angle into the batten with18mm/³⁄₄in moulding pins.

Wall fixings

Wall switches and outlets that are not proud of the wall surface must be replaced with surface boxes. But first, remember to isolate electrical fittings from the supply before attempting to work on them. Fix battens in a square around the box, and measure the position of the box relative to your panel and its dimensions. Mark this with a pencil, then drill a pilot hole in one corner. Cut out the shape with a padsaw, and secure the panel, ensuring that the cut hole fits neatly over the surface box. Fit the cover plate, so that it overlaps neatly.

Wood ceilings

Wooden ceilings look wonderful, particularly in older houses, cottage-style properties and unusually shaped rooms. Converted lofts with roof windows as a natural light source and interestingly shaped shadow areas can show off quality timber cladding to great advantage. And you can either paint the wood or use a natural finish to show the texture.

Shiplap or TGV matchings can be used on ceilings, in much the same way as they are on walls. Battening supports are used as before, and light fittings should present no difficulty. Varnished wooden ceilings can have an architrave surround, similar to a cornice, and even a ceiling rose cut to a plain circle or a wavy edged design with a coping saw. The ceiling will appear, and in fact be, lower. The wood finish will advance towards the eye, and physically it will be 32mm/1¼in closer, that measurement being the depth of the timber.

Two difficulties you may encounter are locating the joists (hidden ceiling beams) to which you fix the battens, and the fact that all the fixing work goes on over your head. To locate the joists, measure accurately from the floor above. If it is the loft, and the wood beams are exposed, your task is straightforward; otherwise you must lift a floorboard. Note the direction of run, measure the distance between joist centres, and draw the positions onto the ceiling. If you are unable to reach the joists from above, the only solution is to tap the ceiling with a screwdriver handle and listen for the sound to change from a hollow ring to a solid tone. When you think you have found a joist, probe with a bradawl to check. Decide which way the TGV is to run, and offer up a first batten length (cut to size) at right angles to that direction. Mark the drilling centres with a bradawl, and drill the battens on the bench to accept 76mm/3in countersunk number 8 screws. Mount the battens on the ceiling, and invisibly pin the TGV through the tongues as described above. You will need to isolate the light fitting from the electrical supply and remove it along with the rose assembly. Cut a hole in the wood and thread the wires through, reassembling and repositioning on the finished side of the wood length. Cornicing or architrave, if desired, should be wall mounted, butting up to the new ceiling.

When teamed with exposed roof beams, a TGV ceiling provides an interesting decorative feature.

Adequate support for the boards is essential, as their combined weight will be considerable.

In this loft room TGV runs at right angles to the rafters.

Storage units can be incorporated to make the most of the space.

Loft areas

Extending your living space up into the roof is a reasonably economical proposition compared with alternatives like ground extensions, conservatories and moving to a bigger house. Although loft conversions must be left to a qualified builder, the decorative finishing is in your hands. Consider a wood finish for the inside of the loft. TGV fixed horizontally across the rafters not only strengthens the entire roof structure, but also gives a natural, relaxed feel to the area.

Have your builder tackle all structural work, leaving the roof area as a shell. The roof needs to be lined inside by 10mm/³⁄₈in thick plasterboard first. Use a board with metallised polyester on one side as an insulator, which should face the rafters. Mark their

seats. Screw them through the insulating plasterboard to the marked rafters. These screws have the appearance of studs, creating an almost marine feel. Loft window recesses can be lined with timber, and chamfered or decorative architrave can be used as an internal lining border. The short vertical support studs hide the eaves storage space.

To allow access, a small door needs to be made up to fit, preferably in the same style as the TGV panelling work. TGV can be run horizontally each side of this access. If the insulation is continued on the inside of the rafters down to joist level, inside the eaves space, then invisible pinning directly onto the studs is best. However, if the studs carry the insulation, then you must screw the TGV into position as you did on the rafters.

Make a feature of the board fixings by using screws and screw cups rather than nails.

Boards can be fixed horizontally across the rafters and vertically to battens attached to the studs.

Timber cladding is an excellent means of providing finished wall/ceiling surfaces in lofts and

can make use of much of the roof support structure. It is also ideal for lightweight partitioning.

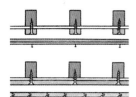
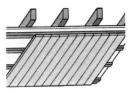

Establish the direction of ceiling joists before deciding on the method of batten attachment.

Regardless of the direction of the boards, the support battens must always be at right-angles to them.

positions in pencil as you go. Fix it in place with plasterboard nails, using as few as you can get away with. With the insulation in place, line the roof area with TGV, starting at the apex and working down to the short vertical support studs tied into the rafters. Fix the wood with 38mm/1½in number 8 brass screws with screw

Loft floor

If you intend opting for this type of wood finish, it is a good idea to ask your builder to fit a chipboard floor. A natural fibre woven floorcovering is the perfect finishing touch, fitted so that the floor is not seen. This solves the problem of wood overkill, which would result if wood were used to floor the loft, and because chipboard is a great deal cheaper than wood floorboards, this option is economical too. Make sure you have access to underfloor services, however.

Basic skills: brick

An exposed brick finish on one wall, often the chimney breast, adds a new visual dimension to a room, and can complement natural wood panelling or a flagstone or tiled floor. It is worthwhile getting to know more about the bricks available and how finishes are achieved, even if you don't do the hard work yourself and have to call in the professionals.

You don't need a bricklayer's skills when decorating or refurbishing the rooms of a structurally sound property. However, a knowledge of brick types and their use, pointing and the method of knocking up a mortar mix is useful. It will also help if you can recognise bondings and the different form of mortar joints available for decorative duties, should you decide to take a wall back to the brick. Although the same basic principles apply to walls constructed of local stone, the irregular stone formation of the wall requires only an examination of quality of construction, and the number of gaps and crevices that need filling.

Bricks

You may encounter three types of brick as you investigate what your house is made of.

Facing bricks

These are well made, often have a textured finish that allows their use as an exposed internal wall and come in a variety of colours.

Common bricks

These have no special finish, and are intended to be covered up, usually by plaster or render. They can be identified by their mottled pinkish appearance.

Engineering bricks

These are super-smooth and are often used as damp-proof, non-absorbent foundation courses due to their density and strength.

If you think an exposed brick wall will add to the character of your room, investigate the type of brick and bonding before starting work, because normally only an outside or load-bearing wall will be suitable. Carefully remove a small patch of plaster from your chosen wall, using a bolster and club hammer, to uncover the bricks. If they are consistent with the rest of the house, the bond is uniformly well laid and the mortar a regular depth, the wall is suitable. If you find pink common bricks that are badly laid and inconsistent with the house finish, stud walls where brick debris is laid between wooden uprights, or lightweight, aerated or dense solid blocks, do not proceed. This wall was never meant to be seen. Your only option is to repair the exploratory hole in the plaster and rethink the plan.

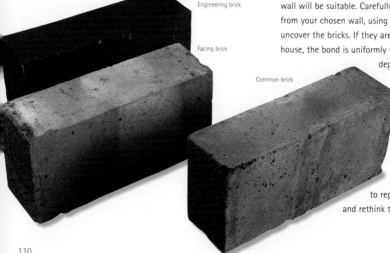

Engineering brick

Facing brick

Common brick

Removing plaster

Assuming your wall is suitable, remove the plaster with
a bolster as before. This is a dirty, dusty process, so it is a good
idea to wear protective clothing, eye protection and a dustmask.
At the top of the wall carry down lumps of plaster if you can, but
don't drop them. Try to remove smaller pieces directly into a waste
sack. This will keep the amount of dust to a minimum. Remove the
skirting and clean up around the base of the wall.

A cornice needs care; cut in with a small bolster directly
underneath and proceed very carefully; a stable moulding (one that
is not cracked) should remain in position as you remove the plaster
below it, even though you will damage the bottom curve slightly.

Repair and smooth off the bottom edge of the moulding as soon
as possible. It will be ultra-absorbent, so a solution of water-
diluted PVA should be applied, wetting the edge. Allow this to dry,
repeat the process and carefully smooth off with multi-finish
plaster. It is not a good idea to use filler in this instance, because it
isn't strong enough.

Glass bricks can be used in external and internal walls as a means of allowing light to pass through, *but without the clarity of a normal window. They are normally square in shape.*

The parts of a standard brick

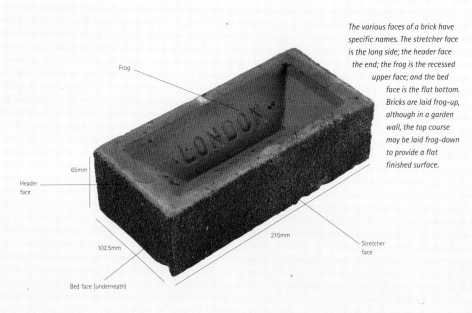

The various faces of a brick have specific names. The stretcher face is the long side; the header face the end; the frog is the recessed upper face; and the bed face is the flat bottom. Bricks are laid frog-up, although in a garden wall, the top course may be laid frog-down to provide a flat finished surface.

Frog

65mm

Header
face

102.5mm

Bed face (underneath)

215mm

Stretcher
face

Cleaning down

As the plaster repairing the cornice starts to dry, wash the wall down with warm water, beginning where the plaster ties the cornice into the brick, achieving a smooth line. Continue down the wall, washing away the surface dust to reveal the state of the brick pointing, and leave the wall to dry out. If the wall is absorbent, or the surface of the brickwork is flaky or floury, brush on a coat of masonry stabiliser. This solution has an unpleasant, sticky finish. Always wear gloves and protect your eyes from splashes.

Pointing the wall

Now you have revealed the bare brick face of a plastered wall. At best the mortar joints will be roughly and haphazardly finished, and probably recessed slightly. For this wall to become a 'display' surface, it needs pointing and shaped, decorative mortar joints. Pointing compresses the original mortar and waterproofs the brick joints when used on an external wall. For an internal wall compression and angular decoration are the aims.

Preparation

Assuming you have washed down, and stabilised the surface if necessary, make room for the new pointing by raking out the old, crumbling mortar to a depth of 25mm/1in. You will need a cold chisel for this, preferably a plugging chisel with a slanted head, sometimes with a groove cut in it, to clear out the waste faster. You may find a highly useful tool known as a seaming or chasing chisel or seam drill. If you use a chasing bit in a power drill for this task, particularly if it has hammer action, take care not to damage the brick corners because any damage done to the bricks now will spoil the effect of displaying the wall.

Mortar – proportions and mixing

Knocking up a mortar mix may seem simple, but accurate measuring is vital. Proportions are designated by volume, not by weight, so use a bucket. Don't be tempted to 'measure' by using a spade as a yardstick; this is only guesswork because sand and cement will not 'sit' on the spade the same way. Avoid the use of washing-up liquid instead of a plasticiser. A liquid plasticiser is a liquid air entraining admixture that forms air bubbles in the final

The four main types of bond

English bond
The courses of bricks alternate stretcher-on and header-on.

Flemish bond
Bricks in each course alternate header-on and stretcher-on.

Header bond
Bricks in every course are laid header-on, the wall being a full brick wide.

Stretcher bond
Bricks in every course are laid stretcher-on, the wall being half a brick wide.

Left: Raking out with a plugging chisel.

Measure out the correct amounts of sand and cement. Accuracy is essential for strong mortar.

Adding plasticiser to the mix will make it more workable and prevent cracking as it dries.

Turn the ingredients over dry until they are mixed completely. Form a crater in the middle of the pile.

Gradually add water to the crater and mix well. Take care not to make it too sloppy.

mix. These bubbles are spaces into which the water expands, stopping cracks appearing. Plasticisers are available from builders' merchants in multiples of 1 litre. Add to your sand and cement mix in the quantity specified on the container. Traditionally, hydrated lime was used as an additive. It made the mix more workable and smoother, retarded the setting time and prevented shrinkage. Lime is still in use, but plasticisers that do the same job have become more popular. Use soft sand, also called builders' sand, and ordinary portland cement in a mix of 5½ to 1, plus plasticiser, if you buy separate ingredients. Otherwise use a dry ready-mix and add plasticiser, or a dry masonry mix (containing plasticiser) and add sand. Carefully measure the correct proportions, and blend the dry mix well, using a 25cm/10in bricklayers' trowel. You will need about the same amount of water as cement. Add the correct amount of plasticiser, and pour half the water into a crater in the middle of the dry mix. Mix from the outside inwards, slowly filling in the crater, adding more water as absorption takes place and turning the mixture several times. When you can chop firm, smooth fillets into the surface with the trowel, the mix is ready.

The mix is correct when it holds ridges formed by chopping the spade across it.

Fill the vertical joints first, using the tip of the pointing trowel to form a neat profile.

Finish off by pointing the horizontal joints, creating your preferred decorative profile.

edge, and draw it into the vertical then horizontal joint. Flush pointing is finished with the side of the trowel; vee or struck pointing is finished with a backward sliding action of the trowel point; concave pointing is finished with the trowel handle or similar, and recessed pointing is finished by pressing a sized length of wood into the joint. For internal joints, concave pointing shows off the bricks to advantage, and flush pointing is a good idea if the brick edges and corners are damaged. Recessed pointing should only be attempted on brickwork in near-perfect condition, and weatherstruck finishes are, as the name implies, for external walls.

On the hawk

Use a small brush to dampen the recessed joints with water. Attend to only a small area at a time or the joints will dry out. Put some mortar on a hawk, select a slither with the pointing trowel

Top joint: flush pointing
Bottom joint: struck pointing

Top joint: concave pointing
Bottom joint: weatherstruck pointing

Top joint: vee pointing
Bottom joint: recessed pointing

Tools and equipment

Tools for brickwork and wall surfaces can be categorised as implements of either destruction or construction, in the form of breaking and shaping tools, such as brick bolsters and masons' chisels, measuring and mixing tools, and application and finishing tools. A few may already be in your general toolkit, but most will have to be bought specifically for the job.

Plumb line

Wall brush
Wetting brush

Remove old plaster or render with a bolster or mason's chisel, driven by a club or lump hammer weighing at least 1kg/2½lb. Lesser weights will cause vibrations, making the chisel difficult to control. A crowbar will be needed if a fireplace has to be taken out.

Chop out old mortar with a plugging chisel. Clean the wall with a large paintbrush and wet the joint areas with a small paint brush. Measure out your materials in a bucket, or a small plastic container depending on the required amount, mix them with a bricklayer's trowel on a mixing or spot board, and carry smaller amounts to the job on a bat or hawk.

Ensure the wall is plumb and level with a spirit level and plumb bob. Use a pointing trowel to insert slivers of mortar and finish joints. Render or plaster larger areas with a plasterer's trowel, use a straightedge for levelling the floating coat and obtain a flat finish by polishing the area with a wooden float. Damp down the wall and splash water on the trowel with a brush.

Buying materials

Buying in bulk is generally more economical than buying small amounts because storing items for future use reduces the unit price. Materials that degrade, however, become a liability. Cement bought in a 25kg pack is not economical if you have to throw three-quarters of it away, which will happen if it gets even slightly damp. A cement binder sets by water action, and must be completely dry when mixing starts.

Storing badly sealed, partly used packs on concrete floors, in cellars or in outbuildings is pointless. A better proposition is available from DIY stores, in the form of dry ready-mixes, sand and cement pre-bagged in quantities of 5kg, and multiples thereof. Be sure to pick the correct pre-mix.

Bricklayers' mortar mix contains the soft sand you need for pointing. A sand-and-cement mix for general use, like flooring screeds, will contain sharp sand, which is not suitable. Plasticisers to add to the mix come in powder and liquid form. Usually the liquid is easier to measure and use, and is available in litre containers.

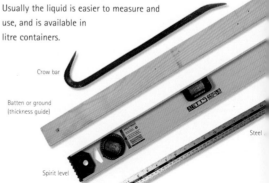
Crow bar

Batten or ground
(thickness guide)

Steel

Spirit level

Basic toolkit

Bricklayer's trowel

Plastic float

Pointing trowel

Club hammer

Hawk

Steel float

Bucket

Brick bolster with hand protector

Mason's chisel with hand protector

Plugging chisel

Mason's chisel

Bat

Plastering

You may never need to plaster an entire wall in your property, but a knowledge of basic techniques is useful. Different plaster types and their uses, preparation and application onto a wall are not trade secrets, nor is the use of the hawk and trowel. Practice can improve your technique and make smaller 'patching' jobs and improving parts of a wall surface easier.

Preparation and plaster types

Absorbent old brick walls draw water out of a plaster coat too quickly, resulting in severe cracking. Absorbency can be tested by brushing on water. If it disappears immediately, it is a high-suction surface. If it sits on the surface or partly runs off, it is a low-suction surface. For jobs around the house, coating the wall with water-diluted PVA will seal and stabilise the surface. Walls should be damp prior to plastering, and smooth surfaces must be roughened or 'keyed'. Mixed plaster is applied to the wall surface in two consecutive coats. First, apply a thick backing or floating coat, known as bonding. Follow this within two hours by a thin skim coat, known as the finish. Don't confuse the finishing skim with thistle board finish, which is a single skim coat for use on plasterboard partition walls.

Test the suction of the wall by brushing on water. Choose a plaster to suit.

Nail timber battens, known as 'grounds', to the wall to provide a guide to the depth of plaster.

Mix the plaster with water in a bucket; a mixing attachment in an electric drill speeds the job.

Practise lifting plaster from the hawk until you are happy that you can do it well.

Remove all old plaster by hacking it off with a hammer and bolster. Wear eye protection to guard against flying particles. This is a very dirty and dusty process, so protect adjacent surfaces.

Hold the hawk close to the wall and scoop the plaster from it onto the wall with the trowel.

Spread the plaster up the wall, keeping the lower edge of the blade pressed in.

Mixing

In a bucket, mix equal amounts of water and plaster. Crumble any lumps, and wait while the plaster absorbs the water. Stir well. The backing coat should be stiff. The finish should be thinner, and easier to work. Empty the bucket onto your spot board and knead the mix into ridges with a plasterer's trowel. The bonding should hold the ridges, but the finish should be slightly too liquid to do so.

Look for any gaps, hollows and imperfections in the surface and fill with more plaster.

Key the backing coat by scoring the plaster surface as it begins to go off. Spread on a thin finish coat (a thinner plaster), working from the bottom of the wall to the top.

On the hawk

Position the hawk under the spot board, and push some plaster onto it with the trowel. Hold your trowel at right angles to the hawk, and push the plaster mound away from you, while tilting the hawk upright. Scrape the trowel up the surface and off, loading the plaster onto the trowel ready for application onto the wall.

On the wall

The required depth of plaster is usually marked out on the wall by timber battens, called grounds, stuck or nailed to the wall. Battens should be about 12mm/½in thick, and spaced roughly a metre/yard apart. Plaster between them and, when the bonding coat has partially set, remove a batten and reposition it further along the wall. Continue the plaster up to the batten, repeating the process until the wall is covered. Start the plaster at the base of the wall, hold the hawk against the right-hand timber ground and scoop the plaster onto the wall, with the bottom edge of the trowel on the batten, tilting up. Push the trowel up the wall slowly to unload the plaster, spreading it evenly. Subsequent plaster loads can be spread parallel to the first, keeping to the same thickness throughout, until the whole area between the grounds is covered.

A straightedge resting on the two grounds will scrape off excess plaster. As the backing coat goes off, it needs to be keyed to accept the finish coat. You can do this by scratching the surface lightly with a couple of nails hammered through a wood offcut.

Skimming

The finishing coat comprises thinner plaster. This is spread onto the wall from bottom to top in a thin coating. Work an area you can easily reach in one arm movement, trowelling evenly. Return to the starting position, and apply a second, thinner coat over the top. Cover the wall in this way. Dip the trowel blade in water, hold it at an angle to the surface, skim off any splashes and leave it to harden. Polish the wall to a flat finish with the trowel surface.

Wall tiles

If you think wall tiles are suitable only for kitchens and bathrooms, think again. There is now a tile for every purpose and situation, be it decorative or protective. There is an amazingly diverse choice, and you can stick tiles on tables and cupboard units, in alcoves and storage shelves.

Ceramic tiles have been used as wall decoration for centuries, as these classical designs show.

Choosing wall tiles

The history of tiles can be traced further back than the birth of Christ, to the eastern Mediterranean and beyond. Early techniques of ceramic decoration were carried from the shores of this sea to Northern Africa and Western Europe, where an important centre was established in Holland. Stone, marble and glass, particularly in mosaic form, were features of Roman buildings, and many of their decorations are preserved on historical sites today.

An interest in this history has led many independent designers to experiment in limited editions of distinctive handmade tiles. Now tiles for wall decoration and protection can be chosen from an array of glazed and unglazed ceramic, glass, iridescent glass, mirrored glass, mosaic, stoneware, relief, metallic and cork.

Small independent workshops have abandoned the familiar sizes too: just about any dimension and proportion can be found or ordered. For example, a tile range of 7.5 x 15cm/3 x 6in is available, which was inspired by London tube stations. A happy compromise between the old imperial 4¼ and 6in square choices is found at 13 x 13cm/5 x 5in. As a consequence, it is a better idea to select tiles before working out areas, as handmade designs can differ in their dimensions.

Whatever tile size you favour, you will find that the border tile, glazed over two edges, and used at the edges or corners of the wall design, is no longer made. Today's universal tiles or square edge tiles have at least two edges finished and glazed, so that they can be placed either in the middle of a tile run, or at a corner. These tiles were often called field tiles in the past and were fitted with spacing lugs at each edge. Now, they have either a universal joining system based on bevelled edges, which butt at the base, or are squared up and require separate spacers. In both cases the resultant surface gap is then filled with grout.

A splashback behind a washbasin is the ideal first project in tiling. By combining tiles with different patterns and colours, you can create an eye-catching decorative feature that is practical too.

Practical and decorative uses

Kitchen areas, bathrooms, shower units and splashbacks are traditional places for tiling. A vast range is available today to replace or upgrade your existing finish. Don't neglect other areas, though. Handcrafted tile sets complete with a choice of matching or contrasting border tiles and a ceramic dado rail will give a traditional welcome to your visitors in the entrance hall.

Internal windowsills and surrounds that receive a lot of light will look better if you fix tiles that do not reflect it. Try a finish quality similar to stone, containing muted, subdued colours with an almost satin-like sheen. Stoneware tiles are also suitable for work surfaces in kitchens; they can often provide an attractive alternative to dreary mass-produced worktops. Their slightly uneven surface causes imperfection in colour and variation, which breaks up large areas visually. In a food preparation area, however, you will need a waterproof adhesive and a special grout, for hygienic reasons.

Glass tiles

On smaller areas of wall, such as splashbacks, wafer-thin metal designs that are sandwiched between layers of glass give a particularly unusual light effect, with the colours in the metals

Cork tiles

Cork has been around a long time, mainly as thin floor tiles. However, it is unsuitable for flooring because it is easily damaged by heels and heavy furniture. It will serve well on a complete wall surface, though, or as part of a half-and-half wall. Thick cork tiles (about 12mm/½in thick) make a good studio or home office pinboard. You can apply them to form a square or make a shape out of the tiles, then edge them with mitred timber battens.

Tiles are perfect in a kitchen, providing a hard-wearing, hygienic surface for walls and worktops.

Use them on large areas such as walls or splashbacks behind basins and work surfaces.

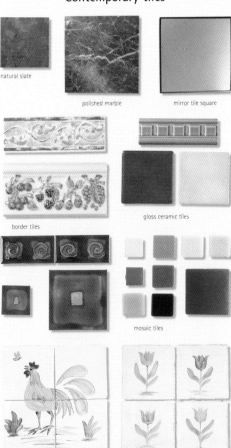

Contemporary tiles

natural slate

polished marble

mirror tile square

border tiles

gloss ceramic tiles

mosaic tiles

hand-painted tiles

appearing almost lost inside their tile. Glass is transparent, so the tile adhesive must be evenly applied on a good, flat surface. If you use a notched spreader, the ridges will show through.

For partitioning off small areas without reducing the light levels try glass blocks. They can be bought as a kit, which includes spacers, reinforcing rods and mortar. The last can be coloured to appear as a grid.

It is important to remember, however, that glass blocks tend to be heavy and will therefore need to be positioned on a substantial foundation. They cannot be built onto a suspended wooden floor.

Tools and equipment

A number of items needed for tiling will be used for other jobs and so may be in your tool kit already. Some of them are 'homemade', such as the tiling gauge or marker. Starter kits available from DIY superstores may supply all you need for small tiling jobs and the more expensive items, like tile-cutting jigs, can be hired.

Starter kits

If you are contemplating just a simple tiling job on a straight wall, it may only be necessary to buy a tiling starter kit, comprising:
• a cutter and snapper
• a tile edge sander
• adhesive spreader
• tile spacers
• a grout spreader and finisher.
More advanced kits are available; they include:
• tile-cutting machines that incorporate a measuring guide
• angle jig, which works with universal or square-edged tiles.
Ceramic tiles are cut by simple 'pencil' scorers, fitted into a tile cutting guide if required, or by a heavy-duty cutter and snapper with a tungsten carbide wheel. In both cases the scored tile is

and sizes. Space and plan using tile spacers, a tile gauge and marker battens, a spirit level, a retractable steel tape, a pencil (for the wall), waterproof pen (for the tile), and hammer and masonry nails to attach the battens. Masking tape will be useful for holding insert tiles (like soap dishes) in position while the adhesive sets. Adhesive and grout are supplied in ready-to-use plastic containers, often with the required spreader. Use water-resistant adhesive and grout where tiles may be splashed, but in shower cubicles and sunken bath surrounds a waterproof adhesive and grout are needed. Worktops need a special two-part epoxy resin grout if they are to be used for food preparation. If one is not provided with the adhesive, you will need a notched plastic spreader. For large areas, use a notched trowel. A grout remover, flexible spreader and finisher will complete the job. Keep a supply of cloths for cleaning and polishing to hand at all times.

Tile scorer, pencil and waterproof pen

Tile cutter

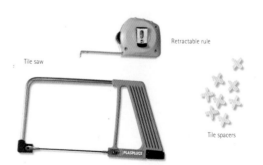

Retractable rule

Tile saw

Tile spacers

snapped over a match or thin edging strip. Cutting machines with measuring guides and heavy-duty cutting machines capable of cutting tiles up to 18mm/¾in thick are ideal for large jobs. Tile files will keep the edges smooth, and a tile saw with a tungsten carbide blade will cut in any direction. This will prove essential when pipework must be tiled around. Tile nippers nibble out odd shapes

Spirit level

Adhesives and cloths

Motorised tile cutter

Cork tiles do not require any special tools for cutting. A sharp craft knife, steel straightedge and accurate measuring are all that are needed when using 12mm/½in cork. A special ready-to use water-based adhesive with a notched applicator binds the tiles to the wall. Wooden batten frames used as a decorative border for these tiles also protect the vulnerable outside edges from damage. Finished timber 12 x 42mm/½ x 1¾in can be bought in DIY packs, and will fit the edge depth. You will need to mitre the corners to fit. Secure the battens to the wall with 30mm/1¼in number 8 countersunk head screws. You can easily disguise the heads by overlaying the same timber size 12mm/½in to the inside, overlapping the cork edge, and pinning or gluing it into position. If you are using cork floor tiles on a wall for a decorative effect, you can apply polyurethane varnish as a sealing finish, or simply leave them unsealed.

Heavy-duty snips and cutter

Notched spreader

Bucket

Tile side nippers

Masonry nails

Cloths

Sponge

Claw hammer

Home-made tiling gauge and batten

121

Basic skills: preparation

Grout lines between tiles form very obvious geometric patterns and are often emphasised by coloured grouts for decorative purposes. For this reason you need to be sure that the patterning will fit square to the walls. Thus accurate measuring and marking out are vital, for nothing looks worse than sloping tiling.

Preparing surfaces

As with all decorating jobs, the eventual finish will only be as good as the preparation, so examine the surface carefully. It must be flat and sound, and clean and dry without being too absorbent. Bare plaster surfaces are ideal, but if they are porous they will draw moisture from the adhesive very quickly, and the tiles will become loose. Brush on a coat of stabilising primer or a diluted PVA solution. If the plaster is unsound or cracked in part, then it must

be filled. Rake out all loose material and brush the surface down well. Coat the area with diluted PVA as before, to stabilise the cracked edges, before making good the damage. New plaster must dry out completely, and an entire wall should be left for about six weeks before a stabilising solution is brushed on.

Man-made boards present no problem, provided their surfaces are sealed and dirt, grease and fingermarks are cleaned off. Plasterboard is likely to be found as a wall surface. If you are

erecting your own, use the rougher side of the board as an outer surface because it will provide a better 'key'. Smooth, man-made worktops will need abrading by hand or with an orbital sander.

All sound, previously painted surfaces need is a 'key' for the adhesive, but flaking paint must be removed. Never attempt to tile on top of wallpaper, no matter how well it appears to adhere. You must strip the surface and treat the bare plaster as described above.

Previously tiled surfaces are a good base for new tiles, but, as usual, the surface must be sound. Re-stick any loose tiles, and clean the whole surface thoroughly. It is not necessary to fill small cracks or defects because the new adhesive will span any gaps. Bare brick and rough concrete walls will be uneven and need to be treated as you would floor surfaces. You need to level the surface using a cement render and then set the tiles in a thick bedding adhesive.

Tiled surfaces are traditional for bathrooms. In this instance oblong tiles have been laid with an overlapping bond much like brickwork, rather than the normal grid layout.

Estimating, marking and setting out

The number of tiles needed to cover a wall area depends on their dimensions. Manufacturers issue tables indicating tiles per square metre based on standard sizes. For example, 86 tiles of 108 x 108mm/4¼ x 4¼in are needed to cover a square metre, 72 of them to fill a square yard. However, with the availability of limited edition and handmade tiles of varying sizes on the market, it is a much better idea to make your own calculation from a homemade measuring gauge.

Select your tile and two lengths of (straight) timber battening. Mark out the tile positions on the battens with a pencil, remembering to include the grout lines, for the horizontal and vertical rows. If your chosen tile is square, then one tiling gauge will suffice. Place the gauge against the wall and count the number of tiles in each direction, then multiply the

When you have decided on your starting position, check the walls for square with a spirit level and plumb line. If the skirting is a true level, it can be used as a starting point, otherwise nail on a support batten so that it is level, its top edge just under a tile height from the skirting, or from the floor if the skirting is not part of your plan. That way you can accommodate any unevenness in the skirting or floor by cutting tiles to fit the gap between it and the first row of whole tiles.

At the tile vertical line nearest to the corner, nail a vertical batten; place a loose tile at the right-angled join to confirm accuracy. These battens support the tiles while the adhesive goes off. Use masonry nails to fix the battens in place, but don't knock them all the way in because you will need to pull them out later with a claw hammer and remove the battens. The remaining gaps are filled with cut tiles.

Mark a guide line for the horizontal support batten a tile's height above the skirting.

Check the adjoining wall for plumb with a spirit level. If it is vertical you can use it as a tiling guide.

Otherwise, nail a vertical batten to the wall in line with the last whole tile position before the corner.

Check the skirting with a spirit level; if truly horizontal you can use it as a tiling guide.

horizontal number by the vertical number. Always add a few extra tiles to guard against mishaps, such as breakages and cutting errors.

Now that you have worked out the numbers, consider your next move carefully, because it is crucial. Tiling must start in the correct position on the wall, and lines must be level and plumb, not necessarily following skirting or architraves. Set out and mark the wall area using the tiling gauge to plan exactly where complete tiles will lie, and where you will need to cut to size. On a plain wall, start in the middle, but if the wall has a window or a door, it is a good idea to centre the tile layout on the opening, so that the pattern formed by the tiles does not make the room seem unbalanced. Move the starting point if necessary.

Otherwise, nail a horizontal batten to the wall as a support for the first row of tiles.

Check that the two battens meet at an exact right-angle by holding a tile in the corner.

Basic tiling

Tiling is not a difficult skill to master, but if you've not done any before it's a good idea to start with a small, simple 'squared-up' area, such as a wall splashback behind a basin. When you are happy with an elementary project, you will have the confidence to move on to a more taxing job involving corners and cuts.

Basin splashback

The easiest way to get used to tiling surfaces is to start with a basin splashback. All you have to do is centre the tile design over the basin, and make sure that it is level.

Measure up one tile height from where the basin joins the wall, and mark a level line with a pencil – don't assume the basin is square or level.

Use your tile gauge, resting on the pencil line, to find the centre, and mark the tile grid on the wall. Then nail on a support batten, with the top edge butting the pencil line. Cover the marked area with adhesive (a notched spreader is usually supplied with the tub), applying firm pressure against the wall. You need to make even, equal ridges over the tiling area, so that the tiles sit uniformly when positioned. Use a twisting action of the wrist to press the tiles into place, separating them with small plastic spacers. Leave the adhesive to set for 24 hours.

Lever off the support batten and complete the last row of tiles. You may need to adjust the tile size slightly with the tile file if the

basin is not level. The final step is to apply the grout. Use the flexible spreader supplied to push the grout between the tiles, pulling the spreader firmly across the face of the tiles. Gently scrape off the grout left on the surface of the tiles. Run the grout finisher along the joints to smooth them off, achieving a consistent appearance. Clean the tiles with a damp sponge. Finally, polish with a soft cloth.

Tiling a wall

If you have completed a basic tiling job, the only difficulties you are likely to encounter with an entire wall involve accurate setting out and tile cutting. Measure, mark and set out your grid on the wall in such a way that cut tiles appear at the end of the wall, not in the middle, under a window or over a door. Other obstructions, such as bath panels that are to be incorporated into the overall design, may designate a starting point of a different height; a complete row of tiles looks better at the top of the panel rather than at the bottom. If your wall has a recessed window ledge, a

Working on a manageable area at a time, spread adhesive on the wall with a notched trowel.

Place a row of tiles along the batten, then add the second row, pressing them firmly into place.

To ensure uniform grouting gaps, insert plastic cruciform spacers between the tiles.

Check periodically with your spirit level that the rows of tiles maintain a horizontal run.

row of cut tiles will look better next to the window frame rather than butting the main wall surface.

When a basin or sink is positioned under a window, you must consider both. If the gap between basin and sill is not an exact number of tiles, the cut row butts the sill, not the basin. The first line of tiles on the sill is still a complete line, however. Don't be tempted to try to match two tile halves over a corner by starting the sill with the cut row, because the grout lines will become too fragmentary.

The rule is always to attempt a symmetrical layout around doors and windows. Narrow tile strips that have to be cut to fit one side of a frame only will stand out visually, the grout lines emphasising an off-centre arrangement. Centre your layout over a door, using an imaginary vertical line drawn through the middle, and fix guide battens around the frame, to allow all complete rows to be set in place first. Cut tiles can be positioned later, once the adhesive has set and the supports have been removed. Follow this procedure for a single window, but if you have a wall with two openings side by side, imagine a vertical line drawn half-way between the two, and centre your whole tile layout on it.

If you have a wall with a number of features that must be tiled around, draw up a scale plan on tracing paper and lay this over a sheet of squared paper to represent the tiles. By moving the traced plan of the

Ceramic tiles are ideal for creating a small decorative splashback behind a handbasin in a bedroom or cloakroom.

wall and its features around, you can determine the best starting point for the tiling.

The tiling technique is the same as that used for a splashback: start at the battened right-angled corner, and spread just enough adhesive onto the wall to fix about a dozen tiles. Universal bevelled-edge tiles will space themselves, but square-edge tiles need spacers at the corners. Work in level rows, using the batten support, but checking at intervals with a spirit level, until the wall is covered with whole tiles. The adhesive must set for 24 hours before battens are levered off and cut tiles placed into the gaps.

Cutting, completing and finishing

Cutting tiles to fit is easy, but take care to measure each one accurately. Then either score, using a hand-held scriber, and snap over a couple of nails, or use a cutting machine just like the professionals. You can hire one from your specialist supplier very cheaply, and it makes the whole process simpler and speedier.

Cutting

Cutting tiles to fit into the gaps at the ends of whole rows, or to fit around door architraves and other obstructions, can be done very simply, with a 'pencil' scorer, tile cutting guide and a couple of masonry nails. Hold the tile up to the wall, mark the area to be removed using a waterproof pen, and place the tile on a cutting surface. Score a line on the glazed face, with the scorer and guide. Then place a masonry nail under the scored mark at each end and

snap the tile cleanly by applying downward pressure on each side. The guide is especially useful for the accurate cutting of narrow pieces, but where thicker ceramics are being cut to shape, a heavy-duty cutter with a tungsten carbide wheel is a better tool. A cutting machine will save time on major jobs. Some heavy-duty versions have angled jigs as well as measuring guides, enabling you to cut tapers and angles by adjusting a side fence. Angled cut-outs and holes for fitting around pipes can be made by scoring the

Mark tiles for cutting with a waterproof pen, holding them in place over the last whole tile.

Hold a steel straightedge across the face of the tile and score the tile with a scriber.

Place a nail under each end of the line and press down with your thumbs to snap the tile in two.

Use a cutting machine if you have a lot of tiles to cut. Set the tile in place and score it.

Use the integral snapper to cut the tile to size. Some machines allow angled cuts as well.

For small cut-outs, use tile nippers to gradually nibble away the waste area of tile.

A tile saw is useful for cutting intricate shapes, as its rod blade will cut in any direction.

Tile snappers have angled jaws that make it easier to break a tile in two than using your thumbs.

You can butt tiles together at an internal corner or use a plastic corner moulding for a neat finish.

At an external corner apply adhesive and butt the tiles up to those on the adjacent wall.

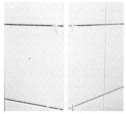

If your tiles don't have rounded edges, use corner trim to finish off an external corner.

As you grout the tiles, wipe off excess grout with a damp sponge. Don't let it dry on the tile face.

Give the grouted joints a neat profile with a grout finisher. Then polish the tiles clean.

You can buy a variety of narrow ceramic border tiles to finish off the edges of tiled areas.

shape of the cut on the glazed surface, then breaking off or 'nipping' the waste part of the tile using nippers or a small pair of pincers. Alternatively, make the cut-out with a tile saw fitted with a tungsten carbide rod saw blade that you can angle in any direction. If the cut is not as smooth as you would like, jagged edges can be removed with a tile file before the piece is offered to the wall.

Completing

Sometimes space is very tight, such as in an internal corner, where small strips of tile must be placed to complete a row. In this instance, spread the adhesive directly onto the tile back, not the wall surface, and push the tile into position. Unless you are using plastic corner trim to finish off an internal corner, the tiles on one wall should fit up to the adjacent wall, then the tiles on that wall should be cut to leave a grouting gap at the corner.

Some cutting machines incorporate a removable cutting gauge that can be used to measure the size of cut tile required and which makes an automatic allowance for the grouting gap. Since the

tiling will always be centred on the wall, or some feature on it, it is extremely unlikely that you will ever finish a row at an internal or external corner with a whole tile. If you have insert tiles as part of the layout, for example a toilet-roll holder, leave the correct space on the wall when tiling. Its extra weight means the insert tile must be fixed when the remainder of the wall has set. Use strips of masking tape to hold it in position while the adhesive sets. Grout the tiled surface and continually wipe the surface with a damp cloth. If your tile kit does not include a suitable finisher, use a small offcut of dowel with the end rounded by abrasive paper. Run it firmly along the grout channels for a uniform grooved finish.

Finishing

Tile trims, beads and rails, slimline borders and dados are often available to add the finishing touch to your design. Workshops that make tiles by hand offer overall schemes with matching border and finishing tiles, and it is a good idea to investigate all the possibilities before making any calculations. You can also edge tiles with hardwood mouldings that use the tile adhesive as a fixing. Try ramin quadrant or mahogany scotia as a top edging on a half wall, or use a hardwood angle moulding pressed into an internal or external corner.

TOP TIP

Most tile grouting is white, but sometimes a plain or very basic patterned tile can be given a new lease of life by using one of the coloured grouts available. Existing white grout can also be transformed by treating with a coloured dye, emphasising the grid lines and linear structure.

Mosaics and mirrors

If small panelled areas of mosaic in a room are purely decorative, then mirror tiles can perform a useful function. Iridescent glass mosaic in pewter or cobalt can be bordered with waxed woodstrip in a small display; mirror tiles in a batten grid can reflect much-needed light patterns along a dull corridor.

The use of wood strips to outline or emphasise specific tiled areas on a wall is particularly apposite when bordering mosaics. This usually decorative technique combines small pieces of ceramic, stone or glass, called tesserae, to make up a larger picture or abstract image. Areas of similarly coloured tesserae that are visually broken up by lines of grout benefit greatly from an external definition in the form of a natural wood border. This border can form any shape around any display; it does not have to be square or rectangular, although floor-to-ceiling strips of mosaic can be very effective on otherwise plain walls.

Using mosaic squares

The easiest way of making up a panel is to buy sheets of mosaic squares, consisting of equally spaced tesserae held in place by a mesh cloth backing or, in some instances, a paper facing. You will find a popular size is 30 x 30cm, about a square foot, although other sizes are available. Specialist manufacturers offer many different colour combinations, from strong greens and pinks to muted yellows, and with a suitable border these will add considerably to any scheme you choose. Being able to position complete sheets of ready spaced tesserae one after the other on the wall surface speeds up the whole process enormously.

Traditionally, the individual pieces would have been laid separately. All you need to do is stick and grout, as you would larger wall tiles. Mark out and prepare the wall as you would for any ceramic tiling job, then spread adhesive onto the surface. Some manufacturers recommend applying grout to the back of the mosaic sheet first, then bedding down on the wall with a homemade tamping block (a piece of plywood with a square of old carpet glued to it). Others ask you to follow tradition, which is to bed to the wall, leave it to set for 24 hours, remove any facing and

then apply the grout. The second method is faster, because you are able to grout the spaces between the tile sheets at the same time as the tesserae, as opposed to grouting twice.

Grids

The grid formed when strong grout lines make a visually distracting pattern can, of course, be used to advantage. Dark grouts

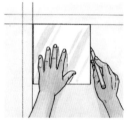

Use a tile to mark out a grid on the wall, allowing spaces for the horizontal and vertical battens.

Screw the framework of softwood battens to the wall and finish them as required.

Attach double-sided pads to the backs of the mirror tiles and press them firmly into place.

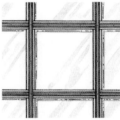

Pin lengths of hardwood moulding to the centres of the battens to conceal the fixing screws.

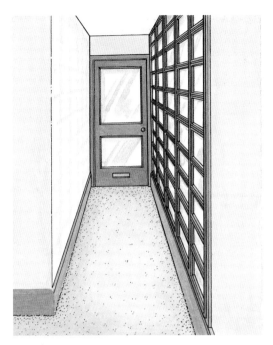

Mosaics are a natural for bathrooms. They are supplied in panels, allowing you to tile large areas quite quickly. What's more, *individual tiles can be removed from the panels for fitting around obstacles. If any do need cutting, this can be done with nippers.*

Use the mirror-tile grid idea to transform a narrow dark corridor. The tiles will reflect any *available light onto the facing wall, giving the impression of greater space and airiness.*

emphasising pale mosaic squares make an interesting reverse image where the lines are almost more important than the squares. You can take the grid theme a stage further by using large tiles spaced by wooden battens, the wood strips doing the same visual job as the grout lines, and forming a grid.

Mirror tiles

Using mirror tiles instead of ceramics inside the grid gives an interesting and practical result. When placed on a wall that receives direct sunlight, the reflected light patterns adjacent walls and increases overall light levels. A short corridor can be lengthened visually by using mirrored light in this way. Simply draw a grid of squares onto the appropriate wall using the mirror tiles and 5cm x 2.5cm/2 x 1in planed timber as a dimensional guide. Fix the timber lengths to the wall following the grid. Screw 5cm/2in number 8 countersunk head screws into wall plugs, or use

TOP TIP

Mosaic artists make up their own grout mix because they feel the grout emphasises the spacing between tesserae, an important part of the design. Use soft sand (3 parts), cement (1 part) and a cement dye to colour the mix before adding water. The colour of the grout can contrast with or complement the tesserae. Current thinking is that white grout lines form a visually distracting grid pattern, as well as appearing to pull colour away from such small pieces. If this is a problem on your wall, ready-mixed grouts are available, but colour choice is limited. Any acrylic paint colour can be added to a water-based mix. Adding colour to the grout after it has set is also an option, although with a large area of mosaic this could be a tedious job. Similarly, attempting to shape the grout joints is not worthwhile, as the grout would dry before you had finished; simply sponge them flush.

a contact adhesive. Position the mirror tiles in the squares formed by the battens and stick them securely with the double-sided fixers. Pin an 18mm/³⁄₄in hardwood moulding strip on top of the battens as both a decorative finish and to hide the screw heads.

Shelving: wood and tile effects

Building shelves into an alcove is easy – they sit on battens screwed to the walls. You could also try something more adventurous like pinning TGV lengths to the battens above and below the back and two sides of each shelf, thereby creating a stylish wood surround that also hides all the batten fixings.

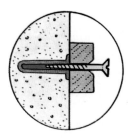

Shelves in alcoves can be supported by screwing battens to the back and end walls. In a solid wall use wall plugs; in a hollow wall, screw to the studwork.

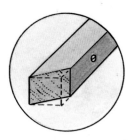

For neatness, mitre the outer ends of the side battens so that they become less obvious. Or hide them with a batten beneath the front edge of the shelf.

Built-in shelving

The need for shelving to hold frequently used items is not confined to kitchens and bathrooms. The modern home has books, tapes, discs and other paraphernalia that must be to hand. These items may still be kept in traditional free-standing bookcases, which were once essential items of room furniture. Their obvious advantage over built-in shelving is that they could be moved from room to room as needs altered. That advantage now seems outweighed by the amount of wall space needlessly taken up by such large pieces of furniture.

Built-in shelving solves storage problems while taking up previously unusable room space, such as small alcoves, chimney-breast recesses and dead-end corridors. When shelving is placed at head height, the shelf fixings are fairly obvious, and support

Cut the shelf support battens to length, drill and plug the wall, and screw the battens to the back and end walls of the alcove. Make sure that they are truly horizontal by checking with a spirit level.

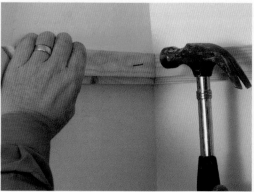

Countersink the fixing screws, then conceal them by pinning on thinner strips of wood or decorative moulding. Make sure this is flush with the top edges of the battens.

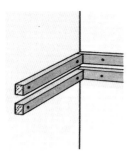
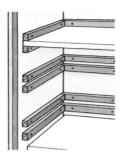
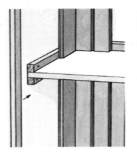
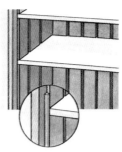

To line the alcove with cladding, fit battens to the walls above and below each shelf position.

Slide the shelves into position and fit a vertical batten to each side of the alcove.

Pin cladding to the battens above and below the shelves, finishing flush with the vertical battens.

Conceal the leading edges of the cladding where it sits on the vertical battens with beading.

battens with exposed screw heads will need a smaller woodstrip pinned on top to hide them. The batten arrangement must then be painted to match the wall. The shelves should be varnished or painted a different colour, so that the eye picks them out first, and the supports appear to be part of the background wall.

Floor-to-ceiling shelving

Ideal for an alcove, this scheme maximises the storage capacity of a small area while taking up the minimum of floor space. If sited next to a chimney breast, for example, the floor line should continue the line of the breast face for the neatest finish. On no account should a previously recessed area be brought out further into the room than the adjacent skirting, because this will destroy the whole visual balance.

If you are considering a floor-to-ceiling scheme, support battens can be disguised slightly by painting them to match the wall, but a more attractive solution is available. Battens supporting shelving can perform an additional task: supporting timber cladding cut to fit between the shelves and giving the entire alcove a rich wood finish.

For this finish run two sets of battens per shelf, instead of one, fix one below the shelf in its usual position, and one above so that the shelf slides in between the two. Position the shelves and fix two vertical timber lengths to the right front and left front, butting the ends of the horizontal side battens. TGV or shiplap boards fit snugly between the shelves, pinned to the battens. Cut the sides level with the shelves, and finish off with a vertical length of beading or moulding pinned to the side uprights and the front of the shelves.

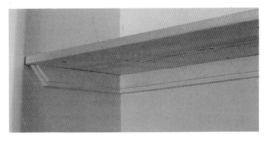

This simple shelf is easy to install, but very effective and practical. When the support battens are painted to match the walls, they become less obvious, as though part of the background wall.

Alternative shelving finishes

Combining different finishes in the same scheme always adds interest, both during the project and as a talking point when it is completed. Plain colour wall tiles may look less than pleasing on a large wall area, but when added to a wood scheme they can act as a perfect partner for the complex grain structure in the timbers. Consider using 15cm/6in tiles as a shelf surface. You need to add 29mm/1⅛in to allow for the back batten and cladding, plus 12mm/½in for a front beading, to the overall width. Allowing for grouting, you need to buy 20 x 2.5cm/8 x 1in PAR. Consider the colours with care; try a dark purple tile in a wood scheme where purple water-based dye has been run into the grain, sanded and clear varnished. Contrasts work well too, such as royal blue with a yellow pine cladding, or a pale green colourwashed wood combined with dark red tiles. Smaller shelves can have mosaic tiles, visually complex areas that offset simple clear varnished woods.

Combination storage

Floor-to-ceiling shelving in any recessed area gives economic storage space, but you can take the principle a stage further. Instead of having open shelves from top to bottom, which only collect dust and partly protect the contents, you can enclose them. You can hang doors on all or some of the shelves, creating a customised unit. Although paired doors can cover the entire front, and obviously give the best protection, most rooms benefit from a combination of base cupboard and face-level shelves.

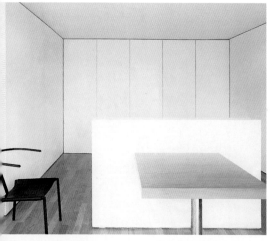

Bulky storage can be accommodated at floor level, and smaller items, such as books and tapes, can be stored on the shelves. Being open, these shelves are also an ideal place for flowering and trailing plants.

Creating cupboard space at the base of your unit is not very different from the floor-to-ceiling shelving project, because the top of the cupboard becomes, in practice, another shelf about 940mm/37in off the floor. You can construct the top of the unit as before (see page 142), using wood cladding between the shelves, and screwing vertical timber supports to right and left. The last shelf, now the cupboard top, needs a support under the front edge and at both sides, at right angles to the vertical side pieces. For these supports, 7.5 x 2.5cm/3 x 1in PAR is an ideal size. A final front piece level with the cupboard top edge acts as a joining length, as the sides and horizontal support can be fixed to it by screwing through from the back. Screw a base batten to the floor to support the back of the side pieces, and consequently the hinges. You have now created the paired door opening. A parting bead, measuring 12 x 25mm/½ x 1in, pinned to the inside with the rounded side facing out is a good finishing touch and accepts a flush hinge.

Cupboard doors

Probably the most intimidating part of the job, doors must be equal in size, square cornered and fit the opening well. The simplest doors are cut from 18mm/¾in blockboard or plywood, and you can have them machined to size at the woodyard. Measure the sizes needed to fit the opening, then deduct 4mm/⅛in from every side. This will allow you to pin a hardwood edging strip around the outside. This protects the outer veneer, and gives a professional finish. If you pin a 25mm/1in edging strip to an 18mm/¾in board door, flush with the back edge, overlapping at the front, a lip is created. A 12mm/½in half-round moulding, pinned on the board face abutting the lip and mitred at each corner, gives a simple, effective border, although many more decorative mouldings are available.

If you have been tempted to tile the shelves used on the open part of the unit, you could try the same tile scheme on the door fronts, as a coordinating effect. The doors are cut as before, and

Floor-to-ceiling shelving can provide a lot of useful storage space. Putting doors in front of the shelves will not only conceal their contents but also protect them from dust and sunlight.

edged with 25mm/1in hardwood strip, overlapping at the front edge. Seal the door surface if needed, and clean off any dirt or grease. Apply tile adhesive and position the tiles centrally, so that any small pieces of tile cut to fit are equally spaced around the edge. Leave this to set for 24 hours, then grout in the usual way. Alternatively, centre complete tiles only, and pin a suitable moulding around them to form an inner border. The door lip can be used to form its own outer border with a half-round mitred moulding as before.

Another way of constructing paired doors is to pin a simple mitred moulding on a man-made board cut to size, imitating a panelled door. The board needs to be edged with a hardwood strip, and looks better painted rather than varnished. The technique used to make wooden shutters (see page 198) can be easily adapted to make smaller cupboard doors. If necessary, the cladding can be fixed to both sides of the frame, making the door extremely strong. Finally, because the cupboard opening can be made any size you like, second-hand doors can be used.

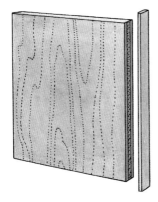

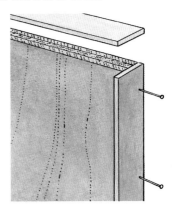

Shelves can be fitted with doors cut from plywood or blockboard sheets. Have them cut undersize and edge them with hardwood strips to provide a neat finish and protect the edge of the veneered face.

To make features of the doors, use edging strips that are wider than the doors' thickness. Pin these to the doors so that they are flush with the rear faces and project beyond the front faces.

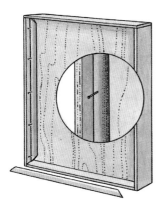

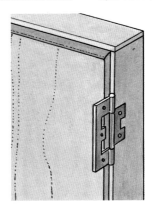

Finish off the doors by pinning a half-round moulding around the inside of the projecting edging strips. Mitre the ends of the moulding so that they fit together neatly in the corners.

Fit the doors with flush hinges top and bottom (add a third if the doors are floor-to-ceiling height) and screw these to the framework surrounding the shelves. Finally, add suitable catches.

Customised fire surrounds

After a period of unpopularity following the advent of central heating, the fireplace as a decorative room feature is back in fashion. Whether you have a surround that you don't like, one that needs refurbishing or merely a boarded-up hole, the focal point that a fire surround provides can be custom-built to fit or custom-decorated to match your decor.

Take it out...

Although they had been a functional part of room design for centuries, the fireplace and surround really came into their own as a decorative feature in Victorian times. They were a piece of built-in room furniture, a multi-faceted talking point that contributed much more to the living space than just its primary function, the supply of heat. With the introduction of central heating (a cleaner, more efficient way of heating the home) came a new style of living where the fireplace was no longer the centre of attention.

Designers had created a more modern environment, and the fireplace became part of history. Cast iron, tiled, marble, slate and wood surrounds alike were thrown into builders' skips.

...and put it back

Recent interior design principles do not entirely hark back to Victorian thinking, but they have resulted in a revival and reinstatement of the fireplace. Contemporary design and period fixtures are no longer considered to be mutually exclusive. Original

Above: A fireplace often provides a focal point in a room. This period bedroom would be lost without its fireplace, which gives a feeling of warmth despite the tall ceiling.

Right: Simple tiled fire surrounds are common to many pre- and post-war houses. Although basic, they can look good when teamed with sympathetic decor.

features can be updated with different colour and paint finishes, giving them a new lease of life, and ensuring they co-exist happily alongside modern schemes and furniture.

Replacing the fire surround is not a difficult task, but first you need to establish the state of the chimney breast. The mantlepiece and surround may have been removed, but the opening and fireback left in place, battened, covered with plasterboard and skimmed with plaster. If this is the case, there ought to be a ventilation grill, but if there isn't, you still need to investigate further by stripping back the wallcovering. Look for a join in the

The dramatic pillars supporting the mantleshelf turn this plain modern fireplace into a dramatic statement. Always integrate the fireplace into the room's overall decorative scheme.

plasterwork, then chisel away to reveal the wood frame fixed inside the opening. Then remove the battens, plasterboard and the resultant mess. If you are unlucky, however, and the opening has been professionally bricked up (the new brickwork will have been 'toothed-in' to the original bond), then you need to consult a builder or fireplace specialist.

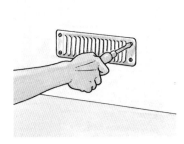

If your fireplace has been boarded up, there should be a ventilation grille in the closing panel to prevent condensation in the flue. Remove it.

Cut the plaster back from around the opening and lever the closing panel from its supporting framework in the fireplace.

Remove the wooden framework and clean up the opening ready for a new fire surround. Be prepared for a lot of mess.

Tiled finishes in working areas

When you select tiles for decorative purposes, lining walls in living quarters or tiling surfaces that reflect light patterns, the choice is almost unlimited. Handmade and decorated terracotta, unglazed, iridescent glass, stoneware, three-dimensional, metallic and retro are all available; the challenge is to match into your colour scheme.

Tiles for use in a working area, in particular on preparation surfaces in a kitchen, need to be both decorative and functional, and not all tiles are suitable. Tiles that are intended to be part of a work surface must not stain easily, must be strong and not crack, must be suitable for wet areas and be easily cleaned. In addition, crazed and cracked tiles that harbour dirt and germs must be avoided because they are a health hazard.

Tile selection

Tile makers – mass manufacturers and individual craftspeople alike – use many different clay types and glazes. The density of the clay and the glaze used affects the strength of the finished tile. For example, white and near-white glazes are much stronger than coloured ones. For this reason most specialist suppliers have a 'suitability chart', grading their tiles in terms of strength and colour, to ensure that you make an appropriate selection. Before you make this selection, consider carefully the function the tile will have to perform. On working surfaces in a kitchen you will need

the strongest tiles available in a colour that will resist staining by food and its preparation. Special-effect tiles, such as iridescent glass or metallic, are not practical, however attractive they may look. Mosaic sheets need careful consideration, too. They are easy to install on a work surface because the backing sheet can be shaped to fit, but again, you will need the strongest tiles available. They require a lot of grouting, too, with a special epoxy grout recommended for kitchen surfaces.

Updating your kitchen

Refurbishing a kitchen or working area is not simply a matter of decorating walls. Storage areas and worktops must be upgraded as well, or they will detract from the finished scheme. Storage units can be fitted with new doors that are simple to make. Plywood cut to size and edged can be tiled to match a worktop style in the same way that the combination storage doors matched the tiled shelves (see page 144). TGV doors pinned to a softwood frame will help create the feel of a country kitchen. Even a partial paint job

When adding a tiled finish to an old worktop, work over the surface with coarse abrasive paper to provide a key for the adhesive.

Set out the tiles 'dry' so that you can determine the best arrangement of colours and work out where you will have to cut tiles to fit.

Be prepared to revise your arrangement; change colours and patterns until you achieve the best layout before bedding the tiles down.

Mosaic panels can be used to good, colourful effect in a kitchen, although they do not provide the ideal surface for a worktop since they are unlikely to be thick enough.

- Allow space at the front edges for a wood edging strip if desired, although edging strips fixed at the sides of the worktop are best, protecting the top better and allowing tiles to be set flush against the edge.
- Spread the waterproof adhesive and bed down the tiles as you would on a wall, cutting to fit as needed.
- Leave to set for 24 hours.
- Before you grout the surface, make sure that your retailer has supplied the correct epoxy grout essential for these surfaces.

Finishing with wood
- Select a wood strip for the worktop edge. An astragal moulding is ideal; it has no right-angled edge to knock against.
- Mark and mitre to fit.
- Fix into position with 30mm/1¼in number 8 countersunk screws. Drive home the screws, setting them well below the surface of the wood.
- Fill the hole with a plastic wood filler that can be sanded flush when dry.
- Alternatively, bore each pilot and shank hole in one go with a combination screwsink that leaves a counterbored hole, and drive the screw in.
- The hole is filled by a wooden plug, cut to the correct screw size from the same wood by a plug cutter, and glued in place.
- When set, cut the plug as flush as possible with a sharp chisel, and sand to leave a professional finish.

on the original doors can suffice, if it is combined with a new wood stain or a simple stencilled motif. The really noticeable difference, though, will result from a new worktop surface, and tiling over the existing top will be the most effective economically.

A new top
Select your tiles carefully. A tough glazed stoneware tile with a good colour range would be ideal, but, depending on your surface size, they ought not to be too large.
- To avoid unpleasant visual discrepancies when cutting strips to fill, 10cm/4in square would be small enough yet still allow for fairly simple grouting.
- Make sure the worktop is clean and dry.
- Abrade the surface with coarse aluminium oxide (40 grit) to provide a 'key' if it is very smooth.
- Using a tile as a template, set out on the surface so that you achieve the best arrangement.
- Ensure cut tiles are at the back, where the wall meets the surface, not at the front.

Protect the perimeter of the worktop with wood strips the same depth as the tiles. Cut to size, mitring the ends and check the fit.

Pin the strips in place, overhanging the edge. Fix a reinforcing strip underneath the lip.

For reasons of hygiene, kitchen worktop tiles must be grouted with a two-part epoxy grout. Use a small trowel to press it into the joints.

Storage box sections

Whether you need to reinforce sagging shelves with vertical supports or make up a self-supporting unit with stepped sides, the same simple wood joint can be used. Halving joints allow the shelves to slot together at right angles, forming a strong, unseen bond which can also be used as a decorative feature.

Weight for support

Shelving systems, constructed from 25mm/1in boards or 18mm/¾in plywood machined to size, are ideal for fixing in an alcove. The recess will generally be less than 1.8m/6ft wide and the shelf length, if supported on battens to the side and rear, will be perfectly stable. Longer lengths, needed to span a gap where, say, two rooms have been knocked into one and the resultant distance

A modular box-section storage system can provide a versatile means of containing and displaying *a wide variety of domestic objects. Such systems can be tailored to meet your specific needs.*

between chimney breasts is over 3m/10ft, are liable to sag, particularly if they are 30cm/12in in width. Front support pieces, glued and screwed under and flush with the front edge of each shelf, will help, but heavy weights will still cause problems.

It is reasonable to assume that a long, wide shelf will be used to hold larger, heavier items than a small shelf, so it must be constructed with more support. Loadbearing shelves can have brackets screwed underneath, either as separate fixed items or as part of an adjustable shelving system, where removable brackets are slotted into steel uprights screwed to the wall. There are numerous adjustable systems on the market, all using the same principle, and the heavy-duty ones are very strong indeed. The wall fixings must involve no less than 56mm/2¼in number 10 countersunk screws driven into heavy-duty wall plugs. The uprights should be spaced 75cm/2½ft apart. Heavy-duty adjustable shelving is available in only very basic colours, however. Although you can paint it yourself, and it may look effective in a workroom, garage or outbuilding, it isn't exactly subtle. There is a better, much more attractive loadbearing support system for a living area, which you can construct yourself.

A self-supporting box system

This is a simple wooden unit that relies on horizontal and vertical boards meeting at a series of halving joints and providing mutual support. A halving joint is simple to cut and, when accurate, extremely strong and virtually invisible. The principle behind halving joints (also called half-and-half joints or half-laps) is that where the timbers meet or overlap at right-angles, one exact half of each timber is cut and removed to allow the pieces to slot together. The timbers can be cramped securely, marked out with a knife and cut together so that the housings are the same width

Cut the first half of the joint in one board. You can subsequently use it as a template to mark the matching half with your marking knife.

Cut the joint by making a series of saw cuts through the waste to the bottom of each of the slots. Then remove the waste with a thin chisel.

Then check the fit of each of the joints. They should all be snug, and making saw cuts on the waste side of each marked line should ensure this.

Glue inside the housings of the corresponding joint halves and carefully assemble the boards.

Cramp and wipe off excess glue. The unit can be strengthened by gluing and pinning on a plywood backing.

as the thickness of the wood, and cut back with a chisel to a shoulder half the width of the timber. Always saw on the waste side of the marked line when cutting halving joints. If you don't, the housings will be too wide by the width of the saw blade, and the joint will be loose.

Custom building

Any size of unit can be constructed in this way, depending on your storage requirements, and the space available. A drawing dividing the wall space into compartments is a good start. These can be any size, but square is easy and uniformly attractive. Consider using measurements that turn the unit into a series of cubes: if your

chosen timber is 30cm/1ft wide, use the same figure for the internal dimensions of each box. A scaled-down model made of card will give you a better idea of how it will look – slots cut in the card will join together in exactly the same way as the timbers.

The top of the unit need not reach the ceiling. A long top shelf for houseplants and ornaments is created by forming external corners, which are simply one-sided halving joints.

Your unit is floor-standing, so you need to consider a plinth for the base, and this should be the height of the skirting. Flush at the front and sides, the plinth can be set forward the width of the skirting at the back of the base, so that the unit back is flush with the wall.

Securing and backing

If you are making a small unit, cramping it square as you glue the joints will ensure it is stable enough. Larger units can be glued in sections as you proceed, but any 'play' in the halving joints will result in undue pressure being placed on the unit's square corners. A support batten glued and screwed under the top back edge of each top corner box will hold that corner square, and allow you to drill through and fix the unit to the wall. If you prefer, you can attach a back panel, placing the unit face-down on the floor, and confirming that it is square.

Cut 6mm/¼in plywood to fit the outside back, and glue and pin into position with panel pins. Make sure that the best side of the plywood is visible from the front. The unit is now stable and free-standing. Screws driven through the backing into the wall can be used to provide extra security, if required (sensible if it is to hold heavy items).

FLOORS

The choice of a floor covering is usually a vote for practicality over style and fashion. Heavy traffic areas, potentially wet areas, outdoor access areas and more intimate, friendly areas all have their own separate requirements which take precedence over decorative style. Expensive wall-to-wall carpeting is not compatible with large, muddy boots, while cold quarry tiling is not suitable for the children's playroom. Given today's lifestyles, versatility must be an important issue when deciding on your flooring; indeed, many modern flooring materials are described as multi-functional. In a modern living environment, choosing which floor covering to put where has never been more important.

Designer's notes

A floor serves a single purpose; it is there to be walked on. Therefore, the first principle of flooring and floor covering is practicality. There is a wide range of flooring materials to choose from. Depending on the purpose of the room, you may want warmth and softness underfoot, or a more hard-wearing surface suitable for heavy traffic.

Above: Fitted carpets provide a soft and comfortable floor covering that creates a harmonious link between one room and another.

Right: Vinyl flooring is very hard-wearing and ideal for use in areas of heavy traffic, such as a hallway. It is also easily cleaned.

To begin, decide on floor plans from a purely cosmetic viewpoint, and then look at the consequences. Stripped boards can allow draughts, especially if the house has a cellar. Light-coloured or plain carpeting shows every mark. Scattered rugs can trip people up. Tiles can be cold in areas where people are likely to walk barefoot, as can lino and vinyl. Stockinged feet slide on polished floors, and thin woodstrip veneers wear out quickly in heavy human traffic. The way you choose to treat your floors has not only a decorative impact, but a noticeable effect on the quality of life around you. Don't overlook the effect a poor decision can have on your bank balance, either, should you be faced with the prospect of replacing expensive flooring that proved unsuitable.

Rugs can be used to provide colourful accents on a floor, but they can also be trip hazards.

Use special rug grippers to prevent them from moving and causing an accident.

Flagstones were often found in the kitchens of period houses. If you want to recreate the look of the past, they are ideal, and you can buy modern imitations, but they will be cold underfoot.

Work with what you have

Replacing a floor is an arduous task, and one that should not be undertaken lightly. Quite apart from the floor surface, the skirtings will have to be removed and possibly replaced, damaging the wall surface and the decorative finish.

Unless you are renovating a property from scratch, or the existing flooring is beyond redemption, try to work with what you have inherited. This need not mean covering up an area with carpet or vinyl, relying on the 'out-of-sight-out-of-mind' theory. Instead, identify the positive and workable characteristics of the floor.

If you have original floorboards, check them for rot and damage. If they are sound, you have an opportunity to sand, varnish, colourwash, stain or simply leave them with a plain scrubbed finish. Broken, damaged or rotted boards need replacing. Note the width and depth of the wood and its type (pine, usually) and seek out a local architectural salvage yard.

Modern floors tend to be chipboard, an artificial board of no visual worth in itself, but which provides a sound base for painted designs. A piece of woven matting placed centrally can be effectively emphasised by a painted border in contrasting colours.

Chipboard is also a good base for vinyl floorcoverings, and for supporting interlocking boards of hardwood veneer on a backing of softwood or plywood, known as woodstrip flooring.

Period houses may have slate, marble or flagstone floors, particularly in kitchen and washroom areas. Slabs are available from specialist suppliers, but they tend to be quite expensive. Imitation flagstones, made of concrete, can be bought at a fraction of the price.

Tiled floors can be refurbished, and encaustic tiles are available from specialist suppliers for repair purposes. Dull floors can be stripped and re-polished. Quarry tiles were also popular throughout the ground floor and outhouses, and if you discover a damaged floor you can easily replace individual tiles.

Start at the bottom

When you have identified the advantages inherent in your existing flooring, try to visualise the rest of the walls and ceiling in a finish that emphasises these qualities. It may seem odd working up from the bottom, but if you can start from the point of a natural and practical asset, then you are much more likely to achieve a pleasing result that benefits the entire household design scheme.

Basic skills: identifying boards

Recognising wooden floor types and sizes is not a particularly difficult skill to acquire, but dealing with defects and problems, sometimes caused by neglect or bad workmanship by previous owners, can be hard and time-consuming. Replacing floorboards may involve sourcing second-hand materials from salvage or reclamation yards.

Basic, traditional floorboards will be made from softwood – usually pine. You may find them as bare wood because many older properties preferred scrubbed floors, or they may have been varnished to imitate a darker, more expensive wood. Using cheap timber and varnishing it to deceive was a Victorian trick. This has found popularity again, although today's colours, stains and varnishes give a much subtler finish. You may also find painted boards, either across the entire floor, or just at the edges where they would be visible if the room had a central carpet.

Boards were laid in a number of sizes, originally 25mm/1in thick timbers, in widths of 13cm/5in, 15cm/6in or 18cm/7in. Genuine old hardwood floors are rare, and the timber width will be significantly less than softwood. Be careful you don't mistake veneer strip flooring for the real thing.

Infestation

Check the condition of the floor carefully. If you have removed old carpets and underlays, or ripped up hardboard pinned or stapled in position, remember that this will have stopped the floor 'breathing'.

Inadequate ventilation, combined with damp conditions, can lead to wood rot, so examine the entire area carefully, including skirtings. Dry rot can often be present in a timber with an apparently unaffected surface, although small splits may be visible close up. If you are suspicious, prod the timber with a blade – dry rot gives easily. Wet rot is found only in saturated conditions, and thus tends to be more obvious. Both cases are solved only by cutting out the infected timbers, drying out the surrounding area and treating it with a wood preservative. You must remove the cause of the damp and ensure proper air circulation or the problem may return. Woodworm is a constant concern in timber-framed properties. If you find tiny flight holes in the floor, inject them with woodworm fluid. If the problem is far-reaching, you must call in a professional.

Repairing and lifting boards

Repairs to basic floorboarding are straightforward, and they do not require many specialist tools. You will need a padsaw and electrician's bolster, but these should be part of your household kit

Far left: Wet rot is caused when timbers are exposed to constant damp conditions. The wood begins to crumble and so loses its strength. The only solution is to cut out the damage and replace it with new wood, after having found and cured the cause of the original damp.

Left: Attack by woodworm can be identified by the small flight holes left when the insects bore their way out of the timber. Small areas of damage can be treated with fluid; large areas should be dealt with by cutting out and renewing the infected timber.

Identify the joist position (the fixing nails will help) and drill a hole at the edge of the board just to one side of the joist.

Insert the blade of a jigsaw through the drilled hole and use it to cut across the floorboard alongside the joist.

Drive the blade of an electrician's bolster into the saw cut and use it to lever the cut end of the board upwards.

Lift the board sufficiently to wedge a length of batten beneath it so that it is held clear while you cut the other end over a joist.

Screw a short length of batten to the side of the first joist, and flush with the top, to support one end of the new board.

Cut the new board to size and set it on the batten and second joist. You can nail it down, but screws will allow easy removal in future.

anyway. A floorboard saw is useful if a lot of board cutting is needed. The first task is always to identify the cause of any particular problem. More floor damage is caused by previous attempts to access pipe systems and wiring runs than any amount of footwear. Access panels that are to be retained in the floor should be screwed down, not nailed. Screwing down a wooden board rather than nailing it should cure any annoying creaks under carpeting that are caused by movement. If the board is man-made (chipboard) it should ideally have been screwed down in the first place.

Check to see if the boards are anchored on all joists, and none is missed. Creaking, exposed floorboards that are to be varnished can also be screwed down, but the screw heads need to be hidden. Either countersink the heads and fill with an appropriate coloured plastic filler, or counterbore a hole and cover the head with a chamfered wooden plug.

To remove a damaged section of board, or to gain new access, locate the nearest joist and mark a pencil line alongside it. The floorboard nails will be your best indicator. Drill a hole to the side of the joist, large enough to start the cut with a padsaw blade, then use a floorboard saw. Alternatively use a jigsaw, cutting the board parallel with the joist.

Lever up the end with the electrician's bolster, lift it and slide a wood batten under as support while you cut the other end, directly in the middle of a joist. Use a tenon saw for this cut; on no account try using a jigsaw, because you have a solid joist underneath and will snap the blade immediately.

Screw a batten to the side of the first joist, to act as a support for the access panel or a new piece of board. It is important to bear in mind that if the boards are tongue-and-groove, you will have to saw down one length to cut through the tongue and release the board.

Preparing exposed floors

Old wooden floors that are re-coloured if necessary and varnished for protection look good in almost any situation. You don't always have to machine sand the boards, either; thorough cleaning is often all that is needed prior to the application of a decorative finish and a coat of varnish to seal them and make them hard-wearing.

The pros and cons of sanding

Sanding floors and varnishing them has become very popular, because the finished floor will look good with any room scheme, and is as versatile an asset as you could wish for. If some of the floorboards are damaged, they can be replaced by new ones. And, since the whole room is being sanded back, there will be no discernible difference in the surface colour. However, one drawback to sanding is that it reduces the thickness of the wood: floorboards

that were once 18 to 20mm/¾ to ⅞in, providing solid support and a fair insulation against sound, are reduced by 3 to 4mm/⅛ to ¼in, depending on the uneven nature of the floor. This may be no problem for you, but in houses with a cellar or exposed beams underneath, the noise level will be increased, as will the draught. If the boards are currently bare and in reasonable condition, consider washing them down and adding colour instead of sanding them back. Replacement second-hand boards can be found at

Clean old boards thoroughly by scrubbing them with hot water and household abrasive cleaner, working with the grain.

When the boards have been allowed to dry, brush on the desired finish, again working with the grain and maintaining a wet edge.

Repeat the brushing process if a paint residue is left, but use wire wool for the best finish and for getting into the grain beneath a stain. You may now be left with a fairly rough board surface. If this is so it is because the water used in cleaning down has raised the wood grain, and the board needs sanding slightly by hand. Wrap a fine grade of aluminium oxide abrasive (120 grit) around a sanding block and gently sand with the grain. It is imperative that the boards are completely dry when you start this job. If the floorboards are smooth after the cleaning process, which they will be if they have been varnished some time previously, they can be 'keyed' to accept a new finish. Gently abrade the surface with a fine grade silicon carbide (wet-and-dry paper) used wet, again working along the grain.

architectural salvage yards, if needed; and even a new board or two can be matched in.

Try experimenting with oil-based stains on a scrap of (new) board, mixing them together, then diluting them with solvent. When you have a reasonable match, brush it onto the new floorboard and sand it down. Oil-based stains penetrate deeper into the wood, so don't try this with water-based stains.

Cleaning and preparing

Plain wooden boards in period properties were scrubbed vigorously with a mix of sand and water, often resulting in a delicate-looking grey sheen. Elbow work is still required, but modern cleaners and abrasives give every assistance and an impressive result. Start as you would any dirty job, using hot water, abrasive cleaning cream and a stiff brush. Work the brush into and with the wood grain, not across it, and clean small areas of board at a time, washing down immediately with clean water. Clean the entire floor, leave it to dry, and repeat the whole process if necessary.

You can now see if any problem areas remain, such as stains, plaster lumps or splashes of paint. Plaster, softened by the cleaning process, will lift off with a flexible bladed knife. Stains and old paint need brushing with a water washable paint remover. Wait until the paint blisters, and then scrape it off with a flexible blade.

The next stage

Take time out to review your plans. Is the floor in good condition? If it is, all you need to do is decide on a wood finish. If it isn't, and the boards have shrunk slightly, leaving gaps, or boards have been carelessly lifted by tradespeople in a hurry, then you have to decide

Left: Removing a ceiling to expose the floor joists of the room above can be very effective.

Bear in mind, however, that sound and draughts can travel up through gaps between the floorboards.

Above: A blue colourwash can look good on washed floor boards, the blue blending with the greyish tint of the old pine. You can use thinned emulsion paint provided it is sealed with a varnish.

whether or not to proceed. Entire board lengths can be replaced, but finding a timber match for second-hand boards is becoming more and more difficult. Gaps between boards can be filled with chamfered wooden fillets glued, hammered into place and left to dry. In both these cases you would do well to consider sanding down the floor with a hired industrial sander, to achieve a level and colour-matched surface.

You may find that the gaps do not bother you. As long as there is no cellar or basement with exposed joists beneath, electric light will not filter up through the gaps, which can ruin the effect of any stripped floor. If you have access to the joists from the cellar, however, it is a simple enough job to nail hardboard to the underside of the floor, between the joists. Cut the hardboard into long strips that fit neatly between the joists. Tack into position with 18mm/³⁄₄in tacks, at 150mm/6in centres. Don't be tempted into using longer tacks, unless you check first to make sure that the points won't break through the surface of the boards of the floor above.

Colours on washed boards

Old scrubbed boards will often have a grey appearance, and you can accentuate this with your colour choice, using a grey-green or pale blue colourwash. A dessertspoonful of emulsion paint stirred into a litre of water will provide you with a wash that sinks into the grain, but can be wiped off the surface if desired. This wash can be repeated until the colour effect is satisfactory. Then, the board can be varnished or left unsealed. If you want to put colour back into the bleached wood, try a wash of dark red, highlighting the grain, followed by an oil-based pine varnish. Dilute the varnish with white spirit so that it can be applied more easily, sinking into the wood surface. Finally, seal with a clear floor varnish.

Machine sanding

Hire centres will rent out two types of sander for your floor: a large machine that looks like an old-fashioned lawnmower with a dust bag attached, for the main floor area, and a small belt or disc sander for getting in close to skirtings. They will supply all the necessary abrasives, and, most importantly, face masks and protective glasses. Make sure you understand how both machines work before you take them home.

Your first job is to hammer down all the nail heads, well below the surface of the floorboards, using a nail set or punch. If you don't take on this tiresome task, the nail heads will rip the abrasive

When sanding a floor, begin by making a series of diagonal passes with coarse abrasive across the boards. Then work diagonally in the other direction with a medium grade of abrasive.

A properly sanded and varnished boarded floor makes the most of the beauty of the wood grain.

sheets on the drum sander. Sanding a floor raises a lot of dust, and although the machine has a collecting bag, a lot gets into the air, so make sure you are wearing a protective mask and goggles when you start up the machine.

- Run the sander diagonally across the floor at 45 degrees to the boards, using coarse abrasive paper.
- Change to a medium-grade abrasive, and again sand across the floor, but this time at right angles to your first run.
- Then sand up and down, following the board direction.
- Change finally to a fine-grade abrasive, and finish off sanding with the grain.
- The small sander reaches into skirting areas, doorways and alcoves where the larger drum cannot reach. Here again, start with the coarser abrasive, finish with the fine.
- Clean dust from the boards before sealing and varnishing.

Sealing and varnishing

Clear varnishes are readily available but they are expensive. Make sure you have the best quality, and that the varnish is recommended for flooring. Cheap polyurethane varnish intended for internal wood work will not put up with everyday wear and tear, and is false economy. It may crack under pressure of furniture castors, and you could be faced with the prospect of a repeat job.

Next work up and down the boards using medium-grade abrasive. Then fit a fine grade of paper to the machine and repeat the process, working in the direction of the grain.

Use an edge sander to work up to the skirtings, using progressively finer grades of abrasive.

After removing all dust and debris, treat the boards with a sealer and apply a varnish.

Fitting a floor, fitting skirting

Renewing a boarded floor should not be undertaken lightly, as it involves a considerable amount of work and disruption. However, replacing a damaged skirting board is a job that can be undertaken as a weekend project. Care and accuracy are required as always, but normal household life can continue around the work.

Fitting a new softwood floor onto joists, replacing one that is too badly damaged to repair, keeping it square with the room sides and finishing with a replacement skirting in the house style, is a major undertaking. This task is best left to a specialist, unless you have some previous experience. Irrespective of whether you tackle the job yourself or not, it is helpful to know what is involved: the room will be out of commission for a considerable time. You must make allowances for time spent not only on the floor itself, but in

making good the room. Wall damage is likely to occur when removing the skirtings, and this may involve plastering or papering. If you have two rooms knocked through into one, measure the size of the skirting board in each half of the new area – they may be two distinctly different styles. Period houses generally had a larger, more ornate skirting in what was referred to as the Sunday room, than in the back or 'living' room. If these rooms are now joined, the skirtings could differ in height by as much as 13cm/5in. A consistent skirting size will be needed. If you fit the larger size to stay in period, you merely need to be as careful as possible during removal. If you are fitting a smaller size, a great deal of making good will be needed to tie in to the wall. Remember the finish, too. Quite apart from any paint effect, three coats of protective varnish will be needed, each requiring 24 hours drying time.

Removal

- Hammer an electrician's bolster between the top edge of the skirting and the wall, near the end of a length, opening up a gap.
- Prise the skirting away from the wall. If excessive levering is required, protect the wall surface with a timber offcut.
- The skirting length may be nailed directly to the masonry, or nailed or screwed to sawn timber blocks inset into the wall, or nailed to vertical studs if you have a stud wall.
- If the boards come away from the wall leaving well-secured nails still in place, it may be easier to hammer them in rather than risk more damage trying to get them out.
- Once the skirting is out of the way, start at one end of the room and prise up the first few boards only.

In period houses skirting boards can be of considerable depth, making a strong visual statement around the edge of the floor. However, they are vulnerable to knocks and may need replacing.

Drive an electrician's bolster behind the skirting board, near one end, to begin freeing it from the base of the wall.

Work along the skirting board, levering it from the wall and trying to minimise the damage to the plasterwork.

If any fixing nails pull through the board as it is removed, hammer them in rather than trying to pull them out.

- Removing boards only as you replace them means that you always have a floor surface to kneel or stand on, lessening the risk of an accident.
- Remove the floorboard or cut nails with the claw of the hammer during the process of removing the board; don't hammer them down.
- Brush dirt and debris off the joist when it is revealed and then you are ready to lay the new floorboards.

New for old

Unless you plan to fit a reclaimed timber floor, possibly utilising some undamaged lengths from the old one, you will find the board widths will not be exactly the same as the ones that you have taken out. Actual metric sizes of finished timber have replaced the old imperial nominal sizes, so board widths will be close, but not exact. Because the entire floor is being replaced, this does not matter, and allows you the opportunity to select TGV boards, giving the floor overall additional strength and minimising the risk of warping and lifting.

Measure the floor carefully, in the direction the boards run, and make sure when you order the wood that there will be enough boards of that length or longer to complete the job. This avoids cutting and shutting on the main part of the floor, and looks much neater because no break appears in the run of the wood grain. If this seems overly fussy, remember that unmatched joins will be more noticeable if you intend to use a decorative paint or stain finish.

Alcoves or bay areas with shorter lengths can be cut from longer stock on

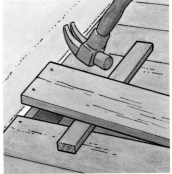

Lift the first floorboard by driving an electrician's bolster into the gap between the boards and levering upwards.

Once you have the end lifted high enough, slip a batten underneath and begin to drive it along below the board, which will be sprung free.

site, but remember when making your calculations that bays may need mitres. Begin at the end of the room; you may be able to use the old boards as templates for cutting the new, particularly if you have to start in a bay. Otherwise, transfer angles for cutting lines directly from a sliding bevel. Notice that the boards stop slightly short of the wall. This allows for any small expansion of the wood and helps air to circulate between the floor and ceiling. This small gap will be covered by the skirting.

Measure the floor carefully to calculate the number and length of new boards required. Try to keep joints in runs to a minimum.

If the ends of boards need to be cut at an angle, use a sliding bevel to transfer the angle accurately to the new boards.

Closing up the floorboards

Whether you use TGV or straight-sided boards, they need to be cramped together tightly. This will not only maximise the strength of the TGV join, but also minimises the gaps that inevitably appear when using conventional boards, as the wood dries out fully even if it has been fitted after acclimatisation. You must help this process by placing the timber lengths in the room for a few days before installation. It still won't stop small gaps appearing over time, but it will tend to reduce the shrinkage.

As with all bought softwoods, the worst problems occur when cold, damp timber is cut and joined, and the central heating is turned on. For this reason, really top-quality floors are relaid, closing up the boards, after six months or so.

• Lay half a dozen boards in position, leave a 5cm/2in gap, and place a timber batten across the joists, either nailed down or held against the old boards yet to be taken up.

• Make up two identical wedges, about 30cm/1ft long. Place them in the gap and hammer them together, tightening up the floor.

• Leave the wedges in place while you nail down the floor. In high-quality TGV work, where the floor is to be left exposed, one board at a time must be laid and wedged tight, so that the invisible fixing (50mm/2in lost-head or finishing nail) can be made through the tongue and then hidden by the subsequent board. With TGV boards it is important not to damage the tongue when wedging, or subsequent grooves won't fit very easily. Cut a scrap piece of TGV in half, fit the grooved half over the tongue as protection, and hammer your wedges against that.

Lay six of the new boards in place, leaving a space between them and the old boards yet to be removed.

Nail a stout wooden batten across the joists about 5cm/2in from the edge of the last new floorboard laid.

Cut two long, narrow wedges and drive them between the batten and floorboard to cramp the boards tightly together for nailing to the joists.

Measure up for the new lengths of skirting, beginning at the door opening and working towards the nearest corner.

Nail the board in place. At an internal corner, mark the profile of the skirting on the adjoining board so that it fits over the first board.

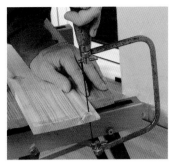

Use a coping saw to cut the profile in the end of the board. Its thin blade will be able to follow any intricate pattern with ease.

At an external corner, mark the board for length against the wall, then mitre the end outwards from this mark. Do the same with its neighbour.

Nail the boards to the wall on each side of an external corner. Then pin through the end of one board into the other.

You can attach the skirting by using the original method, nailing into the wall or timber wedges, or screw it in place.

Putting back a skirting

The size and form of a skirting will often date a property, so make sure the one you pick is suitable, and not at odds with the rest of the decor. Larger, more ornate moulded skirtings give a period feel to the room, and usually appear to be part of the wall, not the floor. Smaller, modern skirtings, often found with a two-sided profile so that they can be fixed either way around, tend to appear as part of the flooring, particularly if they have been treated with the same finish.

- When you have made your choice of moulding, start from the door opening (a right-angled cut).
- Measure and cut right into the first corner, flush against the adjacent wall.

- Butt up the next board, mark the moulding profile onto it and cut it to fit. All internal corners should be cut this way.
- External corner turns should be mitred – after fixing the first length, mark the inside of the next mitre on the reverse side of the next board. Remember that the cutting line should run outwards from the back face of the skirting, as the 45-degree joint with the adjoining board runs out from the corner.
- Fix the skirting in place either re-using the method that was employed in fixing the old one, or screw into position, covering the counterbored heads with wooden plugs, cutting flush with a knife and sanding. This fixing method is recommended if you intend a stain and varnish finish.

Staircases

Staircases come in a range of shapes and styles from the purely functional to the elaborate and ornate. Get to know your staircase type and its functional parts, for example whether it is a straight, sweeping, half-turn, quarter-turn or dog-leg style staircase, and whether it has a closed or open string or open tread.

Types of stairs

Modern staircases tend towards one style, the closed-string stair, which takes up the minimum of space, usually against a wall, and is the most economic to construct. Other styles in timber staircases include the open-string, where the strings are sawn to the profile of the steps, and the stair treads sit on the cut-outs, or the open-tread, where the risers are omitted altogether. Other staircases, such as spirals, are often functional space savers installed to gain access to loft rooms or basements.

If you own a period property, you will already know that, historically, the staircase was much more than a functional way of changing floors – it was a status symbol. The Victorians, in particular, favoured elaborate, decorative stairs and their house design emphasised ornate hallways, where the stairs could be admired by a visitor to the front door. By the time the stairs reached the servants' floors, however, best-quality joinery timbers were replaced by cheap pine, painted or varnished a darker colour as an attempted disguise. Whatever the age of your staircase, it contains the same functional parts, all of which are replaceable.

Basic staircase repairs

Creaking stairs are usually caused by loose-fitting treads or risers. Under foot pressure the loose part moves against an adjacent fixed piece. The repairs are fairly simple, however:

- Locate the source of the creak, and check the wedges that should hold the tread and riser firmly in position.
- If one is loose, remove it, checking that it is not broken or split. If it is, use it as a template to make up a new one. Replace the wedge, hammering it into position with a wooden mallet.
- Check the glue blocks, re-gluing if necessary.
- On troublesome treads, you could try screwing and gluing a batten of 25 x 25mm/1 x 1in underneath the complete width, joining the tread and riser together.
- Countersink 30mm/1¼in number 8 screws – don't use longer ones or you risk them coming through on the other side.
- Still underneath, drive the same screw size up into the bottom edge of the riser through the back edge of the tread.
- If you cannot gain access to the underside (if the soffit is plastered, for example), approach the problem from the front.

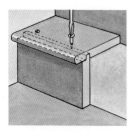

Screws can be driven down through the tread and into the riser below to reinforce the joint.

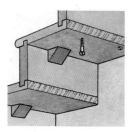

From beneath the stairs, drive more screws through the tread into the riser above.

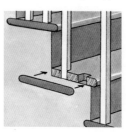

Return nosings can be prised off and replaced. They also give access to the baluster base.

If access to the underside of the stairs is impossible, reinforce the treads and risers with L-brackets.

Staircase terminology

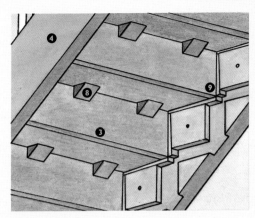

1 **Tread:** the part you stand on as you ascend or descend, usually overlapping the riser with a rounded or semi-rounded front.

2 **Nosing:** separate moulding on the tread front, or the rounded tread front itself. (Return nosing is the same as the nosing, but hiding the end grain of the tread and side base of the baluster on staircases built with open strings).

3 **Riser:** the vertical timber joining the back of one tread to the front of the next.

4 **Strings:** the sides of the staircase. Against the wall side, the inner string forms part of the continuous skirting. The outer string, which can be open or closed, holds the balusters in place.

5 **Balusters:** usually decorative turned sections of wood acting as banister supports. (Balustrade is the collective of balusters.)

6 **Banister:** hand rail, running on top of the balusters.

7 **Newel post:** anchored support post, at the stair foot, and where the stairs turn.

8 **Glue blocks:** positioned at the back of the joint between riser and tread, as reinforcement.

9 **Wedges:** positioned underneath, securing both tread and riser to the string.

- Your only choice at the back of the tread is a right-angled metal support bracket to hold it to the riser.
- Mark the position with a pencil and carefully chisel the depth of the metal out of the wood.
- Screw into position with 12mm/½in number 6 screws.
- At the front of the tread, countersink 30mm/1¼in number 8 screws down through the tread, into the riser edge, at 10cm/4in intervals along the length.

Finishes on wooden staircases

If you have been forced to repair a tread from the front, using visible brackets and screws, you have little choice but to fit a carpet or runner. Functional and conventional, coverings reduce the noise of feet on the stairs. Closed string cases suit a fitted carpet, but open strings encourage the use of a centrally positioned stair runner, allowing both exposed sides to be varnished or painted.

There is no reason why stairs in good constructional condition should not have a paint and varnish finish. Try a combination of royal blue or dark green with a clear varnished natural wood, where the balusters and the risers are painted and the banister, tread and nosings varnished. The different woods of banister and stair contrast well with each other and the painted parts.

Use a top quality floor or yacht varnish on the treads, applying four coats as a minimum and sanding gently between coats. Don't reverse the stair scheme, though. Paint on the treads won't last long unless it is over-varnished, which rather defeats the object.

Overlaying floors

There is no better floor in any home than a timber surface in good condition – it can be the centre of attention. Its good looks ensure that it fits well with any decorative style. Timber flooring, as well as making a statement about your lifestyle, invokes memories of an age when floors were part of the decorative scheme in houses.

A popular choice

Current market research indicates that real wood and real wood veneer flooring will remain as a popular choice with property owners for the foreseeable future, being hard-wearing, stylish and relatively 'low maintenance'. Real wood floors are perceived as warm and inviting in cold winters and as having a cool feel to offset hot summer days. Health is an issue, too, as carpeting of any

The beauty of a real wood floor will set off any room's decor to perfection. The richness of the colour and grain pattern will provide a feeling of warmth in winter and coolness in summer.

kind harbours dust mites, and asthma and hay fever sufferers can benefit from the low dust retention qualities of this replacement flooring. Strip wood manufacturers have been quick to promote good environmental policies, too, claiming not to fell any endangered tropical species, and to take supplies of hardwood only from controlled areas where the rate of replanting equals the rate of harvesting.

Strips and mosaics of real wood

Real hardwood floors can still be laid, using solid boards that are machined from oak, elm, chestnut and ash, among others, often from controlled European stock. Specialist workshops will supply and fit a new floor, and often take on restoration projects. The cost can be prohibitive, though, and the rise in popularity of real veneer timber flooring systems is testament to this fact. Solid hardwood strips will always be the top of the range, expensive to source and very time consuming to lay, but offering a finish that will last a lifetime. Current layering technology now offers a good-looking alternative, at a price closer to the average budget. Real wood veneers form the top layer of a composite construction, which includes a shock absorbing middle layer and a stabilising base. The three different layers comprise wood strips laid at right-angles to each other, to minimise expansion and shrinkage of the floor panel as it experiences different climatic humidities. The veneered panels are finished with up to five coats of varnish offering ultra-violet protection, with a pore sealer, and as a first impression offer the same visual qualities as solid floors. Planks of veneered flooring are tongued and grooved, and are priced per square metre, but often sold in packs covering 3m or more, and they can be fairly simply installed as 'floating floors'. The veneer thickness, about 4 to 5mm, allows the laid floor to be sanded down

Laminate flooring provides an inexpensive alternative to real wood flooring and can be very effective. The panels snap together and have a synthetic finish representing various woods.

Laminate flooring

If real wood veneer panelled flooring is the economic alternative to a traditional hardwood block floor, then laminate 'wood effect' floor panels are the cheap alternative to real wood veneers. The top layer is a photograhic effect, a fairly good plastic representation of a hardwood finish, either in colours pertaining to real woods such as cherry, chestnut and ash, or in plain blues and greens. These easy to fit tongue and grooved panels are sometimes glued and sometimes snapped together, but always need a flooring underlay and a fitting kit. Be aware that the top 'wood effect' layer is very thin, and will not tolerate heavy traffic. Again priced per square metre, laminate flooring is available in packs usually covering about 2 square metres. A fair indication of its quality is the price tag. You will pay about 20 per cent of the price of a real wood veneer floor, and it would be more realistic to offer this product as an alternative to linoleum or vinyl.

Whatever type of flooring you choose, bear in mind that looking at small areas 'in the pack' will not necessarily give you a good idea of the impression produced by the finished floor; some finishes may become overpowering over a large area.

and finished in the same way as a solid floor, and as the years pass, it will age and colour in the same way. The same sanding and varnishing technique is needed for most wood mosaic tile floors, although a few manufacturers supply pre-finished units. Wood mosaic consists of five or more strips of wood joined along their longest edge into a square, then bound together at right angles to similar units on a cloth backing to form a square tile. The small strips may be solid hardwood, but more often than not are veneers on a softwood or man-made backing board. Mosaic tiles offer a wide choice in wood types and are sold in packs, again priced per square metre. The main difference between these tiles and the strip flooring panels is that the tiles are glued into position conventionally, while the panels are joined to each other and not to the sub-floor.

Wood mosaic flooring comprises square panels of wood strips on a cloth backing, which are laid like tiles. The strips may be cut from solid timber or softwood or board faced with veneer, and offer a range of hardwood finishes.

*Plastic laminate flooring
boards offer a cheaper
alternative to real wood.*

*These real oak
laminate boards are
tongued–and–grooved for jointing.*

Locating the right floor

Always consult with your supplier to ensure the flooring panels of
your choice are suitable for the domestic location you have in
mind. Depending on the manufacturer's recommendations, certain
panels may be deemed unsuitable for bathrooms (wet areas) or
kitchens (high-humidity areas), or be classified as suitable for
entrance halls or bedrooms (high- or low-traffic areas). Some
boards are unsuitable for heated floors, such as beech, whereas
some woods are ideal for humid areas where high dimensional
stability is required. Bamboo, for example, has a low moisture
content and works well in bathrooms.

Preparing to lay a floating floor

As usual, the hard work in laying a floor is unseen, being
underneath. Preparation is the key to a good floor, while the actual
laying of the panels should proceed reasonably quickly, permitting
an ever increasing view of the final result. The preparation must
include levelling of the existing floor, if necessary. A basement with

a solid floor may need
screeding with a concrete mix,
or sealing to prevent damp
problems. Slightly uneven or
pitted concrete floors can be
made good by pouring on a
self-levelling compound;

*Parquet flooring strips are
traditionally laid in a herringbone
or basketweave pattern. The latter
lends itself to mosaic panels.*

hardboard can be pinned over floorboards. Battening and fitting a
TGV chipboard under-floor is a good idea in a basement; however
headroom is often a priority in these areas, and if height does not
permit battening then you must work on the concrete floor. If your
room has a skirting, consider whether or not you wish to remove it
for laying, or replace it altogether with a matching wood finish.
Floor panels must have a 10mm/³⁄₈in expansion gap all around the
perimeter of the room, to facilitate absorption and loss of
moisture, either covered by the new skirting or a strip of beading
pinned to the old one. Finally, prepare to lay your hardwood panels
on a dry, level surface called a sub-floor, which is an underlay on a
roll that can be supplied with the boards. The cushioning effect of
this underlay disguises any (small) defects in the old floor surface,
and allows the new floor to 'float' on top.

Floating the floor

When you are happy with the sub-floor, set out the hardwood
panels. Lay the panels with the tongues facing into the room,
following the direction of the longest wall, unless the room is
square, when you should set out in the direction of the incoming
light. Don't lay the panels in a strict grid; offset to make sure the
butt joins do not line up across the floor. Make sure your first row
of boards is straight – remember that the wall may not be – and
use 10mm/³⁄₈in blocks to create the expansion gap. Saw the last
panel in the row to fit, using its offcut to begin row two. Glue the
panels to each other, at the sides and end, by running glue into the
upper side of the groove and gently tapping with a mallet and
protective block. Panels will probably need cutting to fit
lengthways when you reach the final row: mark the cutting line
with a pencil by placing them on top of the previous row.

Remember to include the expansion gap, and that your calculation must include the tongue-and-groove joint. Glue the final row of panels to each other, position the expansion blocks and leave to dry. Finally fit the skirting to cover the expansion gap after removing the 10mm/³⁄₈in blocks or, if the skirting has been left in place, fit a decorative beading such as quarter quadrant or similar.

You may find that you have to fit the flooring around central heating pipes, in which case take careful measurements of each pipe's position and transfer these to the appropriate board. Bore a hole in the board, making it large enough to clear the pipe, then make cuts from the hole to the board edge. Retain the off-cut. Fit the board in place around the pipe and glue the off-cut back behind it. If the flooring is to stop at a doorway, fit a hardwood threshold across the bottom of the frame and lay the boards up to it. Use a profile gauge to copy the shape of the architrave, or make a paper template, and transfer this to the flooring, cutting around the shape with a coping saw.

Lay out the wood panels, working away from one wall with the tongues facing into the room.

Maintain a 10mm/³⁄₈in expansion gap by inserting slivers of wood between the wall and boards.

As you work, glue the panels together by applying a bead of glue into each panel groove.

Tap the panels together, using a hammer and protective block to avoid damaging the edges.

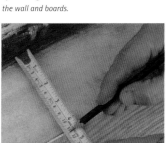

When you reach the far wall, measure for the cut board, allowing for the expansion gap.

Transfer the dimension to a board, making allowance for the tongue-and-groove joint; cut it to width.

Use an angled metal strip to tap the cut boards into place. Then cover the gaps with beading.

Basic skills: Tiled floors

Tiles are more popular than ever before as a decorative floor covering. This is due in part to the array of options now available, from basic ceramics from a discount warehouse to diamond-sawn slate from a specialist supplier. They can be easy to clean, hard-wearing and, of course, very good-looking.

Tiles used for a decorative flooring effect in period houses were well made and extremely hard-wearing, surviving decades of abuse from working boots with nailed soles and heels that tramped in street dirt. Encaustic tiles in basic colours were used to make patterned floors in hallways and corridors; older houses sometimes had flagstones or slate tiles in kitchens and laundry rooms downstairs, but quarry tiles were more common in these areas. If you uncover a tiled floor in an older property that is basically sound, consider using it as a room feature rather than replacing it. Old cleaning principles and techniques can restore the look of a tiled floor simply and cheaply, soda crystals in hot water will take off grime and grease, and traditional polishes are still available

stone tile

natural slate

cork tiles

quarry tiles

marble tile

stone tile

from specialist suppliers. Encaustic (where coloured clays are burnt in) and geometric tiles (natural clay fired into simple shapes and inserts) are available again, and it may be possible to match a tile design if floor damage has occurred. An independent tile workshop or supplier can advise you, or consult a restoration specialist.

Types of tile

If you intend to lay a new floor, several tile options are open to you. Specialist shops offer diamond-sawn slate, marble, and many types of natural stone slabs, and reclaimed terracotta in tile form polishes up beautifully. Quarry tiles are functional, good-looking and easy to keep clean, if rather cold to the touch, and ceramic

Flagstone tiles make for a practical, hard-wearing yet attractive floor in a kitchen or hallway. They are easily cleaned, retain their colour and pattern well and require no maintenance.

Encaustic tiles with simple patterns were commonly used in the hallways of period houses. Modern versions are available, making the restoration of this kind of flooring a viable proposition for those seeking to recreate an original look for their homes.

Repairing and levelling solid floors

No matter what tiling system you intend to lay on a solid floor, the floor itself must be level. Quarry, stone or any tile bedded in mortar will need a homemade strike-off board to level the mortar bed, and this in itself will level a slightly uneven floor as the job proceeds. Otherwise a self-levelling compound can be used. This is a special mortar available from any good builders' merchant and is supplied dry, usually in 25kg packs, for self-mixing. Mix the contents in a bucket, following the manufacturer's instructions, so that the fairly liquid, lump-free compound can be poured onto the floor. The principle is that it finds its own level, but you need to assist it by trowelling out to a thin layer with a plasterer's trowel. The compound dries hard and smooth, and although you can walk on it in a couple of hours you must leave it a day before attempting to lay a floor on it.

Concrete that has cracked or has deeper surface damage can be patched: use a strong mortar mix (3 parts soft sand to 1 part cement), wetting the cracked area first and levelling off with a trowel. Slightly damp floors can be treated by brushing on two or three coats of a proprietary damp-proofing liquid, but if the floor is wet enough to indicate a failure of the damp-proof membrane under the surface this will not solve the problem. A new membrane stretched onto the concrete can be covered with flooring-grade tongue-and-groove chipboard, creating a dry floating floor surface. Ideally, the membrane should be continued up the walls to meet with the damp-proof course.

floor tiles are as easy to lay on a floor as a wall. Other options are pre-sanded cork tiles, laid with adhesive but requiring a sealer, or pre-sealed cork that is easy to maintain. Vinyl floor tiles are usually self-adhesive, and come in a wide variety of colour schemes, but if vinyl is your choice consider loose-laid sheet vinyl, available in many designs and colours but often found as imitation wood or tiling complete with three dimensional effect and coloured grouting. Similar to sheet vinyl is linoleum, sold the same way by linear metre off a wide roll. A wide range of decorative patterning is available, to suit any room area, but particularly a children's play area because it is tough and easy to keep clean. Its drawback is that it is more difficult to fit, being stiffer and less easy to manipulate, and more awkward to cut.

Using a mixing attachment in an electric drill will speed the mixing of self-levelling compound.

Trowel the compound into small shallow depressions, making sure you fill them completely.

Pour the self-levelling compound directly from the bucket into large depressions.

Feather the edges of the compound with the trowel and allow to dry completely.

Heavy tiles

These need to be bedded in mortar, and a concrete (solid) floor is ideal. Floorboards or chipboard over joists (a suspended floor) may not take the extra weight and is not really suitable for this type of tiling. Vinyl, cork or a veneered floating floor would be more sensible, but if you really must have heavy quarry tiles or similar on a suspended floor, check with a professional builder first.

Laying ceramic tiles in adhesive

First set out a dry run: simply place the tiles on the floor to find the best arrangement or sequence before any permanent positioning is done (remember to leave a gap for the grout). Setting out corridor shapes, long and thin, can often be done by eye, following the longer dimension, but regular room shapes should be started at the centre. The room centre can be determined by using lengths of string to join the central points of opposing walls, forming a cross where the strings meet. To confirm that the grout pattern is square when you open the door, run a third string from the door frame to the opposite wall, forming a 90-degree angle. A right angle should occur where all the strings

cross; if it does not, then the room is out of square. If this is the case, use the string from the door frame as the starting guide, and adjust the centre point strings to form the required right angles. When you are happy with the setting out, either chalk the strings and snap them to the floor surface, leaving a guide line, or if you are confident that they are fixed securely, use the strings themselves as guides. Spread the adhesive to the required depth, using a notched spreader. The notch size is designed to spread different thicknesses. Your specialist tile supplier will advise you, and ensure you have the correct adhesive, flexible on a suspended floor, water-resistant in potentially wet areas. Don't spread too much adhesive at one time; start with a square metre or so, until you are confident that you can work more quickly. Line up the first tile with the guides, press firmly into the adhesive bed, and place tile spacers (or match sticks) to ensure correct positioning and spacing of the next tiles.

As you proceed across the floor, check that the work is level, using a straight edge. When the floor is covered with complete tiles, leaving only the borders to cut to fit, clean the joints and remove excess adhesive.

As when tiling a wall, use a notched trowel to spread a layer of adhesive on the floor. The notches ensure a uniform amount is applied.

Only cover a manageable section of floor at a time with the adhesive, otherwise it will begin to go off before you can lay all the tiles.

Set out the tiles dry first to establish a starting point for the rows and determine where cut tiles will be necessary. You may have to re-arrange them several times until you are happy.

Bed the tiles in the adhesive, working away from your guide strings.

Remove excess adhesive from between the tiles. Grout the joints when the adhesive has gone off.

Lay a tile on the last whole tile laid and butt another against the wall to mark the cutting line.

Score along the line and snap the tile in two in the same manner as ceramic wall tiles.

Tile nippers are ideal for making small cut-outs in tiles to fit around pipes and other obstructions.

Spread adhesive on the back of a cut tile and press it into place. This protects adjacent tiles.

When the adhesive has dried, mix up the grout and spread it into the joints.

At the edges of the floor, work the grout into the joint between tiles and wall.

Use a damp sponge to wash off all traces of excess grout before it has a chance to dry.

When all the excess grout has been removed, polish the floor with a soft cloth.

Make sure you remove any powdery deposits left in corners by the sponging.

To measure the border tiles for cutting, lay a complete tile directly on top of the last one laid in that row, place a tile on top, butted to the wall or skirting and mark the gap with a line on the tile underneath. Cut the tile by scoring and snapping, or by using a tile cutting machine which you can hire by the day. Fix the cut tile in place, and follow the same sequence in the next row. When the entire floor is completed, clean down and leave for 24 hours.

Grouting and finishing

Spread the grout on the tiled surface, and force it down between the tile edges into the joint lines using a squeegee. Use a damp cloth to wipe the tile surface clean, rinsing the cloth regularly. The lines of grout now need to be smoothed out, you can ues a grout finisher, available from your specialist supplier, or a short length of dowel will do just as well. When you are happy, and all tiles are free of excess grout, polish the surface with a clean, dry cloth.

The finished floor will give many years' service and will maintain its good looks throughout.

Laying vinyl and cork tiles

Good setting out and a level surface are the keys to successful laying of
cork or vinyl tiles on a suspended timber floor. Gaps between floorboards
will show through the tile, even if level; covering the boards with hardboard
is the only way to achieve the flat surface needed. TGV chipboard floors
that are not uneven need sanding at the joins to ensure a smooth surface.

A hardboard sub-floor

Before you lay hardboard sheets onto conventional floorboards,
you need to punch the existing nail heads below the surface,
otherwise the overlaid sheets will not lie flat.

Use a nail set and hammer, just as you would if you were
sanding down the floor. Use the largest size of sheet that you can
conveniently handle, to cut down the number of joints, and fit
each shiny side down onto the floor. The textured face provides a
good key for the tile adhesive.

You will need to stagger the joints from row to row, so that
you do not create a line across the room, but as hardboard cuts
easily, either with a saw or knife, this is a fairly simple job. Secure
the sheets with hardboard pins, punched in at 100mm/4in centres
and 100mm/4in intervals along all the edges, or use an industrial
staple gun.

Setting out and laying the tiles

Set out the tiles following the guide for solid floors, finding the
room centre and drawing a cross on the floor. This centres the
arrangement in the room, but, if this leaves a narrow border that
does not suit the decorative design on the tile, you can adjust it.
This is easier if you use string to make the initial centred cross,
dividing the area into quarters. The string can be tied to pins
driven into the floor, or secured with tape. If the tiles are
patterned, ensure the design matches up as you place a dry run of
two rows of tiles from the centre to the skirting, butting the tiles
to the stringline. If there is a narrow gap at odds with your tile
design, adjust the strings so that complete tiles butt to the wall in
two directions. When the arrangement is satisfactory, rub chalk
onto the strings and snap them against the floor to leave accurate
marks or leave them in place and use them as guides. Peel off the
backing of the tiles (if they
have one). Position, working
along the guidelines to the
wall. Some cork tiles use
adhesive, which is spread on
the hardboard (not the tile)
with a notched spatula. Lay one
tile at a time, pressing it down
firmly. Cutting tiles to fit is a
matter of overlaying on the gap
and marking the waste, then
cutting the tile with a sharp
craft knife held against a steel
straightedge. Use a tile offcut
as a cutting mat. Unusually
shaped objects such as

*Before cladding a floor with
hardboard sheets, drive all the nail
heads below the surface.*

*Use a panel saw to cut sheets to
size as necessary and stagger the
panels from one row to the next.*

*Staple or nail the hardboard sheets
to the floor, spacing the fixings at
100mm/4in centres.*

Some cork tiles are self-adhesive, so all that is necessary is to peel off the back and press them down.

Press the tiles into place on the floor, aligning the first rows carefully with strings.

Centre the arrangement of tiles on the floor, using two strings at right-angles to maintain the alignment.

To fit a tile around a bathroom fitting, make a paper template and transfer the shape to the tile.

Mark tiles for cutting by laying one over the last tile laid and butting another against the wall.

Using a steel rule or straightedge as a guide, cut the tiles to size with a sharp knife.

Press the cut tiles into place around the edge of the floor to finish the job.

pedestals may need a template of paper to aid fitting. Tape scrap paper to the floor and cut a series of slits into the pedestal shape from the edge. Press a fold line around the shape with scissor points, remove it from the floor and cut out around the fold. Tape the template onto the tile and follow the outline with a craft knife.

Sealing the floor

Plain cork tiles are easy to fit. They need sealing after laying, but vinyl-coated cork does not. When the plain cork floor is finished and the adhesive has set, lightly sand rough areas at the edges of the tiles with fine-grade glasspaper wrapped around a cork block. Brush away dust, and wipe the floor with a rag damped with white spirit. Use two or three coats of cork sealer or clear polyurethane varnish to finish the job.

Cork tiles can provide a stylish, attractive and warm floor covering for almost any part of the house, including the kitchen.

WOODWORK

Wood surfaces about the home need a sympathetic treatment if they are to look their best. Fashionable finishes are beneficial if they add to the character of the original wood, but if they disguise it they are merely doing the same job as a lick of paint, commonly used by builders to cover new timbers with well-marked growth rings and carrying defects. Traditional treatments like colour waxing, intended for the best quality stock, and combinations of paint and stain washes will have a different visual effect depending on the wood surface. They can be used to emphasise and exaggerate timber defects, resulting in a unique, abstract patterning.

Designer's notes

The decorative scheme you apply to the woodwork in your property should be viewed as an important finishing touch – if not exactly reflecting the period of construction, then certainly not being at odds with it. There are so many different finishes to choose from, whether you want to let the natural grain pattern show through or disguise it with solid colour.

Older-style houses have more elaborate mouldings, architraves and frames than modern properties, and the use of bright, glossy, modern paint schemes can detract alarmingly from their intended elegance. Gloss paints of any colour can reflect both natural and controllable artificial light alarmingly, causing flare and highlight in mouldings and recesses where none was intended, often appearing to change the shape of the wood and certainly destroy any of the joiner's intended subtlety. Original period mouldings were painted with 'flat' oil colours and varnishes, the lack of any sheen on the finish emphasising the decorative qualities of the joinery. Today, 'dead flat oil' is again available as a paint finish from specialist suppliers, but attractive alternatives include water-based effects and finishes which can be sealed with a matt varnish, or oil-based eggshells that can be partially rubbed down and 'distressed' before a sealer is applied. In this way, bright colours can be used together without causing light to flare across moulded surfaces, and the original integrity of the joinery can be

maintained as well as updated. Whatever the period, always seek to enhance the natural characteristics of your property, rather than work against them. Modern housing, often having smaller, plain or chamfered wood surrounds, is more suited to simple gloss treatments; often the narrow, minimalist frames match the glossy, plastic feel of PVCu window

Intricate mouldings and panels must be treated with sympathy.

systems. These styles are based around advanced technologies, where expensive woods have been replaced with metals, plastics, laminates and man-made boards. The increased use of metals, and a new awareness of customer interest and demands, have led to innovations like hot skirtings, where metalled snap-on sections carry electric heating next to the floor. Standard panel radiators, so often a room design problem, can now be replaced with a variety of space saving linear sculptures like multicolumns, and heating art designs such as continuous coils. As with period properties, work with the technology, not against it: powerful primary colours on narrow, plain surrounds complement minimalist room sets and provide defining borders for large wall areas.

Panelled doors can be painted with solid colours, which allow the shapes of the panelwork to show through. Too fussy an effect would produce a confusion of shapes and patterns.

Shutters make an interesting addition to any window. In period houses the original shutter boxes may remain, needing only new shutters to be made. However, they can also be added to more modern homes.

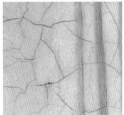

Crackleglaze is a two-part varnish that can be applied to wood to produce an aged look.

Doors offer all sorts of possibilities for decorative finishes, whether they be stains or paint.

Dealing with doors

Modern technology has changed the look and installation of many room features, and paint and decorative systems have adapted along with it. The basic principle behind room entry doors, storage doors and shutters still remains the same, however, and this is an area worth exploiting decoratively.

Entry doors, either new or reclaimed, that are made from solid wood can be colour stained and varnished to emphasise the grain structure. Cheaper modern doors that have plywood panels or other man-made inserts benefit from a combination scheme: insert panels can be painted a solid colour, and the real wood frame washed with a tint of the same colour. Seal or varnish to protect the finish. Try matching up cupboard or storage doors in the same colour system as the main door, or consider commissioning or building shutter doors to replace curtains. They can be constructed

Choose from a variety of paint effects to cheer up old cupboards throughout the home.

A rubbed, oil-based wax-resisting red emulsion and an abraded green colourwash.

to the same basic door style fairly simply, and the same combination paint scheme will result in a co-ordinated wood finish. Bear in mind, too, the other woodwork in the room, such as skirting boards, dado and picture rails, pelmets and wall panelling.

Same technique, different area

Using the same paint effect on different door types and sizes, irrespective of the wood grain or board surface, is fairly logical because it achieves an overall pattern in the room. What isn't quite so obvious is that the majority of effects can be made to work on any wood surface, irrespective of where you may have seen them used, and the only limit is your imagination.

Techniques based on the principle of oil and water not mixing together, for example, as in wax resists used to distress floorboards, can be equally effective on mouldings. Soft solvent-based wax can be rubbed onto the top relief surface of a moulding, and the entire architrave painted with water-based paint. Rubbing down with steel wool takes the paint off the surface moulding, but leaves it in the recesses. Wax resist techniques, often used to distress furniture, can look good on skirtings, especially when an underlying colour is revealed. Likewise crackleglazing, normally associated with small areas such as picture frames, can be used on inset door panels with a matching tint varnish on the frame of the door. Always remember that paint effects on wood can be applied to more than just one area, and, as long as the finishes are practical in the areas that you intend to use them, are versatile and interchangeable.

Basic skills: wood

In any decorating job in the house you must decide what finish you desire before you prepare the surface. Paint on woodwork must cover defects such as holes and knots, therefore they must be filled and sealed; or stains and varnishes can be used creatively to emphasise them, if this is appropriate for your chosen decor.

Preparation of surfaces

The surface preparation for the envisaged job will obviously depend on how you have visualised the finish. Wood only offers two basic choices, putting paint on, or taking it off. If you intend to repaint, and the existing paint surface is sound, you do not need to strip it off, only to remove the sheen completely using a medium-grade silicon carbide paper (wet-and-dry paper) soaked in a hot solution of sugar soap and water. Abrade the surface using plenty of liquid until the area is of a dull matt appearance. Switch to a fine grade of paper to achieve a smooth finish if necessary. It is important, after using wet abrasives and washing down, to allow all surfaces to dry out thoroughly.

You can now overpaint directly with an oil-based gloss if the colour is similar, but a totally different scheme, such as dark blue replacing a pale yellow, will need the paint maker's recommended undercoat. If the existing paint surface is unsound, however, showing obvious visual defects like cracking, flaking, blistering,

Wood may be stripped in two ways: with a chemical paint stripper (left) or a blow torch (above). Both methods need care as they are potentially dangerous.

peeling or chipping, then the paint must be stripped back to reveal the bare wood.

Stripping wood

Stripping paints and varnishes off wood surfaces is a time-consuming, dirty job. Unless you are stripping a door, which can be

Old paintwork should be rubbed down with abrasive paper to provide a key for the new paint.

Wash down the paintwork with a sugar soap solution and allow it to dry completely.

Areas of bare wood should be primed, and the surface sanded back where they join.

After undercoating, apply one or two top coats, keeping a wet edge to ensure no obvious joins.

Panelled walls offer a range of decorative possibilities, whether you stain and varnish them or apply a solid paint scheme.

taken off its hinges, the job must be taken on in situ. Panelling, frames and skirtings are best tackled with a burner and gas bottle; a flexible blade or shavehook follows the flame through softened paint and scrapes it off the surface. Hot-air strippers (or heat guns) are also suitable, but they are heavy, and as they must be held in the 'wrong' hand (the 'right' hand is holding the scraper for greater accuracy) are tiring to use. Paint strippers are another option, the chemical action causing the paint to blister and bubble, so that it can be scraped off easily. They are recommended for architraves where delicate mouldings can be stripped by the use of steel wool, rather than damaged by a clumsy blade. If paint stripper is your choice, use the water washable kind, and keep a bucket of warm water beside you. Liquid chemical strippers are corrosive and must be handled wearing gloves and protective clothing; any splashes must be washed off immediately. Another option for removable doors is dipping in a caustic tank. Small firms offering this service will frequently collect and deliver, solving any transport problems, but the drawback is that caustic solutions tend to eat into the glued joints as well as stripping the paint. When your door is returned, be prepared to re-glue the joints and cramp the door

Any holes can be concealed with filler, which should be left proud and rubbed down when dry.

Treat knots with shellac knotting to prevent them from bleeding resin through your finish.

with sash cramps overnight. The door will need sanding down as the grain will have been raised by the stripping process, and the wood will appear dry and dull. If a natural wood finish is required, use danish oil applied with a soft cloth to replace the natural oils taken out in the caustic tank.

Filling

Wood preparation includes filling or sanding irregularities, old fixing holes, dead knot holes, splits or cracks. If the wood is to be varnished, that is the grain and colour will be part of the finish, the filler applied must match the wood colour. Plastic wood filler can be bought to fill different woods, labelled pine, oak, mahogany and so on. Slightly overfill the hole with a small flexible blade, to allow for some shrinkage and for sanding flush when hard. If the wood is to be painted, decorators' filler can be used, which is easy to sand when dry. When filling window frames and other occasionally exposed wood areas, an oil-based stopper or putty should be used, and this should be applied after the primer coat, not before. Otherwise you risk the unsealed wood surface drawing out the oil, the filler shrinking and consequently falling out.

Knots in painted wood surfaces

The treatment of resinous knots must not be ignored if you are to achieve a first-class finish. Brush the knot with genuine shellac knotting, available from your decorating supplier, and allow to dry before applying the primer coat. Knots literally weeping resin must be scraped clean, and dried out as much as possible with a burner flame before sealing. Note that resin stains already under paint will eventually show through a fresh paint film. To remove the problem you must scrape the paint off back to the bare wood, apply shellac knotting, and repaint. Simply painting over resin stains is no good.

Painting doors and windows

Interior doors that are to be painted or varnished do not need a weatherproof finish. You can use oil-based finishes for protection against knocks, or the water-based variety. Windows, though, are exposed to wet conditions, cold in winter with condensation on the inside, and humid in summer, and they should be given a tough finish.

Door sequence

Panelled doors

Remove the door furniture and paint the door edges first. If you are only painting one side of the door, wedge it open. If the door opens towards you, paint the leading edge only, if it opens away from you, paint the hanging (hinged) edge. Wipe off any paint that has fouled the other face of the door. Now paint the panel mouldings and then the panels, taking care that any excess paint in the moulding channels does not 'run' onto the panels or rails. The horizontal rails are next, followed by the vertical centre rails or muntins, and then the outer stiles.

Flush doors

Remove the door furniture and paint the edges as before, but there the similarity ends. You need to treat flush doors more as you would a small wall area, dividing the area into thirds and painting one third at a time. Lay the paint off towards the edges as you finish each section, and work quickly enough to maintain a wet or 'live' edge so that the sections join together easily without leaving an obvious join. Leave the door wedged open until the paint is dry, and do not raise any dust in the room, as this is liable to stick to the paint film and ruin the finish. When the paint has dried, replace the door furniture.

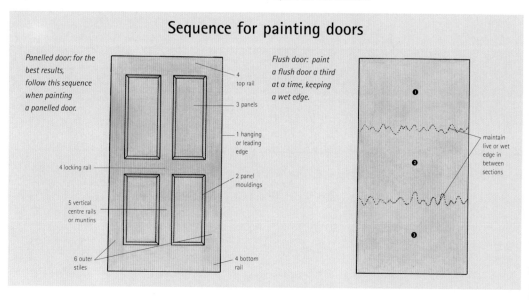

Sequence for painting doors

Panelled door: for the best results, follow this sequence when painting a panelled door.

- 4 top rail
- 3 panels
- 1 hanging or leading edge
- 4 locking rail
- 2 panel mouldings
- 5 vertical centre rails or muntins
- 6 outer stiles
- 4 bottom rail

Flush door: paint a flush door a third at a time, keeping a wet edge.

- ❶
- ❷
- ❸
- maintain live or wet edge in between sections

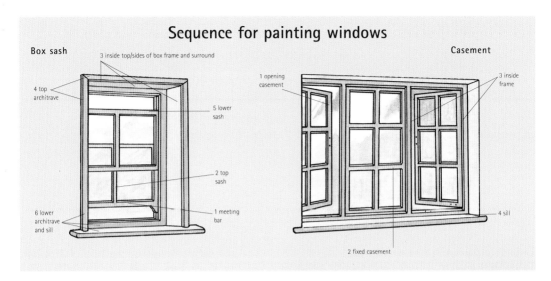

Sequence for painting windows

Box sash

4 top architrave

3 inside top/sides of box frame and surround

5 lower sash

2 top sash

6 lower architrave and sill

1 meeting bar

Casement

1 opening casement

3 inside frame

4 sill

2 fixed casement

Window sequence

Sash windows

Lift the lower sash and pull down the top sash so that the meeting bar can be painted first, ensuring that it has the longest drying time. Paint the top sash then use a pair of steps to reach and paint inside the top of the box frame and side runners, making sure no paint gets on the sash cords. Reverse the sash positions, and paint the architrave and surrounds, completing the stepladder work. Now paint the lower sash, architrave and sill. Be careful when painting up to the glass in the two sashes: the paint should be cut in to overlap the putty slightly, forming a seal and preventing condensation from entering any gap between putty and glass.

Casement windows

Remove the window furniture, and paint the opening window first. Start with the glazing bars and edge mouldings, then the face and hanging edge of the casement. Follow the same sequence for the fixed casement, then paint the external frame and centre frame members, and the rebate for the opening window. Lastly, paint the sill. If you have used masking tape to get a clean edge up to the glass, remove it as soon as the paint is touch dry.

Though functional, like doors, windows can contribute positively to the decor of a room.

Crackleglazing and surface resists

Cracked and crazed finishes are frequently used for special effects, paints and varnishes being specifically applied so that the film tears or breaks during drying. This crazed effect can be used to give an antique-style finish to varnished woods, or, if combined with paints, a rustic appearance that might be found in a country kitchen.

As with all distressed finishes, as they are sometimes called, the aim is to prematurely age timbers, in this case imitating cracked, well worn and weathered surfaces. In the main, distressing techniques rely on the incompatibility of consecutively applied coats. Surface resists also have as their origins a mistake in application, or paint defect, where a second coat will not adhere to the previous layer. Waxes are a prime example – oil-based wax rubbed indiscriminately onto a moulding and then painted with a water-based emulsion will give a patchy torn-up finish that can be further emphasised with wire wool. In this case the oil base has rejected the subsequent coat of water-based paint.

Crackleglazing or cracklefinishing

This is the result of the difference in drying time, elasticity and flexibility between an oil-based varnish and a water-based varnish brushed over it. Artists working usually in either oils or water-based paints found that mixing the two caused problems if they were applied in the wrong order; oil could be brushed over acrylic and water bases but not vice versa. Historically, in the paint-finishing trade, the rule was that consecutive paint films should be of a similar elasticity: a hard drying top coat, such as eggshell or gloss, should not be brushed over a softer, more elastic base coat, or cracking would result. The top coat or finish needed preferably to be slightly more elastic than the preceding coats, unless a crazed finish was specifically required by the client. This generally applied to paints mixed by hand on site.

The introduction of proprietary paint systems where paint-makers supply primers, undercoats and finishing coats ready-mixed has all but eliminated this problem. As a consequence, crackle finishes are rare as mistakes, but commonly employed as special effects, often using oil-and water-based varnishes supplied in kits,

complete with all instructions. In today's decorating marketplace, what concerned yesterday's paint finishers is a practised art form.

Using a cracked finish on wood

Cupboard doors or shutters are a good surface for a cracked finish. They are not too large an area to appear as an overpowering effect, and they provide a choice of cracked colour or wood surface. The surface must be sealed, either by varnish or paint, depending on your scheme. Brush on a coat of oil-based varnish and leave it until it is just touch dry and therefore slightly tacky. Now brush on the water-based varnish, thinly for subtle crazing, more thickly for obvious cracks, and leave the surface near a source of heat, such as a radiator. Some manufacturers recommend the use of a hairdryer at this stage, but care is required not to wrinkle the entire surface accidently as the cracks start to appear. The cracks can be left as they appear on a painted base, or have a contrasting colour rubbed into them, using an artist's oil paint applied with a

Brush on oil-based varnish. While it is tacky, add a water-based varnish. A hairdryer will speed drying.

To make the cracks more obvious, rub a contrasting coloured oil paint into them with a soft cloth.

soft cloth. If the scheme has cracks formed on a natural wood surface they can be emphasised in the same way, using black oil paint, or alternatively a coat of contrasting emulsion can be applied over the top. Use a wide brush or roller, and make one pass only, otherwise the top coat will sink into the cracks, ruining the effect. Whichever of these versions you choose, when the surface is dry, seal with a clear coat of varnish.

Wax resist on wood

Most effectively used on mouldings and architraves, solvent-based wax is rubbed onto the moulding top surfaces, but not into the recesses. Paint the entire surface with water-based paint, and allow it to dry out. Rubbing the waxed areas with steel wool takes the paint off, leaving the top surface mouldings looking as if the paint had worn off during the passage of time. Thinner surface streaks can be removed by substituting a candle for the solvent-based wax.

Small projects

Smaller areas, such as built-in cabinet doors that already have a varnish applied, can be given a period feel without a base coat. Simply 'key' the surface using a fine abrasive paper. Otherwise, seal bare wood with two coats of clear oil-based varnish and leave it to dry. Apply a coat of oil-based crackleglaze, brushing it out well over the surface to give a thin, even coat, and let it dry out until the surface has a 'tacky' feel. This usually takes about two to three hours, depending on conditions. Now brush on the water-based crackleglaze. A thick layer will take longer to dry out than a thin one, and the resultant cracks will be more obvious. You can speed

Wooden furniture can be given an attractive period feel by the use of 'distressing' techniques such as crackleglazing.

the process of drying and crackling by gently warming the surface with a hairdryer if necessary. Don't hold the dryer too close and stop as soon as the cracks start appearing. Rub an oil-based artist's colour into the cracks with a soft cloth to aid definition, selecting a contrast to your original wood colour. Oil- and water-based varnishes and the oil colours used in this technique are available from artists' suppliers.

Basic principle

Crackleglazing is intended as a wood finish, suitable for panelled doors and frames. The basic principle involved, which is the different drying times of water- and oil-based varnishes, can also be applied to large wall areas.

Large projects

For larger areas you will need to substitute colour emulsion for water-based varnish. The oil-based crackleglaze allows the base colour to show through the cracks in the top emulsion coat. This effect works best with contrasting colours, so try brushing on a dark base colour, and leave it to dry. Apply the crackleglaze, followed by a top coat of contrasting pale emulsion, which should be watered down. The effects in this technique vary from the subtle to the obvious. Some experimentation on scrap board will help you decide how far you want to go with your ideas.

Allow the oils to dry for 24 hours, and seal the finish with oil-based varnish to protect it.

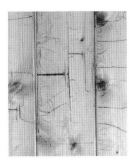

A close look reveals very obvious cracking. Thinner varnish coats can produce more subtle effects.

Crackleglazing effects on timber with contrasting colour cracks.

Waxing and french polishing

Waxing and french polishing, once common practice, are restricted in their use today to small craft studios and homeworkers. Sourcing of materials for traditional practices is more difficult, but still possible, and using the techniques on simple projects is a welcome and challenging alternative to mass-produced finishes.

Completing any joinery project about the house will cause you to consider a choice of decorative and protective finishes, although experienced craftspeople may well have pre-selected a finish, and therefore sourced a wood accordingly. Wood finishes on simple shelving and panelling jobs can vary from straightforward clear varnishes, taking a minimum of effort, to more time-consuming decorative effects. A great number of these can be produced using modern paints and varnishes in a variety of combinations, and all materials can be found in high street stores. While this has the advantage of convenience, it gives no historical perspective to colours and finishes painstakingly crafted by hand in days gone by.

Sand the item to be french polished with fine abrasive paper to ensure a smooth surface.

Prepare the surface by fadding, applying a thin continuous film of polish to seal it.

Waxing

This was once a very popular finish. As well as protecting, it slightly darkened the surface of the wood, and the oils in the wax stopped the wood from becoming dry. A rise in popularity of french polishing sent waxing into decline, but today the versatility of this finish is recognised, and clear, neutral, white and coloured waxes can be found in art suppliers and hardware shops. Original waxes were easy to apply and gave a lustre finish not dissimilar to eggshell; today's waxes should contain a colour that can be worked carefully into the woodgrain and slowly polished off the relief surface. White wax, for example, worked into the raised grain of a rich coloured wood with steel wool and polished, gives a limed finish.

French polishing

This is a considerably more difficult application than waxing, and although it is a finish popular among traditional craftspeople, particularly on bespoke furniture, it is rarely seen elsewhere. Second-hand furniture pieces inherited or sourced from antique shops may be finished in this way, and it may be of interest to know a little about the basic technique, for restoration purposes or even as a matching finish for a bookshelf or bookcase project. French polishing will seal and fill in the woodgrain, stabilising the surface, resulting in an easy-to-clean, hardwearing finish. Kits are available from specialist suppliers.

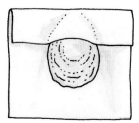

To make a rubber, you need a ball of wadding and a square of clean, lint-free cotton cloth.

Place the wadding in the centre of the square and fold over the top two corners to form a point.

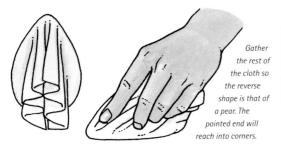

Gather the rest of the cloth so the reverse shape is that of a pear. The pointed end will reach into corners.

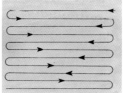

Apply polish with the rubber by working with the grain.

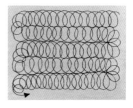

Finish off by bodying-up, applying polish with small circular motions.

Polishing a surface

French polishing involves layering thin films of shellac onto a wood surface. It is a difficult process to master, and you should first select a suitable piece of hardwood to practise on.

Sand the surface flat and smooth with fine glasspaper, and remove any dust. Form a key between wood surface and polish by 'fadding' (the fad is a folded piece of lint-free wadding dipped in polish) covering the surface with a thin, continuous film of polish. Allow the surface to dry completely, then sand down with fine glasspaper, again removing all traces of dust. The next stage, called 'bodying up', is to apply polish with a rubber over the surface,

French polish is a common finish on quality period furniture. It produces a hard glossy finish to wood that allows the beauty of the grain to shine through, but it needs skill to apply properly.

working with the grain. The 'rubber' is used instead of a brush to keep the surface as flat as possible, and is made up of the same lint-free wadding as the fad, wrapped in a square of cotton rag.

Place the wadding in the centre of the rag and fold over the two top corners, forming a point. Fold over the rest of the rag into a ball shape, and shape the top point so that the reverse side of the rubber looks like a pear, the shaped point allowing rebates and mouldings to be polished.

Open the rag, and pour french polish onto the wadding until it is fully 'charged', refold and gather up the rag, squeezing polish through to the rag face in the process.

Now apply polish by passing the rubber over the wood surface, from end to end, with the grain, squeezing the rag ends so that polish comes through in a continuous moist film. Slide the rubber on and off the surface, making sure the runs of polish all join, forming a continuous film. Wait until the polish is dry before applying a second coat; never try to go over a damp surface, or it will tear up. After three coats, allow to dry, and lightly sand down.

Finish bodying-up by polishing in small circles over the surface. If the rubber starts to stick on the polished surface as you work, use a little linseed oil to lubricate the rubber face. As the shine begins to appear the bodying is over, and the surface needs to dry overnight. Lightly sand the surface, and again remove any dust.

Finish by applying polish in the same way, using long gliding strokes with the grain, exerting less pressure each time, and allow the surface to dry for about an hour. Now add a little methylated spirit to the rubber, diluting the polish that is left, and pass lightly and quickly over the finished surface, removing any traces of linseed oil that may remain.

Make sure the finishing rubber is not too wet, glide on and off the surface as before, and don't stop the stroke on the surface, as this will ruin the finish.

Simple wooden shutters

YOU WILL NEED

• 50 x 25mm/2 x 1in
Softwood TGV cladding
boards • 38 x 10mm/1½ x
⅜in Softwood • Decorative
moulding • 50mm/2in
Number 8 screws
• 25mm/1in Number 6
screws • 25mm/1in
Moulding pins • Wood glue
• Wood filler

Internal wooden shutters were an integral part of window design in Georgian and Victorian period houses. The shutters were panelled, often had mouldings that matched the panelwork in and around the bay recess, and folded neatly away into shutter boxes at the sides of the window. They provided security, privacy and noise reduction.

If you have a period property that has had the shutters removed, but still retains the side boxes, seek the advice of a local joiner, for pine shutters can be made up to fit and match, restoring the window area to its former glory. Period shutters are normally associated with sash windows, either full-length and covering the glazed area from floor to ceiling, or more usually covering the lower part of the window only. They look at their best in recessed bays, but were and still can be stylish and functional at any window, and there is no reason why you cannot fit them to modern sashes and casements. Sashes can still be fitted with any height of shutter, but casement window styles look better with full-length screens, having no meeting bar to form a visual parallel to a half- or three-quarter-length shutter.

Made to measure

To install simple shutters to a window, first measure the opening carefully, and look to see if you need to fit timber battens vertically inside the recess to hinge onto. If so, remember to subtract this measurement from the calculation. Small windows can accommodate two shutters easily, which gives you a nicely balanced scheme, but if the window is too large, or you prefer smaller shutters, then measure up for two hinged together on each side, or a total of three with one side doubling up. In this scheme, three shutters span the gap, with one side having two shutters hinged to neatly fold back to back. Check all your measurements twice, then cut to size 50 x 25mm/2 x 1in timber for the inner support frame, TGV cladding for the shutter body, an external frame that overlaps the front edge from 38 x 10mm/1½ x ⅜in wood, and a decorative moulding.

Glue and screw the inner support frame first, using right-angled butt joints, driving home 50mm/2in number 8 screws. Use a combination screwsink to counterbore a hole enabling you to drive the head into the middle of the woodpiece at right angles. Fix a centred cross-piece for extra strength, and then screw the TGV lengths to the front of the frame, using 25mm/1in number 6 screws. Countersink the heads just flush with the surface, and

Begin by assembling the inner support frame, using right-angled butt joints. Glue and screw the joints for maximum strength.

Mark the position of the centred cross-piece on the uprights and drill to accept the reinforcing screws. Glue and screw the piece in place.

Cut lengths of TGV cladding to size and screw them to the front of the frame, countersinking the fixing screw heads, flush with the surface.

Attach the outer frame so it projects at the front, using glue and moulding pins, which should be punched below the surface of the wood.

Cut lengths of panel moulding to fit inside the projecting lip of the outer frame, mitring their ends for neat corners. Pin them in place.

Fill any defects and pin-heads, using a matching wood filler if a clear varnish will be employed, and sand down to a smooth finish.

make sure their position will be covered by the moulding that you will add later. Glue and pin the outer frame in position, counterpunching 25mm/1in moulding pins below the surface, flush at the back and overlapping at the front. Finally, measure and corner-mitre the moulding to fit neatly into the rebate created at the front, pinning it with the same moulding pins.

Fill all pin holes prior to sanding down the surfaces. If you choose to paint the frame and moulding, a decorator's filler is good enough here; if you intend to varnish the work, use a matching wood filler as the wood and grain will show through even if it is coloured. A painted frame and moulding with a similar colour varnished TGV inside makes a good combination effect. Attach the shutters to each other and to the frame with 75mm/3in flush hinges in a brass finish, using brass screws.

You could adapt the basic framework of these shutters to make louvre shutters that will allow cooling air into the room in summer while shading it from the sun. You would need to rout a series of slots into the inside of the frame at an angle to accept the slats.

Louvred shutters are very practical in the heat of summer, shading the interior from the sun. Here they are used to divide a room.

A customised pelmet

It is possible to completely transform a window and curtain arrangement by simply fitting a pelmet. A decorative front and customised wall brackets are easy to make from timber stock. Using solid timber may mean that more support is needed, but you can then pin to the front interchangeable seasonal arrangements, such as dried lavender.

Measuring and cutting

Measure the width of your window, and the drawn curtain positions, then check to see if you have enough space to allow you to fix into the frame surround or whether you need to drill into the wall. In either case, the made-up brackets should be positioned to allow an overhang at each end of 25mm/1in. The principle is that two fixed brackets support, but are not permanently attached to, a pelmet that is designed to be fixed to the wall itself in a hidden position at top dead centre. This allows for easy pelmet removal, for frame painting for example, by taking out one screw and lifting down, rather than removing bracket screws neatly but inconveniently hidden inside the pelmet, a difficult job calling for small hands and a stubby screwdriver. The cut bracket must

be made up to fit exactly inside the internal right-angle of the pelmet. For example, if the pelmet is cut from 100 x 25mm/4 x 1in nominal size wood, planed to a finished size of 95 x18 mm/3¾ x ¾in, the internal dimension is 75mm/3in. Cut the bracket to this

The pelmet comprises a top, front with decorative moulding and short fixing batten.

The upside-down L-shaped brackets take the weight of the pelmet and are screwed to the wall on each side of the window opening.

Glue and pin the top of the pelmet to the front panel, then attach the short fixing batten to the centre of the back edge.

size at the top and part of one side, forming the support, then cut back to form a rebate. A section of wood 18mm/³⁄₄in wide and deep, and 120mm/4³⁄₄in long should be left, and this takes the wall screws, as shown in the diagram. Shape the bottom edge of the pelmet into a design of your choice with a jigsaw. Glue and screw a timber support, 25 x 25 x 100mm/1 x 1 x 4in with a centred fixing hole onto the top centre of the pelmet so that you can screw through into the wall.

Joining together and fixing

Make up the pelmet by gluing the top to the front, and pinning with 38mm/1¹⁄₂in panel pins. On the front face, directly butting the join of top and front, pin a decorative strip moulding, using 18mm/³⁄₄in moulding pins, which disguises the butt join. Now attach the wall brackets, using a suitable length number 8 such as 32mm/1¹⁄₄in if you are fixing to the wood surround, or a countersunk 57mm/2¹⁄₄in number 8 screw into a wall plug if you are driving into the wall. Position the pelmet, and equalise the side

Using seasonal flowers and foliage to decorate a window opening provides a means of extending the garden into the house, blurring the distinction between the two areas.

overhangs, then fix the top centre support to the wall, again countersinking a 57mm/2¹⁄₄in number 8 screw into a wall plug.

Finishing

Fill the screw holes and sand the surfaces smooth. Again, select a filler that is suitable; decorator's fillers are fine if the surface is to be painted, but a matching wood-coloured stopper is needed if the wood grain is going to be visible under a varnish, as this will tend to 'disappear'.

Clear or coloured varnishes will certainly look good on the pelmet, but you could also consider painting the brackets to complement the wall colour, blend in with the wall decoration or to match exactly the wood surround. In this way the brackets are disguised slightly and full prominence is given to the wood finish on the pelmet that will support your choice of seasonal floral decoration.

Position the pelmet on its brackets, screw to the wall through the top batten and varnish.

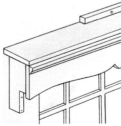

The finished pelmet is designed to accept seasonal floral decoration pinned to the front.

FURNITURE FACELIFTS

Many special decorative finishes are considered unsuitable for large wall surfaces, either because they are messy and difficult to control given the size, or because the result is simply too overpowering. They can be ideal for small projects, though, like table tops, cupboards and chairs, irrespective of age. Bare wood 'flat-packed' self-assembly pieces are suitable, as are traditional auction and flea market finds, but best of all, and the most economical, are those long forgotten items from yesteryear stored in lofts and cellars. So, before you hunt for that expensive new piece to take pride of place in a new environment, consider what a makeover will do for an old friend. You may be surprised at the transformation.

Wooden cupboard

Several different finishes – paint, colourwash, stain, varnish and wax – are used, together with replacement glass and simple brass furniture, to give this well-made but badly neglected cupboard and drawer combination unit a new lease of life.

YOU WILL NEED

- Paint stripper • Steel wool
- Stripping knife • Paint brush • Glasspaper 240 grit aluminium oxide
- Screwdriver • Emulsion
- Colourwash • Varnish
- Liming wax • Clear wax • Brass fittings • Patterned glass • Putty • Beading

Step 1 The old multi-layered paint finish is removed using a scraper to take off blistered paint after applying water-washable paint stripper. Remember to wear gloves!

Step 2 When all the paint is removed, steel wool dipped in sugar soap is used to clean the surface thoroughly. Always rub in the direction of the wood grain.

Step 3 The door is removed and cleaned, and old glass bead and putty discarded. A coat of white emulsion is 'distressed'.

Step 4 The inside of the cupboard needs to reflect a warm, friendly glow; orange emulsion from a sample pot is ideal.

Step 5 Diluted woodwash (available in small tins) is painted onto the base and top of the unit. Turquoise was the chosen colour here.

Step 6 The multi-finish theme continues – diluted ultramarine water-based dye is brushed into the side grain, avoiding the front edge.

Step 7 The front will remain as bare wood, cleaned up with 240 grit aluminium oxide around a sanding block.

Step 8 The waxed drawer is tested to ensure it slides well. Blue and white waxes have been applied and polished.

Step 9 New brass drawer and cupboard door furniture is fitted to replace the old plastic knobs. Small hands and a stubby screwdriver are needed to gain access to the inside of the drawers.

Table mosaic decoration

This table has an interesting top surface; its octagonal shape is emphasised by softwood angles that form corner triangles. The resultant cross is tiled with different shades of blue mosaic, the dark blue pieces matching the triangles, and contrasting with the pale blue colourwash on the softwood.

YOU WILL NEED
- Aluminium oxide
- Sanding block • T-square
- Pencil • Tiles • Hammer
- Rags and cloths • Ruler
- Wood glue • Moulding pins • Counterpunch • Wood filler • Tile adhesive • Grout Spreader • Woodwash
- Clear varnish • Emulsion

Step 1 The top is abraded to remove all traces of sheen and to provide a 'key'. Aluminium oxide is used around a cork block.

Step 2 Guidelines are drawn for the wood pieces, using a soft yellow pencil so that they can be clearly seen.

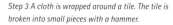

Step 3 A cloth is wrapped around a tile. The tile is broken into small pieces with a hammer.

Step 4 The design is checked to see whether there are enough pieces of the right colours.

Step 5 After mitring the wood pieces, they are glued and pinned following the yellow guidelines.

Step 6 The tile adhesive is spread 3mm deep with a ribbed spreader.

Step 7 The tile pieces are positioned in the adhesive.

Step 8 The spaces are grouted, after the adhesive has set.

Step 9 The mosaic is polished; the table is painted and varnished.

Revamping a wooden chair

YOU WILL NEED
• Sugar soap • Rag
• Glasspaper • Emulsion
• 1in brush • Pencil
• Tracing paper • Artist's
brushes • Artist's acrylic
colours

A small chair found in the loft, dirty from its travels, could be considered ideal for a child's nursery. A distressed paint scheme is envisaged for the chair. The scheme will match the room decor and a hand-painted design on the seat and back support will give the chair its own individual character.

Step 1 The wood surface is sanded down using medium followed by fine glasspaper, to give a smooth finish prior to painting.

The chair was cleaned with sugar soap first, so that dirt and grease wouldn't clog the abrasive and the paint would then go on evenly.

Step 2 The entire chair was painted with a first coat of red emulsion.

Step 3 A second coat (pale blue emulsion) was overpainted.

Step 4 The surface was abraded so the red paint showed through.

Step 5 The seat design (a colourful tree) was traced.

Step 6 The tree design is painted using artist's acrylic paints and a number 5 artist's brush.

Step 7 Flowers and leaves are added using a finer brush and bright acrylic colours.

Step 8 Finally a protective coat of clear satin varnish was brushed on.

STYLISH SPACE SAVERS

The modern living environment and time-specific lifestyles require the best use to be made of limited available space. Traditional lofts and cellars are often converted to form part of the living quarters where once they were dark, cold, long-term storage areas rarely visited. The clamour for personal space in a smaller world is thus one of the contradictions of our time, and householders face a difficult task attempting to maximise potential space while retaining a personal decorative style and concealing everyday items that are unattractive but necessary.

Hanging racks and containers

Hanging racks and wall boxes save space around the home because the floor or worktop space below them can be utilised for another storage purpose. Often cookware was hung on butcher's hooks from ceiling-mounted racks, but modern low ceilings and the dangers of falling pans have relegated even kitchen racks to a wall mounting.

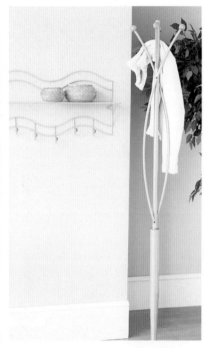

Extra storage space is always useful in the kitchen. Open shelving is easy to fit into small corners and can be used to add an informal country feel. It's also a good way to show off attractive pans and implements, as well as having things close to hand for the cook.

Storage in a hallway should be both practical and look good. In a small space a simple hat stand and shelf unit provides places for guests to hang their coats; in larger spaces cupboards can be built-in for all the family's needs.

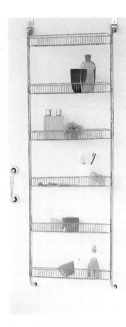

*Open shelves in a bathroom give
you a chance to show off expensive
and beautifully packaged items.*

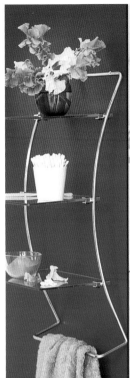

Bathroom shelving comes in
a variety of styles and materials so
you can easily find storage to suit
your bathroom decor.
Wicker cupboards give a natural feel, as well as hiding away the
clutter of personal items. Displaying
towels on open shelves adds a
touch of warmth and softness to
metallic modern design.

Shelving systems

The fittings of the modern home have advanced, none more so than the humble shelf, which has evolved from a rectangular unit holding books and ornaments to a multi-purpose linear structure. Today's systems support all manner of audio and visual electronics, and must display designer qualities themselves, as well as showing off decorative accessories.

Book shelves can be far more than an easy way to store books; they can also act as an attractive means of displaying them and a range of other items.

Modern style shelving can be made out of lighter, less obtrusive material than wood. Lightweight shelving such as this gives the room a modern feel.

Shelf units today are so beautifully designed that they can be used as a feature of the room, not just for *practicality. These small shelves allow you to display mementoes in a stylish and imaginative way.*

Window sills can be used as an alternative to more traditional shelving, but don't think practical think beautiful. Sills can be used not only to display the occasional objet d'art but are a great place to grow things. Allow seedlings to thrive by placing them on a warm sun-filled window ledge, and reap the benefits of bringing your garden indoors at the same time.

Long thin corridors may feel like a waste of valuable space, but with some thought and imagination you can utilise even the narrowest hallway both for storage and to add interest. A clever mix of stored items will provide a talking point to any hallway.

Storage screens: fabric

Fabric screens can be simple lengths under a sink, hiding the household necessities, or complex three-way self-standing frames used as changing screens or simply to indicate an area of privacy. The free-standing, folded fabric screen is both stable and lightweight; its portability and decorative qualities make it functional, fashionable and very versatile.

Fabric screens do so much more than hide ugly clutter, they are also attractive additions to any room. Screens are widely available, but also easy to personalise to suit individual taste and decor. The true versatility in fabric screens, however, lies in the fact that you can position them wherever you want.

Even hard furnishings like wardrobes need no longer be 'hard'. Use lengths of fabric draped over a frame, or hung like curtains round a small space, to add an exotic feel to your bedroom. Choose silks and velvets in bright and luxurious colours to create a spice trail feel, or white muslin to bring a touch of softly flowing colonial days.

Under-the-sink curtains bring a special charm to any kitchen or bathroom, making a sink a feature not just a fixture. An ideal way to add colour to a room, they hide necessities and add a finishing touch to soft furnishings. Choose your fabric carefully and make

sure that you allow enough not just to cover but to drape attractively. Reminiscent of early twentieth century homes, with the right fabric under-the-sink curtains can be brought up-to-date while retaining that country feel.

Boxes and containers

Storage chests are traditional favourites, a fashionable way to store items in a piece of wooden furniture that looks good in any room. Fabric covered boxes, the lid doubling as a seat, can match room decor in a co-ordinated scheme, and wicker laundry baskets will assume a new identity if they are stained in bright colours and sealed with sprayed varnish.

Storage boxes are more than a place to store unwanted clutter.
From coffee tables to seating, strong wooden boxes have become
a fashionable sought-after feature in many modern homes.

Wicker boxes are highly fashionable nowadays and are a distinctive way to store anything from dirty laundry to letters, newspapers and magazines.

The ottoman is the traditional place to keep bedding. Still placed at the bottom of the bed, this ancient piece of furniture has been given a modern make-over through the use of new materials and modern colours.

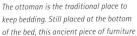

A collection of wicker baskets not only provides storage for nick-nacks and larger items but also makes an attractive feature. They can also offer a handsome hideaway for your dirty laundry if you don't favour the more modern canvas laundry bins (right) that can be equally fetching.

ACCENT ACCESSORIES

If the decorative style of a room is largely dependent upon the characteristics of the building, seeking to emphasise original features and disguise less attractive areas, then the accessories around the room depend on and reflect the character and interests of the occupants. Vases, containers, lamps, boxes and frames can all underline a particular personal curiosity, be it historical or geographical, classical or modern. Accessorising can vary from subtle frame distressing, reflecting an interest in traditional woods, to hand-painted floor coverings that pay homage to other cultures.

Vases

YOU WILL NEED

• Clear sticky-back plastic film • Pencil • Scissors or craft knife • Natural sponge • Range of colours of ceramic paints • Artist's brushes

Enliven a plain vase by decorating it with ceramic paints, available from arts and crafts suppliers. Decant the paint into a small kettle or pot and sponge on tint combinations of the same colour, or be more adventurous and mask out an area for hand-painting a foreground design.

Step 1 Draw a sunflower head on clear sticky-back plastic film and carefully cut out as a mask.

Step 2 Offer up the mask to the vase to check the size and the position.

Step 3 Using a natural sea sponge, put on the first tint of the colour.

Step 4 Sponge on the second tint, to start the build-up of the broken colour effect.

Step 5 Now add the third, darker shade; this gives a three-dimensional feel to the design.

Step 6 *Peel off the sunflower head mask and the vase is ready for hand-painting.*

Step 7 *Paint in bright yellow petals using a number 5 artist's brush. The shadow detail in orange will require a thinner brush.*

Step 8 *On a mid-brown base, touch in the minute black detail in the sunflower centre with a number 1 brush.*

Two-tint distressing

YOU WILL NEED

• Fine glasspaper • Silicon carbide paper • Water-based wood dye • Emulsion • 1 inch brush • Clear satin varnish

A clear-varnished wooden picture frame with rounded moulding creates shadows from sidelighting on its surfaces. In this simple project, two tints of the same colour form half the frame each, and are distressed with white and abraded to emphasise these side shadows.

   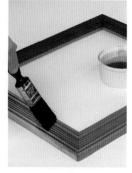

Step 1 Remove the original finish using glasspaper. Fold it over to sand inside the moulding.

Step 2 Brush over two sides of the frame with a strong red water-based dye.

Step 3 Using a more dilute mix of the same colour, complete the other two sides.

Step 4 Distress the frame with fine glasspaper until bare wood appears on the surface of the moulding.

Step 5 Brush on white emulsion diluted half and half with water and leave to dry.

Step 6 Using wet silicon carbide, abrade the surface and inside moulding detail.

Step 7 Apply a coat of satin varnish to darken the distressed wood areas for a subtle finish.

Floor cloth: painting canvas

YOU WILL NEED
• Artist's canvas to size
• Design reference • Ruler
• Pencil • Scissors • Set
square • Combination square
• Straightedge • Iron
• Double sided carpet tape
• Masking tape • Acrylic
prime • Coloured emulsions
in sample pots • 2in brush
• Number 6 flat brush
• Round artist's brushes
• Matt varnish

Hand-painted, individually designed canvas floor coverings owe their origins to the early New World pioneers, who reputedly re-used their boat sails as the raw material. The design on this canvas continues on an historical American theme, using colours and shapes used by native peoples of the South West desert states.

Step 1 'Square up' the raw canvas, leaving a 50mm/2in border to be folded over, and cut the corners diagonally.

Step 2 Fold the border to conceal the rough edges, and iron in the crease after damping down the canvas.

Step 3 Use double-sided carpet tape (available from hardware stores) to secure the folded border permanently in position.

Step 4 Some canvas is sold pre-primed, some raw. If you buy yours raw, give it a coat of white acrylic primer.

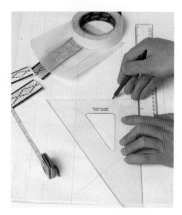

Step 5 Pencil your geometric design onto the canvas, using set square, measure and straightedge to keep it symmetrical.

Step 6 Painting: use a number 0 artist's brush to fill in the corners.

Step 7 Use masking tape to achieve an accurate, straight side stripe.

Step 8 Use brown paper to protect the finished areas as you work.

APPENDICES

D on't skip this section just because it's the last bit at the back of the book before the glossary, because these appendices cover important general safety aspects of decorating work. Many readers will rightly regard the advice as no more than common sense, which it is, but it also contains more specialised tips for protecting people and machines from accidental damage. The acquisition of a basic tool kit, always open to question, and the age-old problem of materials sourcing, particularly in the second-hand marketplace, are discussed at some length, as are the fundamentals and practicalities of artificial lighting.

Safety

Whatever your style or type of property, living and working in it with the minimum of risk to yourself and others is always a priority. Safety issues in the home can vary enormously, from keeping sharp kitchen knives out of the reach of small children, to making sure that your power tools have a circuit-breaking plug fitted between you and the mains supply.

Accidents in the home account for a vast number of out-patient admissions, particularly in the springtime, when there is a rush to take on DIY 'improvements'. To avoid accidents, however, all you need to do is to take sensible precautions and follow some simple guidelines, many of which are little more than common sense.

Working safely in the home

Whatever the task about the house, here are some useful guidelines:

- Move obstructions such as furniture, decorative items and toys – don't 'work around' them. If you were 'on site' elsewhere, you would ask for a clear working space, for fear of damage to the contents of the room, so do the same in your own house. Working in an area that is cluttered and not easily accessible leads to over-reaching and losing control of the tool, and on a stepladder can result in overbalancing.
- Position your stepladder safely, so that you can reach the job height and width without stretching. DIY jobs are not always conveniently sited for a person standing on the floor. The requirement is likely to be of differing tasks at a variety of heights.
- Position the tools for the job on a temporary table surface, never on the floor.
- Route cables from power tools around the sides of the room, not across the middle.
- Clear up as you go.
- Work in a tidy area so that you can easily see and check all aspects of the job in progress.

Different types of glove will help protect your hands from chemicals, paints, stains, splinters and other sharp objects.

Safety in the workshop

- Make sure that small children do not have access to your tools, whether your equipment is left in a cupboard when not in use or is stored in a dedicated workshop in a garage or basement area.
- Store cutting tools and potentially dangerous power equipment sensibly, that is to say, with protective sleeves and guards in place.
- Never leave power tools 'live'; disconnect the supply or remove the battery, and if possible keep them in carrying cases or secure boxes.
- Quality handsaws and chisels come with protective sleeves; if you lose one, make up another from card and adhesive tape.
- Store planes on their sides with the blades retracted, and never leave craft and marking knives with the blades exposed loose in a drawer where they could cut rummaging hands.
- Invest in a good-quality, solid tool box, or a tool bar that can be fixed to a wall to store your valuable equipment.
- Keep the workshop area clean and tidy.
- If you use a bench to cut, plane, shape and drill wood pieces, make sure that a fire extinguisher is within easy reach, as wood shavings burn easily.
- Keep the workshop floor free from obstruction.
- Store bolts, screws, nails and pins by type and size in marked containers so that they can be easily found. Don't leave them lying on the bench. Many a piece of fine woodwork has been accidentally scarred by nails or screws that have been left carelessly in the way.

Power tools

- If the tool has a lead, fit a circuit-breaking plug, and always isolate from the power when changing the bits in a drill or blades in a saw.
- Always make sure you know where the lead is, and keep it behind you if you can.
- If you prefer battery power, remember that the tool is continuously 'live'. Disconnect the battery when changing bits and blades.
- Use the correct bit for drilling, and make sure that the saw blade is suitable for the material you intend to cut, and that both are sharp.
- It is dangerous practice to force bits and blades, and there should be no need.
- When drilling, back off the hole and stop the drill before removing it; likewise with a power saw, back off or stop the cut, and let the blade stop completely.
- Always read the instruction manual carefully before using any tool, and familiarise yourself with its operation.
- Do not switch on any piece of power equipment unless you know how to turn it off.

Safety goggles are essential for some jobs to protect your eyes from flying debris and dust. Some fit over normal spectacles.

Protective clothing

- Site workers always wear safety clothing: protective shoes, overalls and helmets all the time; safety glasses, ear defenders and dust masks when required. As you are doing the same type of work, you should wear the same types of clothing, most of which have obvious functions.
- Shoes need to be strong with reinforced toe caps; trainers may be comfortable but they offer no protection if you drop something heavy on your foot.
- Gloves will protect your hands from chemicals and corrosive liquids as well as from paint and oil stains.
- A helmet may not be needed in the house, but consider wearing one in the loft where the roof clearance is minimal.
- Overalls are better than old clothes, because they are designed in one piece so nothing gets caught up in machinery, and all the pockets are in the right place and can hold useful items.
- Try wearing a tool belt: all the heavier hand tools can be supported around your waist, so they are instantly accessible, and this is very useful on a stepladder.
- Dust masks are recommended in do-it-yourself stores as a matter of course when you buy materials and equipment for a dirty,

dusty job, but wear one even when sweeping out the work area.
- Use ear defenders for heavy-duty masonry drilling and other noisy jobs, but always ensure that you can still hear warning noises.
- Protect your eyes when working; if you find that goggles tend to mist up, impairing your vision, try safety glasses (which can be worn over reading glasses), but make sure they have side protectors. Slivers of wood, particles of rust and lumps of masonry can fly from any angle, not just straight at you.

Take a break

- Plan a sensible working schedule, with breaks for drinks (non-alcoholic) and food.
- Don't start early and finish late in the hope of completing the job quickly; working long hours leads to mistakes and sometimes accidents as the attention wanders. At best, standards drop and the job is put at risk. Pace yourself and take breaks.

Always wear clothing that is appropriate for the job. Overalls will protect your clothes, gloves will save your hands from damage, while a cap will keep dirt and dust out of your hair.

Basic tool kit

This is a somewhat misleading title, as anyone who has attempted to assemble a basic tool kit will testify. It is perfectly possible to put together an impressive array of expensive tools, and still find that your door handle undoes with an allen key that you do not possess, instead of the screwdriver bit that you have in the basic tool box.

This is an unfortunate fact of life, and you must inevitably add items to your kit every time you take on a job around the house. Don't be tempted to 'make do' with what is in the tool kit, either, because DIY disaster lurks just around the corner. Using the wrong tool for the job can result in an accident; at best it can make the problem you are trying to solve considerably worse. Buying the correct tool for the job allows your basic tool kit to grow with your experience and become a comprehensive tool kit, and before too long you will have a kit that you are confident of using.

For starters

A few basic items will be found in all domestic tool kits: measuring and marking tools, cutting tools, a drill and set of screwdrivers, a hammer, pincers or pliers, tools for making good, and basic painting equipment.

Measuring and marking

• A **retractable steel tape** that measures to 5m/16ft is a real asset; measuring shorter distances is simple with smaller tapes, but they won't run the length of a room. This forces you to add dimensions together, which can lead to miscalculations.

• A **small spirit level** can fit comfortably in an overall pocket.

• An **engineer's square** is essential for checking right-angles.

• A **soft pencil** should be included in your basic toolkit for use on timber surfaces.

• A **waterproof pen** offers a very useful way of marking gloss-painted surfaces.

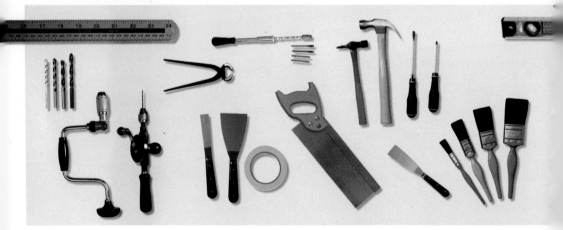

Cutting tools

• A craft or general-purpose knife.

• A small saw: pick a medium-sized tenon saw to start with; it can be identified by a heavy-duty brass or steel strip on the top edge of the blade, keeping it straight. It is a simple saw to use, and can cut across large timbers as well as make smaller, more intricate cuts for joints. Always use the protective teeth guard.

Drills and drivers

These are needed for plugging walls and driving screws.

• Drills: Whether your choice is **mains powered** or **cordless** is entirely personal, but in either case, don't buy cheap. DIY superstores are full of 'bargains', but don't be tempted. Cheap, badly made, noisy, inaccurate equipment is no investment; it will not last and will prevent you from doing a good job. Try to find a tool that will satisfy all requirements – wood, masonry and screwdriving – and which has variable speed control.

• Bits: An extensive range of bits is available for power driving, but consider a quality manual tool as well, such as a small **spiral ratchet driver with interchangeable blades**.

• An electrician's screwdriver.

• Hammer: its role is self-explanatory, but there are several types.

A **claw hammer** would be the most useful starter, the claw able to extract nails and pins. In confined spaces, a **pair of pincers** will do the job of the claw.

Gripping work

• A pair of **combination pliers** and an **adjustable wrench** are called for in gripping work, but it is worth including **long-nosed pliers** because they can sometimes reach where conventional pliers cannot, and are useful when undertaking electrical work.

Tools for making good

Decorating tasks inevitably need tools for making good such as:
• a scraper
• a flexible filling knife
• a putty knife
• a roller and tray combination
• a selection of quality small and medium size brushes.

Boxing clever

Whereas some consumer items are replaceable because they simply wear out, the majority of your tools will be with you a long time, particularly if you buy quality ones.

Invest in a tool box that will protect your equipment, and secure it with a padlock. There is no worse start to any job than a search party attempting to locate lost, borrowed or broken tools. If you store them in a protected, secure environment you will minimise the risk of damage.

Lighting principles

Buildings of every type experience a series of different visual moods as the sun describes an arc from sunrise to sundown. They may be cool and aloof in the morning shade, and warm and friendly in the afternoon sun. Nothing is quite as dramatic, however, as the difference between day and night. Here we discuss how to make the best of the light your room receives.

Lighting-up time

How you see an object, how you define its visual balance and shape, whether or not the angle of the light has caused distortion, or whether the colour is enhanced at all by the light depend on the position of the source. During daylight hours this is the sun, its movement causing long shadows and distortions early and late in the day, and a flattening effect when it is high in the sky. Colours that can seem washed-out at midday intensify at the end of the day as the sun sets, and contrasts temporarily increase before darkness descends. Artificial lighting assumes the same role: that of the source, flattening or emphasising areas, objects and decorations depending on its position in the room.

Add or subtract

As a result of the sun's movement, a house will experience differing visual moods in its south-facing rooms than in its north-facing accommodation. The lighting designer can work with the natural elements, enhancing the effect, or seek to re-balance, adding artificial light to darker, colder areas and throwing highlights onto angles and edges. Just as the afternoon sun casts a warm glow onto a wall, the designer can carefully position wall washers of differing power to throw graduated light onto the area in the same way. Conversely, in rooms where the sun makes only fleeting contact, the designer can employ hidden lighting techniques combined with light-sensitive switching, warming up what was once a cold, unfriendly environment.

Create the right mood

Try to select lighting that enhances the feel of the room and creates the type of environment that suits the family members that use it. Lighting is not merely functional; it is, or should be,

Lighting should set the mood in a room. Using strategically placed table and standard lamps will produce soft pools of light and create an intimate, relaxing atmosphere.

atmospheric. Centrally sited lighting can be used to great advantage in rooms with dark or rich coloured walls, as they absorb a lot of light rather than reflecting it, and the low-key mood can be added to by low-level lamps, up- and downlighters or flicker lamps. Conversely, centrally placed lighting in areas with white or pale coloured walls and ceiling can look austere to the point of unfriendliness; wall lights would throw light and shadow onto each surface simultaneously. Lights recessed in an alcove would create more interest still, adding to the wall's shape. If your decoration has involved a special finish, emphasise it by throwing light on the wall. If it is a textured finish, use the lighting to cast long shadows, increasing the three-dimensional effect.

Practicalities

Each member of the household will remind you of individual needs, be it lighting suitable for working on a computer, or reading by the fire. Your lighting arrangements should allow for all necessities, but at no detriment to anyone else. For example, reading lights positioned behind a bed should allow one partner to read without disturbing the other. Two separately switched directional lamps are needed here.

Areas used by everyone must be well and continuously lit, especially stairwells. Sudden changes in light levels can be hazardous, and for this reason lighting for a stairwell and lights along a corridor should be operated by the same switch. These areas will benefit from a nightlight, too, if you have children or elderly relatives who need to visit a bathroom in the early hours.

Kitchen areas pose a particular problem, in that food preparation and washing-up tasks are usually performed at perimeter units. Consequently a central light will force kitchen users to work in their own shadow. A series of downlighters is a good solution, each positioned over a work area – sink, cooker or hob, work surface and any appliance in regular use, such as a washing machine. Two separately switched parallel tracks of interchangeable, directional spotlights offer another alternative.

The bathroom needs to have a central enclosed light for background illumination, which must be operated by a pull cord if the switch is inside the room. The basin area needs a separate light for shaving or the application of make-up; arrange it so that the user is illuminated, not the mirror. Remember that no one in the house will thank you for installing lighting that has an abrasive and inaccurate fluorescent effect when they are using the bathroom early in the morning.

Lights with a purpose

Always make sure your lights perform the function they should, and review the situation as your needs change. Good planning will ensure that your system is versatile enough to be multi-functional, providing ambient light for background, directional light for atmosphere and decorative highlights, working light for specific jobs around the home, safety light in heavy traffic areas, and security light as a deterrent to crime.

Stairways should always be well lit to prevent anyone from missing their footing in the dark. Placing downlighters beneath a handrail (above) provides the answer without having to resort to harsh overhead lighting. Wall lights (right) create warming pools of light that emphasise decor.

Materials

Quality specialist materials are best sourced from an outlet that trades specifically and knowledgeably in that area of supply, and is therefore in a position to offer help and advice on requirements, amounts, techniques and tools needed, based on experience gained in the field.

Buying materials

The rise of DIY superstores in recent years has led the home improvement enthusiast to believe that all the materials for any job can be found under one roof. However, many of the materials for special projects around the home can be sourced from smaller suppliers who have specialist knowledge in particular areas.

Timber and joinery materials

Superstores and larger hardware or decorating shops often offer 'packs' of shrink wrapped timber, but the packing can make it difficult to check the quality. The alternative is to buy from a wood merchant. Pick a yard that offers a machining service, and that allows you to select and cut your own lengths from properly stored woods. This will allow you to select lengths that are not warped or twisted, and do not suffer from sap or wet stain, or have shakes and splits. Timbers should be racked horizontally, and be kept under cover. If you find a cheap yard with wood open to the elements or stacked upright on its end grain, walk away. Finally, as price is always a consideration, remember that cheap timber can become very expensive if you have to throw half of it away because of defects or substandard machining.

Specialist suppliers

Basic paints and varnishes can be found in your local decorating store, but these shops cater for all tastes, and space is limited. As a result, particular effect paints and glazes are not usually a priority, and you must source from a specialist outlet. Many of these suppliers can be found in the classified pages of consumer magazines and trade journals. The supplier may be nowhere near

you, but will offer a telephone or internet buying service, and a delivery service, except, of course, where the product is a fire risk.

Many small specialist suppliers have the time and the knowledge to advise you, both on the products they sell and the technique you are about to employ. They are usually able to supply materials needed for any project, for example french polishing, in the form of a kit.

Buying economically

Don't automatically assume that you can save money by buying in bulk. True, it costs little more for a 25kg bag of cement than for a small DIY sand/cement mortar mix, but what exactly are you going to do with what's left over? If you store it in even a mildly damp place, it will be useless, and you will end up throwing it away a few weeks later.

Larger quantities of paints, varnishes, plasters, cartridge sealants and adhesives must be sealed and stored correctly to be of any use at a later date. A cellar will be cold and damp, an outside shed prone to frost, and the garage (if it's big enough) probably has no heating. Timber lengths must be racked level, and at room temperatures, too; if you take wood from a cold shed into a warm room you will have no straight lengths to build anything with. So, unless you have the luxury of good storage facilities, think twice before chancing the often false economy of bulk buying.

Reclamation yards

Probably associated more with restoration projects than DIY tasks, the reclamation yard is nonetheless a good bet for stripped doors, old fire surrounds, old pine floorboards and all sizes of second-hand timbers. Old timbers sourced here will be of better seasoned stock than new woods, and if you have access to a machine saw, can be re-sized to live a new life. Don't pass by a builder's skip without having a good look, either; it's amazing what gets thrown in them. Just make sure you ask permission before removing something that takes your fancy.

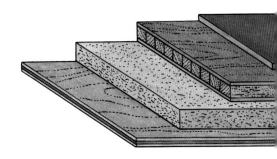

Measurement conversion tables

The timber supply industry is a worldwide industry and you might find you have to convert from metric to imperial measurements or vice versa when you are sourcing materials to redecorate or revamp your home. Here are two tables that might be useful to you. The first shows the metric sizes that wood comes in, with the equivalent imperial measure and the nearest traditional lengths. The second is a general feet/metres conversion table. The figure in the central column refers to metres if you are converting to feet and feet if you are converting to metres. For example, in the first row of figures the number of units is 1. If you look in the left-hand column, you will see that this means 1 metre converts as 3.2808 feet. If you look in the right-hand column, you will see that this means that 1 foot converts as 0.3048 metres.

CONVERSIONS: FEET/METRES

Feet	Number of Units	Metres
3.2808	1	0.3048
6.5617	2	0.6096
9.8425	3	0.9144
13.123	4	1.2192
16.404	5	1.5240
19.685	6	1.8288
22.966	7	2.1336
26.247	8	2.4384
29.528	9	2.7432
32.808	10	3.0480
36.089	11	3.3528
39.370	12	3.6576
42.651	13	3.9624
45.932	14	4.2672
49.213	15	4.5720
52.493	16	4.8768
55.774	17	5.18163
59.055	18	5.48644
62.336	19	5.79125
65.617	20	6.0960
68.898	21	6.4008
72.178	22	6.7056
75.459	23	7.0104
78.740	24	7.3152
82.021	25	7.6200
85.302	26	7.9248
88.583	27	8.2296
91.86	28	8.5344
95.14	29	8.8392
98.42	30	9.1440

WOOD: METRIC AND IMPERIAL LENGTHS

Metric	Equivalent Imperial	Nearest Traditional Length
1.8 m	5' 10⅞"	6'
2.1 m	6' 10⅝"	7'
2.4 m	7' 10½"	8'
2.7 m	8' 10¼"	9'
3.0 m	9' 10⅛"	10'
3.3 m	10' 9⅞"	11'
3.6 m	11' 9¾"	12'
3.9 m	12' 9½"	13'
4.2 m	13' 9⅜"	14'
4.5 m	14' 9⅛"	15'
4.8 m	15' 9"	16'
5.1 m	16' 8¼"	17'
5.4 m	17' 8⅝"	18'
5.7 m	18' 8⅜"	19'
6.0 m	19' 8⅛"	20'
6.3 m	20' 8"	21'

Paint and paper charts

Use the chart on the right to work out how many rolls of wallpaper you'll
need and the chart below to find out what sort of paint(s) will be required
for your redecoration plans.

PAINT: TYPES AND USES

Primers/Undercoats	Base	Thinner (Cleaner)	Surfaces
Knotting solution/primer	Oil	White spirit	Wood knots, resin channels and resin stains
Wood primer	Oil	White spirit	All softwoods; softwood veneered boards
Aluminium wood primer	Oil	White spirit	Hardwoods, oily timbers, resinous woods, powdery surfaces (old plaster)
Alkali-resisting primer	Oil	White spirit	New plaster, fire-resistant boards
Penetrating stabilising primer	Oil	White spirit	Crumbling, powdery surfaces of brick or plaster
Red oxide primer	Oil	White spirit	All ferrous metal surfaces
Acrylic primer/undercoat	Water	Water	Interior softwoods; softwood veneered boards
Oil/resin undercoat	Oil	White spirit	All softwoods, hardwoods and boards

Finishes/Top Coats	Base	Thinner (Cleaner)	Surfaces
Vinyl matt emulsion	Water	Water	Walls and ceilings
Vinyl silk emulsion	Water	Water	Walls and ceilings
Gloss emulsion	Water	Water	Interior wood finishes, small walls
Gloss	Oil	White spirit	All types of wood, metal finishes
Eggshell	Oil	White spirit	Woodwork, walls and all smooth surfaces
Eggshell emulsion	Water	Water	Woodwork, walls and all smooth surfaces
Smooth masonry paint	Water	Water	Brick and mortar finishes
Floor/Tile paint	Oil	White spirit	Concrete, brick, tile, cement, mortar

ESTIMATION OF NUMBER OF ROLLS OF WALLPAPER NEEDED

Height from skirting to coving/ceiling (feet)	Total measurement around walls (feet)							
	28	36	44	52	60	68	76	84
7–7½	4	5	6	7	8	9	9	11
7½–8	4	5	6	7	8	9	10	11
8–8½	4	5	6	7	8	9	10	12
8½–9	4	5	6	8	9	10	11	13
9–9½	4	6	7	8	9	10	12	13
9½–10	5	6	7	9	10	11	12	14
10–10½	5	6	8	9	10	12	13	15
10½–11	5	7	8	9	11	12	13	15

KEY

• *Match height of wall (right-hand column) with total horizontal measurement (top row) to identify number of rolls needed. For example, a 10 feet high room 76 feet around would require 12 rolls.*

• *Each roll is assumed to be 10.05m/33ft long, and 520mm/20½in wide.*

• *Measurement listing includes average window and wall recess (door) areas. Increase/decrease as needed.*

• *Large (wasteful) patterns will need an increase of 1 roll in 5.*

1 litre will cover	Recoatable in	Notes
N/A	N/A	If wood is very resinous, combine with aluminium wood primer.
11–12m²	16–24hrs	Use oil with oil-based undercoat and finish. Clean surface with white spirit before application.
14–16m²	24hrs	Leave for 24 hours before recoating.
9–10m²*	Overnight	* Figure quoted for hard plaster surfaces; more porous surfaces will use more primer.
6–8m²	16–24hrs	Sticky and splashable: wear eye protection and gloves at all times.
9–10m²	16–24hrs	Clean off rust stains with wire wool; best base for oil-based finishes.
12–13m²	1–2hrs	Inside use only; suitable for water-based gloss finishes. Not as durable as oil-based paints.
16–18m²	16–24hrs	All purpose undercoat, use with oil-based gloss. Manufacturers colour matches undercoat with gloss.
12–14m²	2–4hrs	Cannot be wiped clean – unsuitable for kitchens
10–12m²	2–4hrs	Washable/wipeable finish.
9–10m²	3–6hrs	'No undercoat' versions available; not as hard-wearing or as glossy a surface finish as oil-based gloss.
16–18m²	16–24hrs	The ultimate paint finish for wood/metal. Smooth, shiny, tough and permanent. Use inside and out.
19–20m²	16–24hrs	Semi-gloss finish. Also found as silk, lustre or satin finish. Good base for paint effects on walls. Needs no undercoat.
10–12m²	2–4hrs	Not as hard-wearing as oil-based eggshell.
9–10m²	6 hrs	Limited colours; intended for external walls, but ideal for cellar walls.
10–12m²	16–24hrs	Limited colours. Ideal for red ceramic tile floors, conservatories and utility rooms.

Glossary

Abrasives
Sheets of sandpaper of differing grit sizes used for smoothing a surface or removing a finish.

Anchor bolt
A fixing bolt for securing a wood or metal frame to a masonry wall or solid floor.

Auger bit
Large-channelled spiral drill bit for wood-boring.

Backsaw
A small-to-medium-size handsaw for accurate cross-cutting.

Batten
A length of softwood, often used as an invisible support.

Bond
A decorative system for binding bricks together to form a strong and cohesive wall.

Bowing
Wood lengths bent out of true by uneven shrinkage or due to supporting weights too heavy for them.

Butt
As in butt joint: items meeting but not overlapping.

Chalk line
A taught, straight string, fixed at each end and dusted with chalk, which, when 'snapped' against a surface, leaves an accurate guideline.

Chamfer
A 45-degree symmetrical bevel to remove a right-angle.

Chuck
Lockable, adjustable jaws allowing insertion of differing diameters of bit, for rotary drilling applications.

Circuit-breaker
Protective device that disconnects the mains supply to a power tool.

Contact adhesive
A glue that is applied to two surfaces so they bond instantly on meeting.

Counterbore
To drill a straight-sided hole, subsequently filled with a plug, so that a screwhead is concealed below the surface.

Counterpunch
To set a nail below the wood surface, filling the entry hole with a matching coloured filler.

Distemper
Traditional water-based coloured paint with a matt finish that dries to a powdery bloom. Lighter in colour when dry than when applied.

Dry rot
Timber decay, caused by a fungus, due to damp and poor ventilation.

End grain
The exposed wood fibres at the ends of cut lengths, prone to splitting and very absorbent.

Epoxy grout
A two-part, epoxide-resin-based, ceramic-tile grout, with a tough, hygienic waterproof finish needed in food preparation areas, which has to be mixed on site.

Feathering an edge
Using abrasives to sand down the rough, chipped edges of a previous finish for a smooth starting surface.

Floating floor
A thin layer of flooring laid on top of the existing surface.

Flogger
Long-haired, wide, flat brush, used dry to drag through a finish.

Flush fit
An exact and even fit of two joining surfaces.

Half-wall finish
Where the lower part of a wall has a different decorative scheme from the top half.

Halving joint
A simple wood joint, made by joining two halves, or where two rebates meet, each half being the thickness of the timber.

Housing
Also known as mortise, a rectangular piece cut out of timber, across the grain, into which a tenon or tongue is slotted.

Invisible pinning
Where a matchboard or similar is nailed in such a position that the subsequent board will cover up the fixing.

Jamb
(Door jamb) the sides and top of a fixed frame.

Joist
Heavy-duty horizontal support for floors and ceilings.

Kerf
Cutting slot made when a saw-blade passes through wood.

Key
Abrading a smooth surface, so that the roughened face will provide a grip for a paint finish.

Knot
Defect in timber lengths where branches joined the tree.

Laminate
(Flooring) ultra-thin layer of artificial veneer with a photographic wood or other effect, on a plywood base.

Laths
Thin wood strips pinned to studs (walls) or joists (floor or ceiling) to act as supports for the plaster or plasterboard.

Laying off
Final long surface strokes through a paint layer, to smooth the finish and prevent drips and runs.

Locking rail
The central, horizontal support in a panelled door.

Making good
Restoring a surface to its previous standard of finish, after a repair or alteration.

Matt
Surface finish of non-reflective paints and varnishes.

Mitre
The cut-off right-angle corner of a board, removed at a 45-degree angle.

Moulding
Narrow strips of wood or plaster with a decorative, incised surface.

Mortar
Bonding mix for brick and stone, consisting of cement, soft sand, water and any additives.

Muntin
Glazing bar or divider between panes of glass in a window; vertical rail in the centre of a panelled door.

Noggin
Short horizontal plank (stud) used to reinforce uprights in a stud or partition wall.

Nominal size
The sawn size at which timber lengths are specified, as opposed to the finished size.

Out of plumb, out of true
Not truly vertical or horizontal, not straight or level.

Pilot hole
Small drill-hole used as a guide for a larger one, or for a screw thread.

Pointing
Decorative, weather-proof finish for mortared brick joints.

Proud
Surface raised above another, so they are not level with each other.

Ratchet
Screwdriver mechanism allowing movement in one direction only.

Rendering
The first application of a mix (e. g., plaster) to a brick wall.

RSJ
(Rolled steel joist) heavy steel support beam attached to slate, holding up a floor or replacing a lower support wall.

Screed
To lay down a concrete mix to level a floor area.

Skew nailing
Driving nails in at different angles, for a more secure fixing.

Soft jaw
Fibre or softwood pieces used in jaws or clamps to protect the item being clamped.

Template
Shape or pattern used as a guide for cutting or drilling.

Tenon
Projection or tongue cut into timber, intended to slot accurately into a cut housing or groove.

Thread
Continuous spiral groove cut into a screw, enabling it to grip the wood or plug securely.

Transom
A window directly above a door.

Two-way switching
Electrical wiring that enables artificial light be controlled from two different places.

Plasterboard
A thin, manufactured sheet of solid plaster with paper facing both sides, or one side with a damp-resistant shield.

Warped timber
Wood twisted out of true by uneven shrinkage or extreme changes in temperature.

Wet rot
Decay in timber caused by a fungus, due to water saturation and inadequate ventilation.

Yacht varnish
Expensive, superior quality clear varnish intended for outside use and suitable for floors.

Environmental planning
Planned development of towns, cities and rural areas..

Index

Acknowledgments

The author would like to express his grateful thanks to the many working professionals whose advice and time has been willingly given during the preparation of these pages. Special thanks are due to Martin Gowar, whose depth of knowledge in finishing was frequently an inspiration; to Cheryl Owen, for help and advice; to Russell Sadur, Theo Dorou and Steve Tanner, whose photographic studios were virtually taken over at times during shooting; to Diana Cibil, who styled the projects; and to photographer Steve Gorton. Cheerful in all weathers, Steve's commitment to the job and unfailing logistical support made a sometimes difficult task that much easier.

The publishers would like to thank the following for the use of properties:

Oak-engineered laminate flooring on pages 158/159 supplied by EC Forest Product Sales Ltd. Units 5 & 6 The Woodland Centre, Whitesmiths, near Lewes, East Sussex BN8 6JB.

Moran & Co. Builders, ICI Paints, Farrell & Ball, B&Q, Wickes, Brewers & Sons Ltd, Master tiles, Covers, Travis Perkins, Paint Magic.

Picture credits

Anaglypta Wallpaper: p.6, 194L.

Crown Paints: pp. 24B, 30T, 29, 34T, 42, 107, 147.

Elizabeth Whiting & Associates:
pp. 12, 13, 17, 23R, 22, 23B, 34B, 31, 46, 48, 49, 51, 52, 53, 55, 57, 68R, 79, 81, 83, 84, 85, 96L, 97TL & BR, 105, 106, 108T, 118, 119L, 122, 125, 132, 134R, 135, 137, 141, 142, 143, 146, 155, 156, 157, 160, 161, 165, 167, 168, 169, 175, 177, 181, 191, 214R, 194R, 195, 196L, 197R, 209, 214, 215T.

Houses & Interiors: pp. 11, 22BR, 23T, 27, 50, 54, 96R, 97TR, 134L, 171.

Image Bank: p.9.

Jaafar Designs/Florida squares & spirals: p.119BC.

Laura Ashley: pp. 38T, 39B, 173, 197L, 199TL.

Morris & Co.Collection: pp. 68L, 70L, 150.

Next Directory: pp. 22L, 103B, 129R, 138, 148/9, 179B, 214L, 193, 196R, 198, 199TR & B, 215B.

Osborne & Little/V&A The Historic Collection: p. 69T.

Painted Tile Company/Wellington Tile Co/Crazy Chicken & Tulips: p.119B.

Sanderson: pp. 23T.

Stock Market: p. 2.

Front cover: Elizabeth Whiting & Associates, CB;